STALIN'S
MASTERPIECE

STALIN'S MASTERPIECE

The Show Trials and Purges of the Thirties — the Consolidation of the Bolshevik Dictatorship

Joel Carmichael

St. Martin's Press
New York

Printed in Great Britain

Library of Congress Catalog Card Number:
75-39517

First published in the United States of America
in 1976

Contents

Foreword

This book began as an enquiry into events in the Soviet Union during the second half of the thirties, when a number of prominent 'Old Bolsheviks' were publicly accused of extravagant acts of treason and defection. In court they vehemently confessed to the charges; nearly all of them were executed.

The 'Moscow Trials' were given great publicity throughout the world as well as in the Soviet Union; beginning in August 1936 there were three major 'Trials' over a period of one-and-a-half years.

During the same period there also took place – more or less clandestinely – what came to be known as the Great Purge, in which literally millions of people were imprisoned on similar charges. They, too, confessed; they were either killed or sent to forced labour camps, where they generally soon died.

Both in the well-publicized Moscow Trials and in the subterranean Great Purge the indictments established as arch-criminal, indeed arch-fiend, Leon Trotsky, together with Lenin the co-architect of the Bolshevik regime. Trotsky, in exile since 1929, had been out of power since the early twenties.

Many sympathizers of the Soviet Union, a major bulwark against Nazi Germany, were stunned by the Moscow Trials.

I spent part of my adolescence discussing them: could the Old Bolsheviks have been monsters? Why had they confessed? Were the Trials authentic? What could it all mean?

It was an enigma that aroused the most ferocious passions.

The Show Trials and Purges are generally thought of as a grotesque episode of the dead past, yet they epitomized the consummation of a new social order.

Stalin, author of this masterpiece, macabre and unacknowledged, performed an act of creativity as potent as the secret act of coupling that creates a new life.

The pattern laid down during this era of Soviet history still guides action within the Soviet sphere – 'trials' in which accusations of unbelievable duplicity are spliced with bizarre 'confessions'. Not merely have the Moscow Trials never been publicly repudiated, but the various trials after the Second World War, in the Soviet satellites especially, and the routine charges of complicity in worldwide conspiracies sporadically levelled at various rivals or opponents of ruling factions within the regime, are clearly modelled on the events of the thirties in the Soviet Union.

When I started out to do a study of the Moscow Trials and the Great Purge I intended to explain to the contemporary reader what had brought them about and what effects they have had on the world of today.

There has been a considerable literature on this phenomenon, most of it fragmentary (personal memoirs and partial studies). The very few general accounts are defective largely through their omission of three factors: the historical background, the meaning of 'Trotskyism', and Stalin's motivation.

Yet filling in these gaps within the chronological framework of the Trials and Purges alone proved impossible. I found myself going back to the original act of genesis – the Bolshevik putsch in 1917.

I found I had to explain the emergence of a secular religion – the Marxist cult still dominant in the Soviet bloc, a cult that after being paralleled for a quarter of a century by the quasi-deification of Stalin has survived his death with no apparent loss of solidity.

I found myself giving a thematic analysis of Soviet history – the Bolshevik seizure of power, the Bolsheviks' decision to try some form of socialism in a backward country, the institution of terror to man-handle the population, and the establishment of a dogmatic orthodoxy that engendered a new world-view, heightened morale, and sanctioned repressions.

To lay bare the grand theme arising out of the disentanglement of these complex events I have had to omit the mention of their countless victims. The names of only a few key figures are referred to; the rest are subordinated to the articulation of the theme.

J. C.

1
Introduction: Apparatus, Orthodoxy, Divinity

For technical brilliance, the October 1917 putsch of the Bolshevik Party can hardly have been surpassed. Camouflaged by demagogy masquerading as ideology, framed by the war and the democratic order established through the Tsarist breakdown of February 1917, and propped up by immense secret funds from the German Imperial Government,[1] the Bolshevik putsch placed a handful of men in control of the biggest country in the world. They managed, moreover, to mask the entire enterprise with a matchlessly successful mythology.

In that mythology the putsch was not a putsch at all, but the end-phase of a groundswell in the life of mankind: the Proletariat, represented by the Bolshevik Party, had finally burst through conventional politics in order to undertake the radical overhauling of human society – to replace the malignant anarchy of capitalism by an orderly, moral organization. Society could become, at last, the expression of man's true nature – kind, humane, rational.

Marxist tradition had always assumed that the transition to socialism would necessarily occur in an advanced capitalist country, where the high level of technology and productivity, paralleled by a concomitant social transformation, would engender a proletariat strong enough to disrupt and replace the bourgeoisie. Nothing of the sort happened; the capitalist order in Europe, and still more so in America, emerged from the strains of the First World War stronger than ever.

For a few years the Bolshevik leaders consoled themselves with the prospect of an upset elsewhere. The turmoil in Germany following the extinction of the monarchy could be interpreted as a ripening medium for the Revolution. The notion that things were about to be whirled aloft once more by the irresistible movement of History, as foretold by the Dialectic, for a while remained plausible within the Soviet milieu.

The success of the New Economic Policy, initiated in 1921, sharpened the Bolshevik dilemma still further: if the Bolshevik Party, having taken power in 1917 on the 'theory' that it was merely the vanguard of a

I

general revolutionary upsurge, was now confined within a country too backward to ensure the economy of abundance needed for socialism, and if capitalism in Russia was now reviving through the New Economic Policy, what could the Party do about it? Could socialism be created in Russia *at all*?

The Bolsheviks had assumed the government of a vast country: they were committed to the day-to-day tasks involved in national administration. The very fact that they had taken power in the name of an ideal meant that they were obliged to reorganize society on a commensurate scale. The Party, formerly a coterie of theorists, agitators, propagandists and conspirators, became a bureaucracy. Ideology became incarnate in an 'apparatus'. This fundamental process was carried out through the agency of Joseph Stalin, General Secretary of the Party.

Stalin was already in actual control of the Party in Lenin's lifetime: he had achieved this in the course of 1923. His magnification had taken place almost imperceptibly; none of the Bolshevik intellectuals, including Lenin and Trotsky, seemed to grasp its consequences. Stalin, regarded by them as a lowly, though energetic and efficient 'practical' – i.e., not a thinker – was, in harmony with his role as a wheel-horse of the Party, modest and unassuming in manner. Very short, like Lenin, with a slightly withered left arm, pock-marked face, yellow eyes, sallow complexion and webbed feet, Stalin had devoted most of his career to 'practical' tasks – holding up trains, editing Party newspapers, organizing. His diffident, quiet manner masked a temperament at once wily, perverse and vindictive.

For some years during the twenties, at a time when open discussion seemed to revolve around broad philosophical themes, Stalin was not so 'evident' as the voluble intellectuals.

His practical functions assumed titanic dimensions. As the bureaucracy, geared to the outsize goals of the Party, expanded fantastically, so the office of General Secretary, the hub of the Party, grew accordingly.

As General Secretary Stalin built up a network of strong points within the Party apparatus: he did this so pervasively, so organically and naturally, through the patronage inherent in the office, that it was always possible for him to attain his aims in a way that was formally unobtrusive: a vote would confirm his own decision. The functionaries he nominated as secretaries of regional, district or local Party branches realized that their jobs came straight from him; as the number of people directly dependent on his patronage gradually swelled, his power swelled with them.

From this functional point of view, the Bolshevik Party had never really been sovereign at all. How, indeed, could a group of thousands exercise power? Nor had the Central Committee of the Party ever really wielded power: its executive functions were concentrated in the Politburo.

Nor was the Politburo ever a fully empowered collective either; even during Lenin's lifetime he himself would form a decision after mere consultation with a sort of inner core. As Stalin's appointees filled the apparatus, the power of decision came to rest more and more exclusively within his own hands. He merely formalized the *de facto* situation within the Party.

Stalin's success was guaranteed by a still broader phenomenon – the general passivity of the Party, especially on the levels just below the summit. This was itself the result of the Party purges that had started very early on, in April 1922, while Lenin was still very much in evidence; Stalin had embarked on them without opposition. At that time they had been, as it were, technical; but beginning in 1924 the Party purges, spasmodically staged by Stalin, systematically excluded all Communists interested in theory, ensuring the docility of the new bureaucratic caste throughout the wrangling that characterized Bolshevik rule until the end of the twenties.

Thus the original Party membership – devoted, idealistic, 'conscious' – was swamped by masses of passive, careerist novices. It was against this background that the phenomenon of 'Trotskyism' emerged.

'Permanent Revolution', Trotsky's major contribution to Marxism, had been incorporated in the Marxist 'justification' of the October putsch in a country unfit for socialism; without action by the industrial working class in an advanced country, it was impossible to devise a programme for socialists holding power in an agricultural country.

With the failure of all Bolshevik hopes to materialize outside Russia, however, Permanent Revolution became a liability. It was replaced by the dogma of socialism in one country – the contention that in a big country like the Soviet Union socialism could be realized in spite of 'classical Marxism'.

In the general discussion of industrialization no question of principle was involved at first. All Bolsheviks believed in State planning, as the only method of controlling the industrialization of the country. Planning, as such, was taken for granted, but only under different conditions – namely, in a highly advanced, concentrated and efficient economy – not in a country like Russia, with more than twenty million small farms dispersed all over a huge countryside, with industry pulverized and private trade still rudimentary.

With the decision to forget at least the immediate perspective of a big revolution throughout the capitalist world, Trotsky became an indigestible element. His destruction, moreover, was bound to take a theological form: he became the target of an adjunct indispensable for the parvenu regime – doctrine. A newly established orthodoxy encased the apparatus.

The Bolshevik Party, Guardian of the Faith, was obliged to stretch that faith to encompass an inherently contradictory position. Its mythology, designed to salvage revolutionary idealism, the pretensions of Marxism, and, most particularly, the ruling caste that had so swiftly clambered out of the bloody mire of Soviet Russia, was institutionalized. A cult of orthodoxy was established.

The creation of such a cult was inevitable if only because Marxism in Russia had to be transformed, and that transformation could not be acknowledged.

With no revolution in the industrial West, and with a socialist party in control of a country unfit for socialism, it was plain that the situation had to be reassessed.

Could Marx be wrong? Or at least irrelevant? That was out of the question – he just had to be interpreted.

It was just here, in the interpretation needed by the regime to tailor Marxism to its unique embodiment in the Soviet State, that the apparatus was to play a decisive role.

The claim to infallibility is derived from faith in Marxism as a science. It naturally has all the scientific prerequisites – certainty, predictability, *assurance*. Marxist discourse, beginning with Marx himself, streamlined by Engels and given a scholastic rigidity by the Russian Marxists, abounds in phrases like 'iron laws', and 'astronomical certainty', describing the working-out of a natural process that only the Right Thinker with the Right Key is capable of penetrating.

Unfortunately, however, one of the distressing aspects of Marxism as a science is that it is very hard to get the hang of it. Unlike other sciences, whose principles can first be acquired and then applied, Marxism, while stiff with 'iron laws' of all kinds, is at the same time extraordinarily subtle.

Accordingly, a Marxist party in power must find a means independent of its beliefs for reaching a decision that it can claim to harmonize with them. Thus in the Bolshevik Party, during the twenties, the 'General Line' functioned, bureaucratically, as a sanction for all decisions. The Bolshevik regime was embarking on countless zigzags, from the point of view of its professed Marxism; this necessarily generated the contrary notion of a *straight* General Line, since it was just such zigzags that had to be denied. All decisions were invested with the mystical authority of the State, implemented by the Political Police: both Party and State, ostensibly grounded in the 'scientific' methodology of Marxism, became a kind of Holy Inquisition.

Trotsky, a 'classical Marxist' who still believed in the imminent 'explosion' of capitalist society and the consequent Dictatorship of the Proletariat throughout the industrialized world, had to cling to the conviction that the Bolshevik monopoly in Russia was a mere preamble to the imminent collapse of capitalism everywhere. The measures he proposed for the Bolshevik regime were, to his mind, mere makeshifts, meaningless, ultimately, unless the Bolshevik fortress was relieved by a cosmic upsurge.

Quite incapable of organizing a following, Trotsky never had a faction, and had, in fact, been powerless since long before Lenin's death. He remained a celebrity; within the Party it merely seemed that he was being outvoted. He had no effective say in Party decisions from the end of the Civil War on.

Despite his panache and abilities, Trotsky remained strangely passive. Aloof, haughty, indeed, *shy*, perhaps partly because of his Jewish origins, he was incapable of presenting himself in public *on his own authority*.

He had, moreover, a crippling inhibition: he was completely committed to the ikonization not only of the Marxist scriptures but of the Bolshevik Party itself. Individual Bolsheviks were not much – obtuse, cowardly, passive – the Party was everything!

He had accepted wholeheartedly the dogma of 'Party unity': he had subscribed to the formal banning of 'factionalism' secretly instituted by Lenin in 1921; he acquiesced in the apotheosis of Lenin; he never contested the absolute legitimacy of the Bolshevik dictatorship, which he considered essential for the 'besieged fortress' of the Soviet Union. It was impossible for him to criticize the Party seriously.

Oppositionists might maintain that the Party was making incorrect decisions, yet those decisions were wholly legitimate; they were *the Party's decisions*. It was always possible for Stalin to speak *in the name* of the Party; there was a razor-sharp edge between carping at the correctness of the decision and challenging its legitimacy. Trotsky could not attack the legitimacy of the Stalin faction's claim to be the Party, either; hence he was necessarily inhibited in appealing away from its decisions to the fictitious 'masses'.

This curious ambivalence was evident in detail as well. The Oppositionists, for example, were in a position where they had both to emphasize and to disregard the significance of Stalin's infringements on legality within the Party. While claiming that Stalin was creating a new regime within the Party, at the same time they acknowledged the authority of the Central Committee, a body that even in the struggles against the early Oppositionists of the twenties had been turned by Stalin into a rubber stamp.

Hence it was difficult for them to make much of Stalin's manifest duplicity whenever he expressed his humility *vis-à-vis* the Party, or even to castigate his hypocrisy, since either would have been an insult to the Party – *the Party!*

There was no real 'struggle for power' within the Party at all during the twenties. Trotsky did not fight, nor did the other Oppositionists: what they produced was an immense amount of verbiage, incapable of influencing the summit of the Party. Later on, to be sure, Trotsky was to write, quite sincerely, that he had 'lost power' because his revolutionary *ideas* were submerged by the tide of bureaucratic reaction; it was also in the interest of Stalin's apologists to explain his victory by intellectual factors.

But Stalin merely utilized theory to buttress a position of power. Thus it became 'realistic' for Party members to forget the romantic delusions of early Bolshevism and create a party that would be 'monolithic' in a new sense – obedient, zealous, *efficient*. And above all obedient to the centre – Stalin.

Part of the point of this whole transformation was that it had to be accomplished behind slogans that *sounded* the same, so that in the very midst of what reactionary philistines took to be change, the Party was more identical than ever – in short, that Stalin was Lenin and better. It was this retention of traditional phraseology that was, and has remained, the most misleading factor in the evolution of the Communist Party. Instead of a style of analysis, a style of thinking, Marxism became a style of ritual and a style of action, and the Party first an apparatus, then a church.

Back in 1902, Lenin, paraphrasing Archimedes, had boasted: 'Give us organized professional revolutionaries and we shall turn Russia upside down.'[2] He thought such groups had to be infused by 'spirit'. For Stalin the organization was to be bound together by socio-material interests and the consequent *esprit de corps*: it was no longer a band of brothers but an *élite* caste.

He further extracted the implication of the word professional; he coined a phrase of his own: Party activists. '. . . Activists, if rightly used, can represent an enormous force capable of working miracles.'[3] Through these activists Stalin ousted all his opponents. No enemies, or *potential* enemies were to be allowed: the question of personal convictions or past services became irrelevant.

The reverential treatment of the Party past naturally encompassed

Trotsky's biography. Since Trotsky had joined the Party so late, his non-Bolshevik past was disinterred and picked to pieces. As the frictions within the leadership began bubbling to the surface after the Civil War, that non-Bolshevik past could easily be made to outweigh his brief affiliation with the Party.

Nothing was easier than to stir up the violent polemics he had engaged in with everyone else in the Russian revolutionary movement, including, alas, Lenin himself. Before the putsch polemics, characterized by unusual ferocity, had been the medium of the movement. It proved to be child's play to ram a wedge between Trotsky and the Bolshevik Party. All that had to be done was to circulate his bona-fide writings – his description, for instance, of Lenin as a 'shyster' with a 'repulsive style', a 'dishonest accountant', an 'intriguer, a disorganizer and an exploiter of Russian backwardness'. All such polemical routine belonged, of course, to an era, long since past, when opinions could be freely expressed. Hence exhuming such remarks in an era when hagiographical immobility was replacing the elastic interchanges of real life, put them into a totally different context, and transformed polemics into a device in a factional contest guided by the victors.

It was more difficult to undermine Trotsky's reputation in the minds of the newer Party. In the early twenties Trotsky was considered authoritative and, with respect to his personal talents, unique. Among the Party people, especially the rank-and-file, it was taken for granted that Trotsky, who had stage-managed the October putsch and the establishment of the Soviet State, towered above the other Bolsheviks as a candidate for leadership after Lenin's death. Thus in the public arena Trotsky had to be undermined far more tactfully and on the basis of apparent principle.

Yet this too proved remarkably simple. To outsiders the disputes between the leaders could be presented as theoretical divergences; within the topmost institutions of the Party theory was a mere adjunct to Stalin's majority control. Thus he could conceal behind the veil of committee action what in fact were chess moves.

The abruptness of the switch in the official estimates of Trotsky's career is strikingly illustrated in two contrasting quotations from Stalin himself; in 1918 he wrote an article in which, in spite of his otherwise obvious intent to slight Trotsky's role he nevertheless found it expedient, in the atmosphere of the time, to say this:

All the work of practical organization of the insurrection was carried out under the immediate leadership of the chairman of the Petrograd Soviet, Comrade Trotsky. We can say with certainty that the swift passing of the garrison to the side of the Soviet and the bold execution of the work of the

Military Revolutionary Committee the Party owes principally and above all to Comrade Trotsky.[5]

At the time this was, if anything, a quite minimal, indeed somewhat hostile way of summing up Trotsky's role. Only six years later, Stalin could write the following: 'Comrade Trotsky, a comparatively new man in our Party in the period of October, neither did nor could play a *special* part, either in the Party or in the October Revolution.'[6]

Stalin, like all Marxists, had opposed the concept of 'socialism in one country' as late as April 1924; yet in the autumn of that same year he enunciated this idea as having the status not only of a theory, but as being the *official* theory, which from then on it was to remain. Since it was the specific switch away from traditional Marxism, it was Trotsky's contrary theory – Permanent Revolution – that triggered his obliteration.

And since this had to be brought about by Marxist Dialectics, the ideological campaign within the Party turned into a deluge of casuistry and logic-chopping required to obscure the transition from traditional Marxism to the Marxism-Leninism of the new Soviet orthodoxy. The Party membership as well as the *élite* were all reduced to numbness by the obsessional verbiage and the stupefying tediousness of 'Marxist' discourse. In this process Trotsky was the loser, since a loss of interest in the very debate implied the disappearance of the only audience his arguments might have appealed to.

The venom discharged against Stalin's opponents became torrential; from the middle of the twenties, meetings were mere slanging matches. As Stalin's control enveloped the membership of the Party his authority was used to stifle discussion entirely and to destroy opponents by personal abuse. A catchword was created to cover the expulsion of all those with some Trotskyite tinge in their pasts. They were discharged not as such, but as 'bureaucrats' and 'babblers'. The concept of babbling could naturally be stretched to cover any kind of discussion at all. Anyone who was ousted from an actual office within the Party was automatically expelled as a member, too, regardless of any past role.

From the very beginning Stalin had complete control of the Secretariat, a key organ that actually composed the programme of the Party and of the State: both the Politburo and the Orgburo (organizational bureau) were called upon simply to confirm all decisions already made by the Secretariat. Stalin was thus in a position to make all fundamental decisions with respect to the topmost posts in the Party apparatus, the national economy, the army, the trade unions and even the Foreign Affairs Commissariat. Functionally speaking, of course, this assumption of the competence of the Orgburo was tantamount to the absorption of the functions of the Politburo, which thus became no more than a mask for the omnipotence of the Secretariat. It even got to the point where Politburo members were told by external sources what was being done within the Secretariat.

This was a very natural, indeed, an inevitable development, since both the Politburo and the Orgburo were bodies that came together only at stated intervals whereas the huge governmental apparatus had to function daily. Hence, even if the Politburo and Orgburo had been able to overcome the inherent impotence of large committees, they would not have been fit to decide on countless current questions.

The whole of society was now the enemy of the regime. With the peasantry (proprietors, real or potential) four-fifths of the population to begin with, and with the working class a small fraction of it, to say nothing of the surviving members of the middle classes, the intelligentsia, former functionaries, the clergy, and so on – the Bolshevik Party was obliged to manipulate the population of a huge country.

Even before the Civil War it was manifest that an instrument for handling the people was imperative; with the bilateral Terror that sprang up during the Civil War, and with the profound churning up of the population that was soon to follow, the Political Police, under a variety of successive names – Cheka, OGPU, GPU, NKVD, MVD – became the paramount factor in Soviet life.

It became a matter of course for all appointments both to the Party staff and to the State administration – the same thing – to be carried out without even informing the Politburo. It was quite legal, since a statute had been framed for this very purpose, to the effect that 'current executive and organizational work is directed by the Secretariat'.

Yet it was evidently not enough for Stalin to have in his hands the mere instrument of the Secretariat; he also contrived an assumption of authority beyond legality, by infiltrating, purging and thus dominating the Central Committee itself. As General Secretary he had taken pains to select the personnel of the Central Committee: after he had got rid of all members with a definable past (Old Bolsheviks and so on) he proceeded to reconstruct the Central Committee itself.

Before Stalin the Secretariat and the working staff of the Central Committee had had merely technical and administrative functions, revolving around control measures to ensure that all resolutions passed by the topmost organizations of the State – the Central Committee plenum, the Politburo and the Orgburo – were in fact implemented. Theoretically the Secretariat and the Central Committee were not supposed to take independent action at all; they were wholly dependent

on specific instructions issued by the three above-mentioned organs.
Just because of this it was natural to appoint people with the reputation of 'administrators', 'executors' – a reputation that had been Stalin's,
too, from his earliest days.

Having purged the Central Committee of all individuals not specifically subservient to him, Stalin was reconstructing it, fitting it out with
a variety of supplementary divisions (organization, personnel, culture
and propaganda, agitation and mass campaigns, etc.). All these new
sections were generally headed by well-known Central Committee
members also selected by Stalin.

At the same time, however, Stalin was creating *another* special
instrument of his own, his 'unofficial cabinet', later officially sanctioned
in Party documents as 'Comrade Stalin's secretariat'. This purely
personal cabinet was scarcely even noticed. Its members, who were not
on the Central Committee at all, were usually younger people, regarded
by the run-of-the-mill Party people as zealous workers with no personal
ambitions or aspirations to the stratosphere of statesmanship or
ideology. They were visible flitting about everywhere, preoccupied by
what seemed to be the chores of bureaucratic life – writing minutes,
giving technical information, passing round snacks at conferences,
tidying their superiors' desks – doing the donkey work, in short, with
an air of ostentatious obsequiousness.

'Comrade Stalin's secretariat' was quite distinct from the Secretariat
of the Central Committee, which Stalin had *also* hand-picked by
exercising one of his authorized functions. All questions touching on
policy, both internal and external, had to be scrutinized and in fact
decided by 'Comrade Stalin's secretariat' even before being handed up
to the chief organs of the Central Committee and allocated to the
relevant sections. All the sections had to do, in fact, was to confirm
whatever had been recommended by the technical people in Stalin's
cabinet, and then pass it on to be ratified by the topmost Party
authorities – the Central Committee Secretariat, the Politburo and the
Orgburo.

All moot questions had to be passed on to various Politburo committees – either permanent or *ad hoc*. But even though these committees
generally consisted of Central Committee members who were not part
of Stalin's cabinet they were dependent on it anyhow, since it was
Stalin's cabinet that saw to two vital matters – the drafting of the
various proposals and their circulation through the appropriate
superior Party organs.

This bureaucratic control was supplemented by something more
immediate – the control of individuals.

Towards the end of the twenties Stalin proclaimed that: 'Everything depends on personnel.' This meant that Stalin's cabinet, which became essentially a 'laboratory for filtering personnel', could govern, under Stalin's eye, both the domestic and the foreign policy of the Soviet Union through the manipulation of personnel in the topmost posts – the Party, the State and the army. Hence the career of every Party member, beginning with the secretary of the smallest local Party committee, up to a People's Commissar, was in the hands of one branch or another of Stalin's private cabinet.

The mechanism of this whole process was simple.

There had once been a 'Secret Section' of the Central Committee; it held the confidential dossiers of the Party and of the government. As Stalin's apparatus took shape, the Secret Section, after subsiding, apparently, for a while, was revived again and incorporated in his *private* cabinet as the 'Special Section'. This time its activities were not only *really* secret, but even its existence was not officially known until 1934; at no time was it confirmed or discussed in any official Party papers.

The Special Section was set up in order to control the Soviet summits – the Party, the government, the army and the Political Police itself. It had a ramified staff of clandestine agents, and a separate subsection dealing with personnel on the highest Party level. At a moment's notice it could tell Stalin anything he wanted to know about all aspects, both private and political, of the lives of all the Party and State heads. It exercised a meticulous censorship over the private correspondence of the most important functionaries, some of them Stalin's most intimate colleagues.

The Special Section was supposed to watch over every move and if possible every thought of everyone in Stalin's closest circle; as soon as enough notations were put into their personal dossiers the Special Section could decide what was to be done with them. Anyone about to be ousted would be handled in accordance with his position in the hierarchy by the relevant segment of the Central Committee: a topmost government functionary who was not on the Central Committee would simply be dislodged by the relevant department of the Central Committee; if a member he would be handled by the Secretariat itself or sometimes by the Orgburo.

The Special Section was thus in a position to eliminate anyone from any post; the post would then be filled by an immediate replacement from the Personnel Section. Because of this fundamental, life-and-death organizational power of the Special Section, even the highest State officials – People's Commissars, Central Committee men and so on –

went about in awe of the 'technical employees' of the Central Committee. If technology is conceived of, in the modern age, as a decisive factor in everything – as Stalin himself once said – his use of completely subordinate, faceless subalterns as 'technical employees' who through his own personal authority were in a position to decide the fate of literally everyone in the country, illustrates the technology of personnel management at its most effective.

After 1928 there was no longer such a thing as a secretary of any Party organization anywhere in the Soviet Union who had been put in office in accordance with legal Party procedure, to say nothing of what had once been boasted of as 'intra-Party democracy'. A wide range of pretexts was used to dislodge all secretaries elected under the old official procedures, including a form of kicking upstairs into important-sounding industrial or agricultural positions, or even, more rarely, administrative or diplomatic positions. Vacant posts were then occupied by appointees of Stalin's Personnel Section.

Miniature duplicates of the central Special Section of Stalin's private cabinet were attached to the Party staffs throughout the country; these were always under people sent out from Moscow, from Stalin's agencies, and though theoretically they were supposed to be under the local secretaries they were in fact responsible to no one but Stalin's private cabinet. These miniature, local Special Sections had no administrative authority, but were supposed to concentrate on furnishing comprehensive and sound information to the Special Section in Moscow. Each one had its own string of informers on the spot and functioned independently of the Party committee; it was also given a small staff, from three to ten, of highly trained office personnel within the Party committee apparatus itself.

The local Special Section had to be represented at all meetings of the local Party Committee's bureau and secretariat, by a recording secretary together with his special typist, who was a stenographer as well. The special sections in the provinces were used as the channel between the Central Committee of the Party in Moscow and the local committees; they took charge of coded wires and confidential instructions coming from the Central Committee; they deciphered and distributed them while the local committee secretary had to use the local Special Sections in order to send on his own confidential material to Moscow. In addition the Special Section had the use of special couriers on the staff of the Political Police; these couriers transported important documents back and forth between Moscow and the rest of the country and were less bothered by outside interference than a governmental minister. They had commissions bearing the signature of the minister in charge of State

Security giving them personal immunity from arrest and also authorizing them to demand all kinds of assistance from all Party and State authorities.

To put all this in a nutshell, Stalin had managed in the space of a few years to create a bona-fide government responsible to him alone, and to do so very nearly without the knowledge of the vast apparatus taken as a whole. He had accomplished all this by the beginning of 1929.

Politics simmered now well beneath the surface; above, the only thing visible was the tip of the iceberg – the cult of Soviet orthodoxy and Stalin's personal pre-eminence, possibly the most extraordinary personal cult in history.

It swiftly overshadowed all facets of life in the Soviet Union and loomed throughout the universe of the Communist Parties of the world. Perhaps the most striking single element in this cult, aside from its monstrous extravagance, was the rapidity with which, in the full light of day, it achieved its full dimensions. The pace of Stalin's apotheosis directly reflected the pace with which the Soviet apparatus expanded to keep up with its staggering socio-economic undertakings. Only a short time before his unique pre-eminence became manifest – a time to be reckoned, no doubt, in mere months – Stalin had been known to the Party as no more than an 'organizer', a concept that did not seem to mean much until the organization itself became so big. It was in fact a rather vague term, looked down upon by the 'ideological' Bolsheviks – the thinkers, speakers and writers.

What had originally been Stalin's practical, humble attributes – punctuality, zeal, an ability to work hard, plus a natural taciturnity, in the beginning, indeed, almost muteness – were eventually magnified by the coefficient, so to speak, of the magnification of the Party machine. They became attributes of *power*.

In harmony with the monolithic regime launched formally at the April Plenum and the Sixteenth Party Conference in 1929, the cult was all-pervasive. It established Stalin's worship not only in the Party itself and in politics, hence throughout the country – that went without saying – but also in history. It was a concept that broadened out at once to take in all aspects of life – sciences, the arts, the humanities, philosophy.

A new formula was coined: 'The Leader of our Party – Comrade Stalin'. The Party ceased being referred to as the 'Party of Lenin', but became the 'Party of Lenin-Stalin'. Soon Stalin was the 'greatest'; Lenin, sadly outdistanced, was merely 'great'.

Stalin became the paramount Marxist theoretician (only two years before he had been unanimously excluded from the Communist Academy because he lacked 'specialized research in the domain of Marxism');

economists transformed Stalin into the Paramount Economist; historians into the Paramount Historian. Deep thinkers confessed themselves flabbergasted by his terrific Dialectics.

By the time of Stalin's fiftieth birthday, 21 December 1929, he was the paramount, and for that matter unique authority on almost literally every known area of knowledge. It was clearly he who authorized the whole campaign, which until the end of his life – nearly a quarter of a century later – was to be unflaggingly promoted.

It is impossible to do more than suggest the flavour of Stalin's apotheosis. What must be imagined is its overwhelming amplitude, due to the government control of all media in a huge country. The sheer magnitude of the phenomenon cannot be encompassed by a book.

Stalin's glorification went far beyond that of Marx and Engels, far beyond Lenin's. Though he fell just short of technical deification, he can fairly be compared with Muhammad and the Buddha.

At its lowest level, 'genius' became the epithet indissolubly associated with his name. The phrase 'Stalin the Genius' became so routine, from 1930 on, that its omission was *ipso facto* suspect; only furtive hostility was thought to explain it. Stalin was endlessly painted and depicted in outsize, heroic attitudes; his effigy was broadcast ubiquitously, at the very least on medals. Countless cities were named for him, as was a specially hard steel; his features, his name, his person permeated the life of the Soviet Union.

Writers as a class proved adept at formulating dithyrambs. Stalin, combining his love of power with a feeling, perhaps, of inherent worthlessness, must have felt reassured by the constant praise: the writers obliged with extravagant suppleness. Here is a tiny sampling of characteristic quotations from the Soviet press during the thirties:

Alexis Tolstoy:
I want to howl, roar, shriek, bawl with rapture at the thought that we are living in the days of the most glorious, the one and only, the incomparable Stalin! Our breath, our blood, our life – here take it, O great Stalin!
Thou art the bright Sun of the people, the Sun of our times that never sets, and more than our Sun, for in the Sun there is no wisdom.

Pravda 27 May, 1938
[Stalin is among the] profound connoisseurs and critics of Hegel, [one of the] most authoritative experts on the problems of contemporary philosophy.

Revolution & Culture
At bottom certain prognostications of Aristotle have been incarnated and deciphered in their full amplitude only by Stalin.

Cultural Front
Socrates and Stalin are the summits of intelligence.

The full significance of Kantian theories in contemporary science can be definitely understood only in the light of the last letter of Comrade Stalin. (By a professor of the Communist Academy.)

Literaturnaya Gazeta
I write books, I am an author; I dream of creating lasting work. I love a girl in a new way, I am perpetuated in my children. . . . All this is thanks to thee, O great teacher Stalin. Our love, our devotion, our strength, our hearts, our heroism, our life – all are thine. Take them, great Stalin. . . .

Izvestiya
Can anyone really write on anything unless he knows his Stalin? Never! Without Stalin no one can understand anything or write anything of interest.

Kalinin
Ask me who best understands the Russian language, and I reply – Stalin. [This was all the more piquant since Stalin's Russian speech was well-known to be foreign; he had a poor accent and worse diction.]

When the tercentenary of Spinoza's birth was commemorated in the Soviet Union – rather curiously, perhaps – not merely the usual quotations were given from Marx, Engels and Lenin but also several from Stalin, which had, if possible, even less relationship to Spinoza or for that matter to philosophy in general.

The Seventeenth Party Congress in 1934 opened with the extravagant language that had become routine.

Bukharin referred to Stalin as the 'field-marshal of the revolution'; every other sentence began with: 'Stalin was right . . .'; 'As Stalin said . . .' The old epithets 'shock-brigader', 'legendary figure', 'beloved commander', 'thinker of genius', 'adored Stalin' – had become a little stale, so others were newly coined: 'the steel colossus', 'the great engineer', 'great disciple', 'greatest of theorists', 'finest of Leninists', 'Our great wise Leader', 'Leader of the workers of the whole world', 'Engineer in the Locomotive of the World Revolution', 'Wise leader of the peoples', 'Father of the Peoples'. They were consummated by 'greatest of the greatest'. The note of manufactured ecstasy, of penetrating obsequiousness became the most characteristic element of Soviet prose.

The custom spread of an audience rising to its feet and bursting into applause whenever Stalin's name was mentioned at public assemblies; all speeches had set introductions and conclusions, incantations to Stalin's uniqueness; they could barely be heard above the constant hysterical clamour for more, amidst spontaneous ovations and tumultuous applause.

Stalin's response to this torrential sycophancy was modest: 'I am ready to give to the cause of the Party in the future, as in the past, all my strength and my talents, and if necessary, all my blood, drop by drop.'

Plainly, this collided both with Soviet doctrine and for that matter with Marxism, since Stalin's paramountcy was never formulated as a principle: the Soviet dictatorship did not evolve a *theory* of leadership; it simply deified Stalin while paying lip-service as usual to Soviet democracy and even to the fiction of the Party's collective authority.

This was against the background of the nightmarish famine of the early thirties, the destruction of the German working-class movement and the triumph of Hitlerism, not to mention the various defeats of the Communist movement and the Communist International all over Europe and in China.

Against all this fawning, Stalin successfully projected the image of a spartan, selfless leader. Like most of the Bolshevik leaders Stalin, too, lived on a scale that would be called modest: he had a two-room flat in the Kremlin; his habits were frugal; he owned practically nothing. As General Secretary he got perhaps about 1,000 roubles a month (in purchasing power about £15 at the time). The ruler of a sixth of the earth's surface got less than an American family on relief.

Of his dozen secretaries at this time, one would accept this salary on Stalin's behalf. On the first of the month Stalin's secretary would receive a small bill for rent, another bill for his board. When he took a rest in the Caucasus his secretary would send in the regulation payment for a sojourn in a rest house; every month his secretary would send 3 per cent of Stalin's salary to the Party to pay his dues. As a member of the government, he naturally had a pass for free train rides; he also had the use of a car, in fact, any number of cars, which he did not, of course, own. Owning nothing, Stalin had no bank account, no savings deposits, no wallet. It was all on the public account: the roads built for him, the cars from State garages, the countless servants. In fact Stalin never touched money at all. Frugal living with a vengeance!

2
Kirov's Murder and the Great Charades

The Seventeenth Party Congress in 1934 seemed to have put the seal on the cult of Stalin the Genius. At the same time, behind the façade of the Congress, Stalin's position was being eroded by a potential rival – Sergei Kirov, head of the Leningrad section of the Party. Stalin's power was threatened at the very moment he seemed to be more authoritative than ever; the result was the launching of the entire vast enterprise of the 'Show Trials' and the 'Purge'.

At the end of the twenties, with his victory over Left and Right factions consolidated, Stalin had embarked on the twin programmes of industrialization and collectivization. He did so rather off-handedly.

The decree of collectivization, which was to bring about the death of millions, was announced by Stalin on his own initiative, quite unexpectedly on 27 December 1929, a few days after his fiftieth birthday, without even going through the formality of a Central Committee decision. 'We are at a new turning point in our policy and are beginning the liquidation of the kulaks as a class on the basis of total collectivization.'[1]

'Kulak' (*fist*) was slang for a rich peasant; in Soviet statistics it took in some five million people; extended, it included about thirteen million quasi-kulaks, the well-to-do and the sub-kulaks.[2] During collectivization the word was arbitrarily manipulated to cover any peasants who fell foul of the decree for any reason whatever.

The drive for agricultural reorganization was linked to the general aim of increasing the economic output of the country by a maximum degree of industrialization. The basis for industrialization – a form of 'primitive socialist accumulation' as Trotsky had put it – initially had to be the labour of the peasantry followed by the labour of the workers in the projected industrial plant. The labour of both categories had to be underpaid to allow for the surplus to be poured into an industrial plant that naturally had to take a little time to become profitable.

The initial idea for a systematic acceleration of the process of industrializing Russia had been expressed by Trotsky directly the Civil War was over; at that time it had been rejected as too extreme. The specific form of a Five-Year-Plan had been outlined as early as the end of 1925 or the beginning of 1926: its discussion was restricted at first to the Politburo.

When Stalin took up the programme of accelerated industrialization, in conjunction with the policy of collectivization, Trotsky's original estimates seemed far too timid. Stalin, having first hung back on the tempo of industrialization on the basis of Trotsky's formula, now lunged forward with a crash programme, perhaps recognizing the general psychological longing for an heroic effort that would transcend the deep depression caused by the increasingly savage reprisals within the Party and the feeling of siege weighing on the country during the middle twenties.

The forcible collectivization of agriculture required immense factories to supply farming equipment. This called for so much production that the regime began outbidding itself in its attempt not merely to fulfil but to overfulfil the original Five-Year-Plan: the slogan of the period was to 'overtake and pass America', the obvious model. Government departments slipped into the game of creating plans – often fantastic – in what was to be called, retroactively, 'administrative ecstasy'.

By the end of the Plan about 20–22 per cent of the peasants were originally supposed to be in collective farms; but it was decided as early as the first year of the already over-accelerated Plan, amidst the general euphoria, that more than 60 per cent of the peasants should be put in collective farms by the *third year* of the Plan; finally *all* peasants were supposed to be collectivized by the end of the Plan.

The pace was remarkable. The percentage of collectives went up from 4.1 per cent (of households) in October 1929 to 21 per cent on 20 January 1930. *Less than two months later* (by 10 March 1930) 58 per cent of all farms were collective. In fact, more than half the total number of peasant households were squeezed into the new system within the space of five months.

The peasants resisted with furious obduracy. They even forced the government into a brief, temporary retreat, but the campaign was soon resumed with full force. In 1932 the Stalin government created what was doubtless the largest man-made famine in history.

The immediate cause of the famine was the government's insistence on maintaining its high quotas. When the peasants baulked, thinking – rather naïvely – that the government would never actually seize their food in order to maintain artificially high quotas, the government went ahead and seized the quotas by force.

The peasants turned the countryside into a shambles. In the first few months of collectivization they butchered more than 15,000,000 cattle, almost 40,000,000 goats and sheep, 7,000,000 pigs, and 4,000,000 horses. This continued till the cattle reserves of the country were reduced by more than half.

The peasants ate up the quotas; even the medium peasants and the poor participated in the carnage. There were matchless scenes of mass gluttony, with people stuffing themselves to the point of vomiting, gorging themselves over and over.

The Political Police had to be called in: they slaughtered hundreds of thousands of women and children as well as men. When the government seized its quotas the peasants were simply starved to death.

The campaign generated its own excesses if only because its massive character, reflected in the sheer number of victims, entailed a certain inhumanity of execution, apart from its specific objectives. With countless peasants of all kinds – rich, medium, poor – being arrested and deported and their property confiscated, the campaign was bound to become both chaotic and ferocious. The Political Police itself reported (28 February 1930) the motto of many 'dekulakization' units: 'drink, eat – it's all ours!'[3]

After the horrors of the collectivization programme were over the class that had been revolutionized was now asked to run the new collective institutions that had destroyed so many of them. A heavy mortgage on Soviet agriculture!

From the point of view of the regime, the campaign of starvation was unavoidable, since it had to maintain two vital factors of the Soviet economy – the urban standard of living and the amount of grain to be exported. Politically speaking, moreover, it was essential to smash the morale of the peasants. For this, specific reprisals (execution for stealing grain, etc.) were brought into play.

Winston Churchill reports a conversation with Stalin at the end of the Second World War:

'Tell me,' Churchill asked, 'have the stresses of this war been as bad to you personally as carrying through the policy of the Collective Farms?'

This subject immediately aroused the Marshal. 'Oh, no,' he said, 'the Collective Farm policy was a terrible struggle. . . . Ten millions (of peasants)', he said, holding up his hands. 'It was fearful. Four years it lasted. It was absolutely necessary for Russia . . .'

With characteristic humour Stalin added that of this staggering figure 'the great bulk were very unpopular and were wiped out by their labourers'.[4]

The frightful campaign against the peasantry was accompanied by the industrialization campaign as its twin. The propaganda for the first Five-Year-Plan (1928–33) was euphoric: there would be a stupendously rapid advance leading to general prosperity the moment the country's resources were harnessed by true Bolshevik zeal and boldness. The optimism was not, however, borne out: Stalin had to bend the entire machinery of the State to the falsification of the results. Repression was intensified as workers started staying away from factories, as peasants began flooding the towns, and as the food shortages worsened, especially in the starvation year 1932–3.

The theory of workers' participation was pulverized as the bureaucracy was still further elevated beyond the Party rank-and-file. Piecework was introduced instead of payment by time: towards the end of 1932 it was clear that this classic device for the exploitation of labour (in Marx's phraseology) also applied to the Soviet worker, despite the metaphysical claim that since the State itself 'belonged' to the workers any surplus had to be for their benefit. Had the Plan been successful, of course, the contrast between claims and performance would not have been so acute; but since the first Plan failed to fulfil any predictions, what became glaringly obvious – hence supremely dangerous to say – was that regardless of theory the Soviet working class had fallen into a classic state of exploitation itself.

Consumer goods stopped being imported to allow for the import of machinery and materials for the programme of heavy industry; these had to be paid for by the export of food and raw materials, which consequently had to be taken away from the population. The Soviet regime officially denied the existence of the famine even at its worst; it defended the administrative measures that had led directly to the famine by denouncing the rich peasants – the kulaks – who were supposed to be sabotaging the government programme by persuading the other peasants to kill their cattle and to destroy their seed-corn. The famine of 1933 was far worse than the famine at the end of the Civil War in 1921, but the 1933 famine, due wholly to government policy, is almost forgotten abroad. Foreign observers, who began visiting the Soviet Union in greater and greater numbers from the outset of the thirties, simply visited the towns and took trains around the countryside. The signs of starvation were not obvious, except for children begging; the urban population heard only vague rumours.

The famine came to an end very quickly when a free market was restored for farm produce over and above that for enforced deliveries; a substantial sector of town-dwellers, workers and students were ordered to help out on the land in the spring of 1933. The harvest of that year was excellent. Two years later food rationing was stopped altogether.

What was of special significance was the degree of force that from this period on was to be taken for granted. During the implementation of the first Five-Year-Plan the government succeeded in shattering all public resistance, not only of the peasantry and the working class, but of the intelligentsia as a whole, even in the case of technicians, who learned to give in to all government directives without technical argument.

The device used by Stalin to consolidate his control of the Party – the smashing of the Left wing plus the subsequent borrowing of its programme of industrialization – was a parallel in miniature to the general indispensability of imposing the Party apparatus on the country as a whole. The savagery of the campaign unleashed against the populace made it essential to stamp out any rallying point for opposition. Hence semi-autonomous peasant institutions, which had survived and indeed flourished a little under the NEP, had to be eliminated.

Much later Stalin was to make the primary argument in favour of high-speed industrialization the need for building up an industrial defence base against invasion. This argument, which was given a little plausibility by Soviet resistance to the Hitler attack, was concocted entirely after the fact: there was not the slightest likelihood of any invasion in 1928, and the losses of the industrialization and collectivization campaign were so fantastic that at the time there could have been no way of preferring them to a slower pace in building up industry. Stalin simply miscalculated; he discounted all arguments and went ahead.

These crash programmes of collectivization and industrialization brought the Party to a high pitch of tension. By arousing the rage of the countryside, by incurring the hatred of scores of millions of peasants and workers, the Party had exposed all its members to a life-and-death crisis. Retreat was impossible. Nor was it possible to reorganize in the midst of such a crisis, even if a leader had been around with enough 'ideological' authority – to say nothing of hardware! – to lead a movement against Stalin from within the ranks.

At a plenary session of the Central Committee in January 1933 the mood was tense. A member reported what he had just seen in a famine area: 'They've started eating people!' To which one of Stalin's chief aides, Lazar Kaganovich, retorted: 'If we don't pull ourselves together you and I will be eaten, too . . . will that be any better?'[5]

For a time Stalin's primacy, established, as it seemed, by his blanket victory in 1929 (at the Sixteenth Party Congress), was reinforced by the very crisis his recklessness had plunged the Party into.

But his backing was not yet homogeneous; it was still possible in the early thirties to disagree behind the scenes. Aside from a few smaller oppositions within the Stalin milieu (associated with Syrtsov, Smirnov and Skrypnik), all of them easily quashed, there was another focus of discontent – the Riutin affair.

Of peasant origin, Riutin had been a Menshevik until the Bolsheviks took power; he joined the Party and became known for his toughness towards 'Trotskyites'. After the Trotskyites had vanished as a real political element and lived on only in Stalin's swiftly evolving mythology, Riutin began opposing Stalin more and more violently.

Detained in an *isolator*, Riutin composed a 'draft programme' in 1931–2; its main point called for easing up on the peasants. Riutin demanded the outright elimination of the hated collective farms and even proposed economic autonomy for the peasants. This alone was not so startling: what distinguished the Riutin 'platform' was its savage personal attack on Stalin. Fully a quarter of the 200-page document was a violent onslaught both on Stalin's character and on his performance within the Party.

As long as Stalin was at the helm, in Riutin's eyes, neither the Party nor the country could improve. While remaining a faithful Bolshevik, Riutin denounced Stalin as a vindictive, power-mad monster who had well-nigh destroyed the Revolution. In short – Stalin out!

Riutin's memorandum crystallized the hatred of Stalin that inflamed many people even in his own entourage and generated an immense amount of talk. Stalin instantly launched a campaign of arrests and searching of apartments.

For a while no one knew who the author of the memorandum was; Riutin, finally brought to Moscow for a hearing, admitted his responsibility. Riutin came into the category of those whose lives had until then been protected by Lenin's legacy. In January 1933 the Politburo debated killing him; at Stalin's instigation the Political Police asked for his head.

Stalin urged that the taboo on killing Bolsheviks be broken; the Political Police had reported talk of terrorism among students and young workers. In the past no one had boggled at the idea of killing terrorists, even though the culprits were sometimes members of the Young Communist League. Stalin pointed out, logically enough, that there was not much sense in killing youthful terrorists and leaving unmolested the authors of propaganda that was essentially a justification of terrorism. Hence Riutin, whose programme was bound to be interpreted as a defence of the necessity for physically annihilating Stalin, had to be killed.

The debate was turbulent: it was the first time the notion of snapping the bond of Bolshevik brotherliness had been brought up as a matter of principle.[6] The consensus of the Politburo, confirmed by a plenum of the Central Committee, was against a death penalty for Bolsheviks. Stalin seemed to accept it.

This was the first time Stalin had ever had a parliamentary defeat within these two topmost Party organs. The vote was not wholly unfavourable: Riutin's sympathizers were all summarily expelled from the Party, exiled, and thrown into 'isolators'. The Party organs pounced on them with characteristic extravagance – 'wretched little counterrevolutionaries' with an 'out-and-out blatant programme of capitalist restoration . . .', 'the desperate convulsions of the dying class enemy.'

This hectic period saw the emergence of Sergei Kirov. A protégé of Stalin's, Kirov had replaced Zinoviev as head of the Leningrad Party at the beginning of 1926, after Zinoviev (forced into Opposition together with some of Trotsky's sympathizers) had been ejected from his position as head of the Leningrad Party. Kirov's personal popularity was considerable: unlike Stalin, who had avoided the 'people' from 1928 on,[7] Kirov had made a point of keeping up the old revolutionary tradition of participating in workers' and peasants' meetings – a grotesque anachronism as Stalinism developed. Of proletarian origin, he was a Great Russian to boot, and to top it all a remarkable speaker.

Kirov was determined to conciliate both those defeated by the Stalin faction and the non-Party intelligentsia. During the debate on the killing of Riutin it was he who had done most to swing the Politburo and the Central Committee against Stalin.

Yet he was not particularly tender-hearted. In the implementation of the first Five-Year-Plan, he was one of those directly responsible for the slaughter of the kulaks; he was in charge of the prison-camps on the Kem and Murmansk coasts, and of the construction of the Baltic-White-Sea Canal, a singularly murderous enterprise.

It was because Kirov had played such an important role in the first Five-Year-Plan and in the collectivization drive that he was in a strong position, psychologically, when he spoke up for a moderation of the murderousness during the second Five-Year-Plan.

At the hectic session of the January 1933 Central Committee plenum Kirov's main problem was quasi-tactical; he had to avoid an accusation of faint-heartedness concerning the horrors of the famine. He therefore made a point of emphasizing his identification with Stalin, who had pushed through collectivization: he supported the 'builders of the Five-Year-Plan' against the mollycoddles.

He pointed out the transformation of the Soviet economic base involved in shackling the peasants to collective farms; the time had come

for the Party to take in hand the question of changing the superstructure of society. He took it for granted that the first Five-Year-Plan, as
well as the collectivization campaign, had been successful: he thought
that what were called the 'small proprietor elements' in the villages –
those peasants not utterly destitute – had been exterminated (i.e., that
the 'horrors' were over) and that the collective farms were now firmly
established. Hence there was a strong possibility that the economic position was now going to improve, and as it improved the number of
'internal enemies' would decline.

Accordingly, in the minds of Kirov and others, the time had come to
broaden the base of the Soviet regime. It was now the task of the Party
to find those forces within the country that would help it grapple with
the problems of constructive development in the second Five-Year-Plan
and afterwards.

It was not evident at the time that this policy of 'conciliationism'
might displease Stalin, since he had said nothing formal *against* it; he
was merely thought to be troubled by some of its minor practical
consequences.

Thus, by the winter of 1933–4 Kirov, while loyally clinging to the
General Line in public, had imposed on it a nuance of his own – a reconciliation of the people to the internal policies of the Party. A basic
consideration in Kirov's mind was foreign policy, which with the emergence of the Nazi movement in the early thirties had become critical. In
order to bring about a reconciliation with Western Europe – a natural
riposte to Nazi Germany – the army also had to be strengthened and
reorganized. This was entailed by the need to have the population
united behind the regime when the crisis inevitably came to a head.

In foreign affairs the Party pundits had worked out a 'periodic'
theory: the First Period, lasting through the First World War and until
1923, was supposed to be an epoch of upheaval; the Second Period –
1923–8 – was supposed to have seen the stabilization of capitalism; the
Third Period was now to usher in a new phase of upheaval and revolutionary turbulence. The frictions, setbacks, collisions, and malfunction-
ing of the capitalist 'system' were interpreted with a sort of demented
enthusiasm as harbingers not even of a long-range general decline, but
as tactical guides to the immediate future.

The Communists, ever since the split with the Social-Democrats
brought about by Lenin during the First World War, had been saying
that the Social-Democrats were inherently pro-capitalist; in the 'revolutionary situation' of the Third Period, after 1928, the Social-Democrats
were bound to side with the 'counter-revolution', hence there could be
no compromise with them. They were 'objectively' fascists, or, in the

phrase coined for them, social-fascists – socialist only in words and *really* fascists. They were even worse than the obvious fascists, and were the 'chief enemy' that the Communists had to wipe out. The Left Social-Democrats, who *seemed* to be quite close to the Communists, were more dangerous even than the Right Social-Democrats, and so on.

Hitler's assumption of power gave the Soviet regime a great shock. It reversed the policy of denouncing Social-Democracy as the chief enemy and abruptly launched the policy of the People's Fronts, first in France, then ultimately throughout the world. This policy, which endured until the Second World War, was based on collaboration with socialists of most shades and indeed with liberals as well, against German Nazism and Italian Fascism.

The spirit of conciliation linked to Kirov was naturally stimulated by Hitlerism; but Stalin, though he kept him in Leningrad as much as possible and prevented him, according to rumours, from attending Politburo meetings in Moscow, took no action against him. At the time, with Kirov surrounded by a corps of able aides in Leningrad, it might have been rash for Stalin, his own position a little shaken up by the catastrophes of his peasant programme and his policy on Hitlerism, to risk an open break with Kirov.

In the autumn of 1933, Stalin's prestige rapidly soared, primarily because there was a splendid harvest. It was widely felt that he had got everyone out of a terrible hole. There was a relaxation of political pressure; the political trials that had dotted the late twenties and early thirties seemed to be over; the internal Party purges and check-ups came to an end; political arrests also declined. People of non-proletarian or non-peasant origins could get into universities; in one of Stalin's speeches he seemed to be veering away from the notion of class origins; when he said that 'the son was not responsible for the father' he seemed to imply the freeing of Soviet society from the shackles of biologically interpreted political prejudice. The new Stalin Constitution that began to be talked about around the middle of the thirties lulled suspicion; many people thought the worst was over.

In the summer of 1933 the atmosphere had been fairly relaxed. Some former Oppositionists (notably Zinoviev and Kamenev) were reinstated in the Party; some were allowed to do work they liked, and invited to the Seventeenth Party Congress (held in February 1934), which elected a Central Committee full of Stalin's followers, with a few cowed exceptions. This particular Congress was a great triumph for Kirov; even beforehand, during his election and at various conferences he attended in different sections of the city, he had been given apparently authentic ovations, impressively repeated at the Congress itself, where there was some talk as to who, Stalin or Kirov, had been greeted more noisily.

Kirov was made a secretary of the Central Committee, re-elected a member of the Politiburo; this marked a considerable advance for the policy of reconciliation. A secretaryship of the Central Committee entailed moving to Moscow. Even though that was delayed, Kirov's authority within the Politburo kept rising.

At a Politburo session that took place early in 1934 the 'Riutin affair' popped up again: some young people in the Young Communist League, including students, were reported to be discussing terrorism once again. The Politburo – and the Political Police – proceeded very circumspectly, in accordance with Stalin's pattern. The Politburo handed down very elastic directives to the Political Police: no method was to be applied categorically; each instance was to be dealt with on its merits; killing was to be resorted to only where individuals were demonstrably hopeless. The members of these particular Young Communist groups were handled very gently; they were sent to prison camps and isolators, occasionally exiled to places that were not so far away.

After the Seventeenth Party Congress in February 1934 the policy of reconciliation linked to the name of Kirov was implemented in a number of measures; many more Oppositionists, languishing in prison and in exile from the period of the first Five-Year-Plan, came back; at the same time many 'wreckers' were rehabilitated. The Political Police changed its name (from OGPU to NKVD) and in the enabling resolutions it lost its right to use the supreme penalty. The intelligentsia was energetically wooed: at the Writers' Congress of 1934 Bukharin and Gorky wallowed in 'proletarian humanism'. The Soviet Union also dropped its systematic attacks on the League of Nations as the tool of the 'capitalist democracies' and joined it in September 1934.

These moves in the direction of sweetness and light were led very largely by Kirov, propped up, it seemed, on a new Party majority that had formed in the wake of the Seventeenth Congress both in the Central Committee and the Politburo. The policy, though marking a clearly outlined course of action, was advanced by its sponsors as gently as possible from an organizational point of view; the need for Party solidarity was felt by everyone; every effort was made to avoid clashes.

Because of this general desire for Party unity Stalin could not seriously be attacked. The Party seemed to be rallying around him more ostentatiously than ever while simultaneously modifying his policies. It almost seemed that immediately after the Seventeenth

Party Congress he was being transformed into a figure-head – the symbol of a party controlled by others.

At this Congress, the adulation of Stalin reached new heights precisely at a time when he was being defeated on three basic questions: a soft hand with the Oppositionists, the reconciliation of the non-Party intelligentsia, and foreign policy.

In the fundamental Party sphere – organization – something still more important took place: the Congress moved to dislodge Stalin's bloated personal secretariat from its privileged position. It was to be incorporated within the structure of the Central Committee itself as its 'Special Sector', where a check could be kept on it. Stalin's own activities could, for the first time since he had emerged as effective dictator during the twenties, at last be controlled by a vote of the Central Committee, and with a majority now veering away from him towards Kirov that vote might well be adverse.

There was a still more direct attack on Stalin's position. The plenum of each Party Congress, beginning with the Thirteenth Congress in 1924, had specifically confirmed Stalin as General Secretary of the Party. This specific mention was omitted in the reports of the Seventeenth Party Congress.

The omission was plainly decisive: Stalin was no longer entrenched; he was merely the first, *primus inter pares*, of the four secretaries of the Central Committee. It was a sort of bureaucratic insurrection that, were it to have been extended, would have meant mortal peril for Stalin just at the moment when at the 'Congress of Victors' of 1934 he was the chief victor in the eyes of the public and, no doubt, the Party rank-and-file.

At a plenum of the Central Committee in November 1934, Kirov, chief spokesman of the new mood, was a conquering hero; his transfer to Moscow was thought imminent. He was to be in charge of all the ideological divisions of the Party secretariat; he was about to embark on a major role, with substantial support among the Party summit and backed up by the apparently authentic enthusiasm of rank-and-file people in Leningrad and elsewhere. It might have been thought that the thaw had come to stay: nevertheless an abrupt switch in policy was in the offing.

Kirov was moving nearer the levers of power. His personal integrity made him unsuitable for Stalin's factional requirements: Stalin needed pliability more than competence. Kirov's attitude towards the partisans of Trotsky and Zinoviev, for instance, was illuminating: he was simultaneously for the General Line and for reconciliation. He disagreed with Bukharin on theory while revering him as a theorist.

Kirov could not be arrested as an 'enemy of the people' – unlike the other Party leaders whose Party records could be invoked against them, however unjustly. He could not be 'charged' with any 'deviation' at all, since he had not been a Menshevik, nor belonged to any Party opposition of any kind.

There was only one logical solution – a quiet physical removal: Kirov was killed on 1 December 1934. The assassin was said to have been Leonid Nikolayev, thirty years old, a Party member since the age of sixteen.

The official expressions of grief were even more extravagant than after Lenin's death; for almost a fortnight the newspapers were devoted to the commemoration of Kirov's life and death. Ordinary Party people were stunned; Kirov had been widely regarded as a man who not only stood for a general reconciliation but was outstanding enough, both as a personality and as a bureaucrat, to bring it about.

The measures taken in the wake of the assassination remained substantially incoherent. The first official report responded to the Party's bafflement – Nikolayev was said to have been the agent of a fascist power, and to have confessed to receiving money from a foreign consul in Leningrad. 104 'anti-Soviet plotters' – White Guards who had been in gaol since long before the assassination – were shot out of hand.

This shooting of the 104 White Guards was followed by the trial of Nikolayev, together with his 'accomplices', on 28–9 December. It was reported that fourteen people were executed.

Trotsky's name now appeared: Nikolayev had confessed that a foreign consul in Leningrad had given him 5,000 roubles to commit some terroristic acts; he had asked Nikolayev whether he might not wish to send Trotsky a letter the consul could transmit. The indictment itself did not quote any answer made by Nikolayev; it simply mentioned the consul's offer.[8]

The diplomatic corps in Leningrad immediately asked for the name of the consul: several days later the Soviet government came up with the name of a Latvian consul (Bisseneks), who had already left the country. The proceedings of this trial were never published; the consul was never mentioned again.

Nikolayev had kept a diary that made it clear he had acted alone: it was declared a forgery. It was said that the defendants had been plotting to kill Stalin, Kaganovich and Vyacheslav Molotov, Stalin's long-time right-hand man, as well as Kirov. The White Guards were blurrily implicated by testimony to the effect that Nikolayev had had some contacts with members of a White Guard Army (Denikin's).

A couple of weeks later (15–16 January 1935) another trial was held of Zinoviev and Kamenev on a charge of 'moral responsibility' for Kirov's murder; this was after Kirov's murderer and his accomplices had been executed. Nineteen people were tried on the issue of moral responsibility; all were sentenced to gaol for five to ten years.

The Leningrad Political Police officials who had 'had at their command information on the plot against Kirov', as *Pravda* put it, but had done nothing, were tried and sentenced to gaol for two to ten years; none of them was a witness in any subsequent proceedings. This 'moral' trial was summed up in an official statement that did not include the evidence but simply repeated the general claim that the defendants had known of the preparations for the assassination and had confessed.

At this preliminary 'moral' trial in January 1935 Zinoviev's 'confession' acknowledged only criticisms of the government; these criticisms had given rise to dissatisfaction: dissatisfaction had inspired terrorism. All Kamenev confessed to was his failure to break with Zinoviev.

Half a year later, in July 1935, Kamenev and some others were tried on still another charge, that of plotting against Stalin himself: Kamenev got another five years on top of his original five years' sentence. (There was neither a report nor a communiqué about this trial; the additional sentence of five years given to Kamenev appears, actually, only in the verdict of the first Show Trial more than a year later.)

No one noticed that former Oppositionists were hurt most of all by Kirov's removal, nor was any comment made on the police negligence, quite unprecedented in the Soviet Union, which was scarcely even punished, as compared with the shooting of 104 innocent prisoners, to say nothing of the execution of Nikolayev's accomplices, of whom thirteen denied everything.

The mention at the outset of a fascist power being involved had appealed to knowledgeable insiders, since the idea of Oppositionist responsibility for the murder was plainly preposterous. This view made it easy to believe that no matter how significant the murder of Kirov might have *seemed*, it really had no connexion with internal Soviet affairs at all. Kirov's loss was merely personal, of no political consequence.

At first Stalin seemed to be busy with the enquiry to unearth the history of the conspiracy. The committee of enquiry tried to establish two lines of approach: did Nikolayev have backers? Why wasn't he prevented? What were the authorities up to?

On the first point things looked simple: Nikolayev had no accomplices whatsoever. The totally indiscreet diary mentioned nothing whatever to show any connexion with anyone else. The basic point was far more ticklish – police negligence. How *was* it possible for Nikolayev to get anywhere near someone like Kirov?

This fundamental angle was dropped very quickly. To make up for it the committee of enquiry launched a large-scale investigation of Oppositionists and alleged Oppositionists, and in particular it looked into the leniency that had been shown these Oppositionists by the Leningrad section of the political police.

This was not a legal matter, since the people who came under the heading of 'Oppositionists' were, after all, Soviet citizens who had purged whatever could be called their crime and were now living normally in Leningrad. They were not *doing* anything political at all.

Yet the investigators began by asking why the local authorities had allowed these former Oppositionists to live. The local authorities, in a situation that in any other legal system would surely be anomalous, defended themselves by citing an authoritative person – Kirov himself!

It is true that Kirov had, naturally, taken such a line; it was part of his general advocacy of reconciliation, implemented by specific oral and written instructions to the Party watch-dogs to stop harassing former Oppositionists.

By mid-December a report was ready for the Politburo. But the Party atmosphere was by now altogether different from what it had been during the 1933 harvest; Stalin, with Kirov gone and the food situation relatively tranquil, was an unchallengeable dictator. Now it was simply a question of who could get closest to him. His classic stance – holding himself composedly above the mêlée in a discussion within his entourage – came even more characteristically to the fore.

Before Kirov's murder Stalin's attitude on conciliation had been non-committal. Reports circulated around the Kremlin that the Leader was thinking, thinking. This was considered so momentous that everyone realized he had to hold his breath. It was rumoured that Gorky, the world-famous writer, was exercising a moderating influence over Stalin. Gorky was a gentle, unworldly, old-fashioned, European-style liberal; he favoured not only a soft line on dissidents, but also the reconciliation of even the non-Party intelligentsia to the great work of Bolshevik construction.

The final report on the Kirov murder was presented to the Politburo in a rather tense atmosphere. Two allied questions were discussed. What should be done with the conspirators – those who had 'taken part in' and/or 'instigated' the assassination? More broadly, should any conclusions be drawn from the disclosure of this new conspiracy with respect to the former Oppositionists who were, evidently, no longer ideologically disarmed but constituted a real danger?

The Politburo consensus was that no general conclusions should be drawn, and that the plenum of the Central Committee, which had already projected a series of economic reforms, should be backed up. Stalin concurred in Kirov's reform measures, reserving only one small point: the Oppositionists should all be gone over with a fine-tooth comb.

The Politburo decided the first question: the whole matter was to be turned over to the courts as a mere case of terrorism.

This procedure, by allowing political figures to become criminally involved merely because their words or ideas, real or alleged, could be associated with an actual killer through the vaguest of connexions, plainly cleared the way for a subsequent charge of personal culpability on the broadest possible basis.

The ramified Party machinery started throbbing. The Moscow and the Leningrad Party committees had plenary sessions, all very solemn, with speeches made by members of the Politburo. All the members of the committees were given a copy of the voluminous report, but the actual statement found on Nikolayev himself when he was arrested – which indicated that he had no connexions with anyone – was kept top-secret: hardly anyone at all knew about that.

The resolutions, unanimously adopted, launched a ferocious campaign against all Oppositionists of whatever kind; especially virulent emphasis was laid on 'Trotskyites' and 'Zinovievites'.

Kirov's murder had instantly generated rumours that Stalin had somehow been involved. These rumours could scarcely have been convincing; the ignorance of someone so knowledgeable as Bukharin seems decisive. The circumstances themselves implied a sinister relationship of *some* kind between the Political Police and the assassination, if only because such absurdly light sentences were handed out to the officials who were tried for negligence.

The investigation of Kirov's murder coincided with one of Stalin's most successful operations – the publicizing of the 'most democratic constitution in the world'. This was accompanied, because of the general improvement in the food situation, by a relaxation of some of the economic controls and even by a slight amelioration of the harsh regime in the collective farms; farmers were now allowed to farm a tiny patch of land for their own use and to sell some of their surpluses on the open market.

Simultaneously there was the feeling of general political exhilaration within the country at large, symbolized by a torrent of medals, decorations, awards, and honours. Officers' titles and privileges were established in the Red Army once again, the rank of marshal was set up and all sorts of Orders were given currency – of the Red Star, of Lenin, of the

Red Banner, of the Red Banner of Labour. The wooing of the intelligentsia was heightened still further, if that was possible, by giving them awards, too: National Artist, Scholar of Merit, and so on.

'Life', as Stalin put it in his downright way, 'is getting merrier, comrades.'

The new constitution itself was put forth as the pinnacle of human reason and a guarantee of practically everything – freedom of speech, press, and assembly, freedom from arrest and search without warrant, for that matter even the right to work.

Among the enthusiasts created abroad by the Soviet Union, bastion against Hitler, all these manifestations of the new and joyful spirit were welcomed, often ecstatically. Even in the Soviet Union itself knowledgeable people were not yet aware of what was happening in the Party summits. In the general euphoria the terror within the Party seemed atypical – no more than an anachronistic reaction to Nikolayev's eccentric initiative. Insiders took solace in the hope that the atmosphere of conciliation outside the Party would be duplicated within.

The beginning of 1936 was, in fact, the beginning of a session of benevolence on all sides: Soviet society might easily be considered to have entered the period of the peaceful building of socialism. Life really seemed easier. The dictatorial base, organized as a fusion of a State cult, a bureaucracy, and the Political Police, showed signs of broadening out more representatively.

The main obstacle to this perspective of general harmony seemed at the time, oddly enough, to be the conventional assessment of Stalin's temperament.

It was understood that he was morbidly prickly, excessively mistrustful, perhaps even slightly paranoid – though the taboo on Freudianism made psychoanalytic clichés unfamiliar. Therefore, he had to be mollified. It was vital to display as much loyalty as possible to show him that the crisis in his personal relations was quite unfounded – everyone *loved* him!

This quaint piece of political psychology was elaborated into a small theory. Flattery, in limitless doses, was necessary because of this historical 'accident' – Stalin's nature. The requirement was simply a fact of politics. Stalin had to be adulated to make him feel better; the moment he felt better he would stop terrorizing everyone.

As a whole the Soviet élite could congratulate itself: in the spring and summer of 1936 it seemed to have achieved some self-assurance at last. It had come through the ordeal of the preceding period unmolested, skins and jobs intact. The worst was over; little by little, things were bound to get better. Summer holidays, which had become more important, were looked forward to; the normal dead season in politics was also a pleasurable prospect. Some members of the Politburo had already gone on vacation; Stalin, too, was supposed to be taking a short holiday.

In the midst of this general relaxation there came a bolt from the blue.

On 19 August 1936 Zinoviev, Kamenev and fourteen other Party people and functionaries, with a few unknown individuals, described as the United Trotskyite-Zinovievite Terror Centre, appeared in a courtroom, accused of having killed Kirov on the orders of Leon Trotsky and of plotting to kill Stalin and his aides in order to take power. For five days the proceedings went on at a feverish pace: the prisoners, vying with each other in self-denunciation, admitted all major charges. At the end the man acting as prosecutor shrieked out: 'Death to the mad dogs!'

The presiding judge sentenced them all to death by shooting; the sentence was carried out at once.

Not only the public at large was taken completely by surprise; Party veterans as well as the topmost strata of the bureaucracy were flabbergasted.

Though the regime had already conditioned the Soviet public to the presentation of political crimes in the form of trials, Bolsheviks had never been involved. It was accepted, within the Party, that the various dissenters from the General Line could be handled by any means whatever – lying, rioting, calumny, distortion, expulsion, pressure, blackmail – but no Bolsheviks had yet been killed.

There was the odd exception, such as the execution of a few of Trotsky's sympathizers (notably Blumkin in 1924) who had penetrated the inner sections of the Political Police to warn some friends about their imminent arrest, but that had seemed justified: the execution had punished a specific action; it could be looked on as due to the harshness of the regime. The discussion of the death penalty against Bolsheviks during the Riutin affair of 1932 had been provoked by the tensions of the famine. The Show Trial of August 1936, the first of three, with its ostentatious concentration on Bolsheviks *only*, was a complete novelty.

The first Show Trial was heard by the Military Collegium of the Supreme Court of the USSR with one judge presiding and two others sitting beside him. The tiny courtroom held only a couple of hundred people.

Some six months later (23–30 January 1937) the same court, with the same judicial setting – court, presiding judge, prosecutor – heard the Case of the Anti-Soviet Trotskyite Centre.

The indictment was substantially different: the prisoners, charged with having established, in 1933, a centre 'parallel' with the one mentioned in the first Show Trial and still alleged to be under Trotsky's orders, were further accused of high treason, espionage, and wrecking activities as well as acts of terror. This time the victims were Party leaders (notably Radek, Pyatakov, Serebryakov and Sokolnikov), some active Party members, a few specialists and one otherwise unknown individual. They were all shot except four (including Radek), who got long terms in gaol.

Fifteen months later (2–13 March 1938), in the identical judicial setting, the Anti-Soviet Bloc of Rights and Trotskyites appeared. These were accused of having set up, in 1932–3, a conspiratorial group that had not merely spied on behalf of foreign states, but had actively been working for the defeat and dismemberment of the Soviet Union and the restoration of capitalism. The prisoners were also accused not only of the murder of Kirov but of some other prominent Soviet personalities, including Gorky.

The victims were former Party leaders and prominent government functionaries (notably Bukharin, Krestinsky, Rosengoltz, Rakovsky, Rykov), some assistants to prominent people, some active Party members and functionaries, and a few physicians. They admitted all charges; they were all shot except three (including Rakovsky), who got long terms in gaol.

These three Show Trials, taken together, wiped out the bulk of the leadership of the old Oppositions; in addition many thousands of prominent Bolsheviks vanished in 1936–8 with no publicity; many more who were not killed were gaoled or exiled.

Seen from outside, the Show Trials had a number of arrestingly obvious oddities that raised a pervasive doubt long before there could be any possibility of penetrating their genesis.

Their very setting was altogether singular, with its tiny audience and the handful of strangely docile foreign observers and correspondents.

Here were hundreds of people – the prisoners themselves and those they were alleged to have conspired with in vast organizations – being judged by a military court made up of three robot-like judges, in a trial stage-managed by a prosecutor – Vyshinsky – who as a former Menshevik had been a political enemy of the victims all his life.

There was no defence; no argument whatever, in fact, was allowed. No material proofs, though referred to, were ever submitted. No witnesses mentioned by either the prosecution or the prisoners themselves were ever questioned; the two chief subjects of the indictment – Trotsky and his son – were neither told about the Show Trials in advance, nor given any chance to respond anywhere, despite their offer to stand trial for extradition in any country on the same charges.

The 'openness' and 'correctness' of the procedure, naïvely praised by a number of stooges and dupes, display all these glaringly obvious defects. The almost entirely harmonious series of questions and answers indicates, in fact, the artificiality of the whole operation, considered as a judicial procedure.

The outstanding oddity of the Show Trials – the use of confessions as *sole* evidence – was explained away by the general formula that plotters naturally hide their traces.

In connexion with Russia's long-drawn-out history of plots, terrorism and assassinations, with decades full of the liveliest conspiracies and trials, this explanation looks especially silly. Though real conspirators did not discuss their conspiracies in open letters, they did, of course, write letters – seizable, understandable, and demonstrable – and even in chemical ink. Such things were displayed any number of times by the Tsarist police. Stool-pigeons and provocateurs among the conspirators also played a useful and thoroughly demonstrable role; the police could get perfectly tangible evidence about the course of the plotting and the whereabouts of documents and also, for that matter, of the real conspirators at crucial points, even catching them redhanded.

Yet in the Show Trials, despite the most remarkable indictments, claiming the most titanic conspiracies in history, stretching over a period of many years, with threads all over the country and well beyond its borders, and despite the practical omnipotence of the Political Police and its incessant arrests, perquisitions, and stealing of documents, the court was offered nothing tangible whatever.

Conversely, there was never a single situation in which scores of veteran political activists, many of them bona-fide conspirators, kept up a course of subversive action over a period of years and then abruptly, after arrest, suddenly turned on each other and on their 'leader' in exile, furthermore singing the praises of the head of the regime they were supposed to be trying to destroy.

Why, after all, if they had been spending their whole time preparing assassinations *en masse*, blowing up trains, wrecking factories, poisoning armies of workers and peasants, should they suddenly have become so docile?

These two attributes of the Show Trials demonstrated their contrived quality. One might have thought this so obvious that some trouble would have been taken to provide some evidential confirmation of these 'confessions', the sole support of the indictments; it was this objective confirmation, fitting in with the oddity of the two points just made above, that was strikingly absent.

Psychologically, moreover, there was an added curiosity in the self-flagellation of the prisoners; they not only enthusiastically confirmed their formal denunciation in court but vilified themselves in a style that gave the impression of hysteria.

The extravagance of Trotsky's role was doubtless the most extraordinary single element of the Show Trials.

Utterly powerless, as it seemed, an exile isolated successively in Turkey, France, Norway and Mexico, he was abruptly presented to the public as the master criminal on whose orders the prisoners and their countless accomplices had been toiling to undo the Soviet Union.

This indictment of Trotsky was the linchpin of all three Show Trials: beginning with the mere terrorism outlined in the first one, it assumed ever more gigantic dimensions, Trotsky ultimately being denounced as the accomplice of Hitler and the Mikado of Japan.

A nightmarish aspect of the three indictments was their indifference to motivation. On the one hand the prisoners were supposed to be involved in a 'struggle for power' within the Soviet regime, on the other to be struggling for a 'restoration of capitalism'.

They themselves did not seem upset by this: in the dialogue of the courtroom scenes they simply carried along the line laid down by the prosecutor. For that matter none of the methods ascribed to them could bring about either the upsetting of the Soviet leadership or the restoration of capitalism.

Thus, an attempt was made to show that Trotsky, who had demonstrably spent many years of his life talking and writing against terrorism as a political tactic, had changed his mind because of his embitterment at losing power and had suddenly switched to terrorism in spite of everything. Yet no evidence was offered beyond the testimony of stooges that Trotsky even in exile could demolish with ease. Those writings of Trotsky that had been broadcast to millions of people for decades during his career were claimed by the prosecution to be mere camouflage; his *real* thoughts had been imparted to one or two unknown persons.

But even more amazing – still other Marxists, all of them bitter opponents of Trotsky for years, with no occasion to be influenced by him, without deriving the smallest advantage, had suddenly begun docilely taking his orders.

An analysis of the Kirov assassination, the only concrete achievement of the vast network of alleged terrorist plotters, shows that it could not have had the smallest sense.

What could have been achieved? How would getting rid of a secondary figure in the huge Soviet bureaucracy help Zinoviev and Kamenev? Even had Zinoviev and Kamenev taken to terror, it would have been obvious to them that killing Kirov would have done nothing but panic the Soviet leadership into taking ferocious vengeance against their own Oppositionist milieu. Had there been such a tactic of personal terror its only sensible target would have been Stalin – a very easy one, since the prisoners included Central Committee members and government functionaries who were seeing him constantly.

A strange inconsistency was the way a principal charge – sabotage – was dealt with. It seemed that the 'Trotskyites', a mere handful of vermin, controlled the entire network of Soviet industry and transportation. If one took the indictments seriously, one would have had to believe that the whole of Soviet economy was not in the hands of the 'infallible genius' but in those of a helpless exile who had been out of touch with the country for almost a decade.

The idea that Trotsky was prompted by a mad lust for power sounds bizarre: if he were actually to help Hitler and the Mikado to dismember the Soviet Union, why would they put him in power afterwards? For that matter, how could this vast conspiracy, involving thousands of people, be concealed at all?

Even if Trotsky lusted for power, what could have been the motivation of the smaller fry? Not the leaders who, let us say, hoped that Hitler would keep them in power, but the lesser agents supposed to perpetrate such acts of sabotage and terrorism, who were not only risking their lives but going to an almost certain death?

This obvious, common-sense question was never raised at all: the audience were obliged to assume that various witnesses were losing their lives for love of Trotsky, love of the Japanese militarists, love of Hitler, and so on.

Yet, even in a farce, motives are essential.

There is no longer any need to make a point of the incoherence of the Show Trials. They are now known to have been fabrications: both Khrushchev's celebrated Secret Speech to the Twentieth Party Congress in 1956,[9] and many of his statements since, as well as the revelations of a number of Soviet defectors,[10] merely confirm the results of the most cursory scrutiny of the publication of Stalin's government.

There is also other official Soviet evidence, less direct, in the second edition of the *Great Soviet Encyclopedia*,[11] which, in a history of the Communist Party, no longer refers to the principal 'defendants' of the Show Trials as traitors and spies; it also makes it clear that the Political Police had the power to torture its prisoners and did in fact do so.

It will be seen that Kirov's murder was contrived by Stalin as the first stage in a complex, unitary operation, perhaps the most massive, murderous political enterprise ever recorded. Though the inwardness of the assassination did not emerge for more than twenty years, and to this day many details remain obscure, there can be no doubt of Stalin's role.

After an interval of tentative, inchoate manoeuvres, Stalin used Kirov's murder as the pretext for the Show Trials of 1936–8: these served as an umbrella for an enterprise of enormous scope. This was the Great Purge, the campaign of systematized terror, launched by the decapitation of the Red Army (the killing of Tukhachevsky and other generals), carried out some months after the second Show Trial in 1937, that was directed initially against the summits of the Party, State and army apparatuses and then against the populace at large.

The murder of Kirov served, in short, as the pretext under which Stalin transformed the institutional complex of the Soviet Union, wiped out millions of people, and consolidated his personal dictatorship.

The Show Trials were intensively, indeed hysterically, publicized by the regime; the Great Purge was never admitted.

It will be illuminating to discuss both the public impact of the Show Trials and the background against which they were conceived and shaped – the private office of Stalin the Genius.

To do so it will be necessary to use a different vocabulary: part of Stalin's hoax was the use of normal language – 'trial', 'purge', 'defendant', 'prosecutor'. All these words are profoundly and intentionally misleading: even when used, as they must be, in inverted commas, they imply a surrender to the basic hoax.

The Show Trials were not trials even in the sense of being phoney trials; the Purge was not a purge. The Show Trials were a form of propaganda whose aim was to place all potential opponents under an absolute moral ban. The Great Purge, ostensibly based on the same false charges, was devised as a means of transforming the Soviet Union in a certain way.

The Show Trials were, very precisely, theatrical productions presented in a courtroom with certain characters playing certain roles – 'court', 'defendants', 'witnesses', 'judges', and 'audience'.

They were, in short, charades of a special kind; the Great Purge is properly described as the Deep Comb-out.

3
Backstage

Stalin had begun preparing a comeback after his defeat, due largely to Kirov's influence, on the question of killing Riutin in 1932. Publicly this defeat had seemed trivial; it was in no sense a setback even within the small 'public' of the Party; Stalin had acted as he always did – *moderately*.

Indeed, during the period preceding Kirov's murder Stalin had become far sweeter – gentle, affable, taking pleasure in the talk of painters, writers, and so on. He even relaxed with respect to people with a slightly Oppositionist past, like Bukharin, even Kamenev.[1] Kamenev by this time had been expelled from the Party three times and had just as often recanted. His last blunder had been in the winter of 1932–3, in connexion with Riutin's 'programme', when Kamenev had actually been caught 'reading and not reporting' it.

At a meeting arranged by Gorky, Stalin and Kamenev practically fell into each other's arms.[2] Kamenev was rumoured to have made, in a manly way, a clean breast of things: why he had previously thought Stalin no good, why he thought so no longer. He was supposed to have given Stalin his 'word of honour' to steer clear of any Oppositional activity, and to have been promised top-flight political assignments in return.[3]

Kamenev had already been permitted to make a speech at the Seventeenth Party Congress in February 1934, on the one hand, and in that speech, on the other hand, to give the theoretical explanation of why a dictatorship was needed: not merely a Dictatorship of the Proletariat, but a purely personal one. Democracy was all very well when things were going peacefully, but in a crisis you had to have a strong man – Stalin!

It might have seemed that Kamenev was tying himself in knots to please Stalin, but he was not, as it appears, energetic enough. Many insiders thought his speech, if scrutinized, showed traces of malignity that indicated some reserve after all – i.e., the speech meant the opposite of what it said.

While presenting his usual face to the world, Stalin had begun his bureaucratic preparations. Though details were naturally not recorded, a sort of inner logic, fortified by Khrushchev's Secret Speech and some informed memoirs,[4] make its outlines clear.

Stalin had been *de facto* chief of the Political Police ever since the establishment of his primacy; in the course of 1933–4 he bypassed the ordinary Party and Police machinery through the use of his own men. One of the functions of his personal secretariat was the collection of materials on the Political Police. After the Riutin affair his secretariat extruded a special tentacle: the Special Secret Political Department of State Security. The date of its formation is obscure; it was genuinely secret and never referred to in print. It is known primarily from interviews with Soviet refugees and, less reliably, from occasional reports by foreign newspaper correspondents. By the summer of 1933 it was surely in operation.

Its paramount function was the clandestine surveillance of the Political Police. It put its own men into all local branches, most often as deputies to the department heads, themselves appointed by the governing board of the Political Police. This parallel network of the Special Department, originating in Stalin's personal secretariat, was later to provide the backbone of the Political Police apparatus after its regular personnel had been wiped out in the Deep Comb-out.

Stalin's initial assignment in this eminently clandestine operation was the murder of Kirov. His aim was the elimination of any curb on his conduct by legal, intra-Party action; Kirov's removal enabled him both to expand what had hitherto been the process of purging the Party and to transform it from a peaceful procedure into an instrument of terror.

Beforehand the periodical Party purges were carried on openly by committees of the Central Control Commission of the Party. After Kirov's murder it was the Party apparatus itself, in the beginning, that carried on its own purge, operating in secret in the secluded offices of the Party secretaries in the Central Committee itself and throughout the country in local committees. Then, as the Comb-out swelled to encompass the whole population, this was insufficient; the Comb-out of the Party itself was also put in the hands of the Political Police.

This was the germ of the Deep Comb-out – the terror proper.

The reconstruction of Stalin's move against Kirov sounds like the plot of a crime-thriller. Nikolayev, the dupe selected to carry out the assassination, made his first attempt around 20 November 1934; it was timed to take place just before the plenary session of the Central Committee for 25–8 November in Moscow. The would-be assassin was arrested by a bodyguard of Kirov's; a loaded revolver was found in his brief-case. Nikolayev was then inexplicably released. Twelve days later he went back to Kirov's headquarters and killed him.

Kirov's murder must have been timed to make sure of his removal on already prepared terrain – Leningrad – a few days in advance of the plenum, precisely in order to prevent his reform schemes from being adopted by a receptive plenum. When the plan for his assassination on 20 November misfired, Kirov, unaware, attended the meeting and carried it against Stalin's supporters.

At two previous plenums, when the question of Kirov's transfer to Moscow had been raised, the suggestion had been shrugged aside, evidently temporarily, by Kirov himself. For Kirov the question of moving to Moscow must have been linked with the adoption of his reforms; he wanted a congenial background. At the November plenum, however, which he attended only through a stroke of luck, he consented at once when the question of his transfer was brought up again. An early date was agreed on.

The prospect of a strong-willed man like Kirov, with a following both among the workers' organizations of his own city, Leningrad, and within the Party summits by now as well, was alarming and from Stalin's point of view all the more ominous in view of the Seventeenth Party Congress resolution that had already driven a wedge into his authority by subordinating his personal secretariat to the Central Committee.

The Leningrad section of the Political Police was headed by one Medved; before Kirov was killed Stalin had tried to replace Medved, but Kirov had intervened in his favour. Stalin had seemed to give in.

Stalin had a confidential agent, Yagoda, whose protégé, Zaporozhets, worked as a deputy of Medved's; Yagoda took Zaporozhets to see Stalin; they discussed the elimination of Kirov and suggested using a recently denounced 'malcontent', Nikolayev, as an assassin.

Nikolayev was very pathetic: during the Civil War he had volunteered at the age of sixteen for the front, where he had joined the Young Communist League. He had attracted no attention. His diary, which covered the two years before he killed Kirov, is a banal account of vexations: his miseries, the suffering of his mother, wife, two children, his hatred for the Party machine.

That machine upset him, it seems, because the old camaraderie had been replaced by the new bureaucratic rigidity: Nikolayev felt betrayed by the Party's moral degeneration.

This feeling of betrayal was given a more personal tinge: he wanted to sacrifice himself. He not only harped, in his diary, on the necessity of sacrifice as a method of holding this terrible bureaucratic development up to the eyes of the public, but he had been reading about a traditional Russian political activity in the past – the heroic terrorism of the Social-Revolutionaries and their predecessors, the generation of self-sacrificing idealists who had been so successful in blowing up various Tsarist officials. As a dupe he was ideal.

When Zaporozhets heard about his resentment of the Party bureaucracy he decided to use him, and got hold of the 'friend', who had first denounced him. This friend purloined Nikolayev's diary, had it photostated, and returned it without his knowledge. Under an assumed name, Zaporozhets was introduced to Nikolayev: seeing he could be used, he instructed Nikolayev's supposed friend to nurse him along, with sympathy and money and to keep on reporting.

Zaporozhets was told to get the friend to focus Nikolayev's hatred for the Party bureaucracy on Kirov; in Leningrad, Zaporozhets learned that Nikolayev was now obsessed with his idea of shooting someone on the Party bureaucracy as a signal for action, and was actively trying to get hold of a revolver.

Zaporozhets told Nikolayev's friend that the situation was very dangerous; it would be better to persuade Nikolayev to attack Kirov, who was guarded twenty-four hours a day, and thus have him caught red-handed: he could be picked up with a revolver in his pocket immediately after going into the headquarters building.

Nikolayev was now inflamed by the idea of killing a member of the Politburo instead of some obscure bureaucrat; all he needed was the actual weapon. The friend arranged this, too. Nikolayev set out to kill Kirov; he was duly stopped by the guards, who found both the loaded gun and his diary in his briefcase. Then they released him, incomprehensibly to him, and even more so to his friend. Zaporozhets, to blame for the botch-up, had had to order his release. He needed Nikolayev more than ever; Stalin was waiting for results.

After a fit of depression Nikolayev recovered his spirits; he was willing to try again. This time Zaporozhets had taken more pains; Nikolayev duly got his pass, was admitted past the first guard station, wandered around the Smolny building, and got to Kirov's quarters. Now there were no guards at all; he entered the corridor without being stopped, to find a slight, middle-aged man, Borisov, Kirov's personal attendant.

Borisov was preparing a tea tray with some snacks for a committee conference in Kirov's office. Nikolayev waited in the corridor, until Kirov was called by Borisov to the phone to talk to the Kremlin; Kirov left the conference room.

A shot rang out in the corridor: the people at the conference rushed to the door, which was hard to open because it was blocked by Kirov's feet; he was lying just outside in his own blood, quite dead. Nikolayev was also lying there, in a swoon. Political Police officers soon came to arrest him.

Zaporozhets, eager to get the credit for a successful operation before Stalin even arrived on the scene, took a chance on confronting Nikolayev personally. By threatening his family he tried to browbeat him into a confession of complicity with Zinoviev and Kamenev: Stalin had made it apparent that Kirov's murder was to be used as a pretext for action against the former Oppositionists.

Zaporozhets had been hoping Nikolayev would have forgotten him, since their previous meeting had been so casual, but when Nikolayev laid eyes on him, he instantly saw he had been duped. He not only refused to cooperate but rushed at Zaporozhets to beat him up; holding a chair high above his head he drove him out of the room screaming.

Snatched back to his cell, Nikolayev flung himself against the wall, beating his head against it over and over in an attempt to kill himself. From then on he was watched carefully.

Stalin arrived before dawn the next day; he instantly removed the Leningrad Political Police from the enquiry and put Agranov, a confidential aide, in sole charge.

Stalin, always escorted by selected troops and countless bodyguards, invariably wore a heavy bullet-proof vest. Whenever he travelled, three-quarters of the population living along his route were evacuated and the empty houses occupied by Political Police. The road to Stalin's villa was some twenty miles long; it was guarded night and day by three shifts of Political Police, each of 1,200 men. Hence his decision to go personally to the scene of the crime in Leningrad, after Nikolayev had been arrested, was incredible, or would have been if the official story about the exposure of a terrorist ring had been true.

That same morning of 2 December, almost immediately after Stalin's arrival, Agranov had Kirov's aide, Borisov, called in for questioning. Some of Stalin's bodyguard under Agranov's orders went for him in a car. Yet Borisov, obviously a key person, was never questioned – there was a motor-car 'accident' in which no one was killed but Borisov. In his Secret Speech Khrushchev called this 'unusually suspicious'.

After questioning Medved, who of course knew nothing, and Zaporozhets, Stalin had Nikolayev brought in: in a friendly voice, at first, he asked him why he had killed 'such a nice man'. Nikolayev retorted arrogantly that he had been firing, *via* Kirov, at the Party itself. Stalin then asked him where he had obtained the revolver; at this Nikolayev said, with 'an insolent sneer': 'Why ask me? Ask

Zaporozhets!' Stalin dropped his amiable manner and shouted: 'Take
him away!' He then hurled Nikolayev's file into Yagoda's face, snarling,
'Bungler!'[5]

Thus the whole initial phase of the machination was a partial failure,
insofar as Stalin had hoped to be able to use Nikolayev in an open trial
that would incriminate Zinoviev and Kamenev: it was plain that
Nikolayev could not be relied on for such a trial, which required
complete docility.

The tracks left by Zaporozhet's clumsiness had to be wiped out:
Nikolayev's friend was eliminated. As an interim measure Stalin
resorted to the fabrication about the 104 anonymous White Guard
terrorists, and for a few days afterwards he seems to have suspended his
manoeuvre against Zinoviev and Kamenev; but as soon as the witnesses
to the authentic operation had been removed he resumed it.

It seems plain that after the Kirov killing Stalin was not sure about
his next move. A mere recapitulation of all the trials, taking their
ostensible starting-point in Kirov's assassination, indicates this. In
addition to the trials mentioned before – that of Nikolayev and his
'associates' on 28–9 December 1934 (the month of the killing), of
Zinoviev and Kamenev the next month (15–16 January 1935) and of the
political officials a little later (23 January 1935) – there were two more
trials: that of Kamenev and others in July 1935 and the so-called
'Novosibirsk trial' on 19–22 November 1936, between the first Show
Trial of August 1936 and the second Show Trial on 23–30 January 1937
plus the final Show Trial of 2–13 March 1938.

Thus eight trials – five in addition to the three Show Trials – were
generated by the Kirov killing. Each of this strange series of improviza-
tions produced different assassins for the same corpse on behalf of
different political aims. They are all quite inconsistent with each other;
individually considered, too, each improvization is incoherent.

In Party circles the assassination was considered genuine, i.e., with a
political motivation; given the conditions of the time, it was natural to
suspect practically anyone, since there were, at a conservative estimate,
about 150,000,000 people in the Soviet Union who would have been
delighted to wipe out the whole Party.

Thus the massacre of the White Guards seemed to Party people a
natural consequence of the assassination, even though the official version was swiftly contradicted when the charge was shifted, with no explanation, to the 'ideological' complicity of Zinoviev and Kamenev.
When Zinoviev, Kamenev and some others were tried in closed session
in the middle of January 1935, the Party's restiveness was intensified.

From Stalin's point of view, however, which we have been able to perceive only relatively recently, the operation must have enabled him to test various recipes; he was performing an experiment both in the field of public relations and in the kindred field of politics. He had, in fact, almost ideal laboratory conditions. Even those like Bukharin, who considered him practically a demon, never dreamed of the possibility of his initiating such a subtle, long-range intrigue as the murder of Kirov. Nor – still more strangely – did it ever cross Trotsky's mind, either in his current comments or in his biography of Stalin.

After Kirov's murder Yagoda's initial task was to wipe out all participants – Nikolayev and his personal connexions. Beyond presumption, to be sure, nothing at all is known of Nikolayev's fate. It is not known what he said or even when he and his 'accomplices' were shot. Yagoda himself was to be dismissed from the Political Police only a month after the prisoners in the first Great Charade were all shot. Replaced by Yezhov, he was to appear himself in the third Great Charade, with Bukharin and others, in 1938.

At this time Stalin still retained many former Oppositionists in influential posts: he let Bukharin, Radek and Sokolnikov work on the draft of the new constitution; apparently Bukharin, on his own say-so, did the bulk of the work. Pyatakov, who played the role of chief performer in the middle Charade, was still in charge of heavy industry; Krestinsky and Rosengoltz, and for that matter Christo Rakovsky, whose political surrender was very belated (1934), were rather high up in the foreign service; Rykov was in charge of communications. Former Oppositionists were not yet being physically annihilated, although from the point of view of what was happening within the bowels of the Party, where Stalin was readying his vast enterprise, none of their jobs had, to be sure, any significance.

The preparation of the judicial mask for the real campaign against the population was not actually set in motion until after everyone connected with the Kirov killing had been eliminated – the assassin, some 'accomplices', and the Political Police officials themselves, who while using Nikolayev as a dupe had themselves been duped by Stalin.

The first trial of Zinoviev and Kamenev at the end of January 1935 was a mere preliminary: the former Oppositionists associated with Zinoviev and Kamenev were simply divided up, some of them being induced to testify against Zinoviev and Kamenev, but their testimony was limited, for the time being, to the charge of 'counter-revolutionary activity' (mere grumbling over the general situation, criticism of Stalin, and so on). This trial, as it appears,[6] was to groom Kamenev for his Charade.

Zinoviev and Kamenev had to save their necks by confessing to moral turpitude only, and not, as they thought, to the more serious charge of killing Kirov. They had been reduced to a position where all they could buy was time – a tiny amount at an exorbitant price.

There is a point of some philosophical interest in Stalin's consolidation of his monopoly.

Despite the upheavals of Soviet life and the matchless brutality of the Soviet government, there had been no important assassination since August 1918, when Social-Revolutionaries had killed a Bolshevik notable (Uritsky) and wounded Lenin.

At that time hundreds of prisoners had been shot by way of reprisal; a frantic appeal for 'mass terror' had been made. Not the smallest pretence was made that such reprisals were directly connected with the assassination or attempted assassination themselves: they were understood, in Bolshevik jargon, to be moves against the 'class enemy'. At that time, with the Bolshevik regime still precarious and a Civil War looming up, the situation had, moreover, been far more nerve-racking.

Under Stalin, however, with the application of mass terror both to the Party and government as well as to the population as a whole, a fictitious causal link was established between those proclaimed to be spies, wreckers, etc. and the equally fictitious crimes they were accused of.

This was the element that gave the trials a form in which all details – charges, evidence, testimony, roles and sentences – were creatively harmonized within the framework of a general idea.

Before Stalin had evolved a rounded theory of the true nature of Oppositionist criminality, the official reason given to the victims – Zinoviev, Kamenev, etc. – that they had better confess to the *substance*, not the details, of the charges – which were relatively innocuous – was similar to, though less grave than the line applied in the Great Charades.

They were told that only if they made a formal appearance in court, admitted they were the leaders of the Opposition, took the whole blame for any terrorist sentiments – not even *acts* – and then denounced those sentiments, could their 'supporters' be curbed. This offer had made many of the accused very apprehensive; it also, naturally, revolted them. Curiously enough, Kamenev was apparently its most vociferous champion.

It was rumoured[7] that Kamenev had been to see Stalin again, to reassure him that he had been behaving well, that is, had avoided seeing other Oppositionists, as he had once promised Stalin. Oppositionists in Moscow, like those in Leningrad, formed a loose coterie; they naturally saw each other from time to time at 'social teas' when their talk was free of the official hypocrisy that in public was *de rigueur*. Stalin had naturally heard that Kamenev had unburdened himself in the bosom of these 'tea-parties': that he had not, despite his promise, changed at heart.

Kamenev started out, according to the rumour, by protesting that he had been misunderstood and ended up by bursting into tears. Stalin had pretended not to believe him (as though he had believed him before!) and said he would, accordingly, let justice take its course, i.e., leave it up to the Political Police.

In discussing this a couple of years later Bukharin pointed out that the spinelessness of the Oppositionists was easy to understand. Life in the Party was unendurable: 'loyalty' would have required everyone to be a full-time informer, since at the summits, as indeed throughout the country, the tension was now such that all sorts of people were constantly saying and even writing things that could certainly be called 'Oppositionist' since they questioned the wisdom of the Stalin coterie. As the Party required such conformity, most of it, evidently, feigned, everyone plainly had to be lying most of the time. 'We are all obliged to lie, it is impossible to manage otherwise.'[8]

But the mendacity of the Oppositionists went beyond traditional bounds. In the Tsarist underground, for instance, it had been very nearly a crime to ask for mercy: it discredited you. Also, no sincere revolutionist was expected to promise not to escape; this was a rigid rule that often constituted a real hardship in Tsarist conditions. On the other hand, if such a pledge not to escape *was* ever given, in exceptional circumstances, that pledge absolutely had to be kept. It was part of the general Code of Honour typical of the old revolutionary movement.

Bolshevik rule changed all this. Perhaps the most confusing element of Soviet Party life, especially under Stalin, was that it could plausibly be maintained that the Communist Party leadership was not at all in the same position as the revolutionaries in the Tsarist underground. Under Stalin, Oppositionists would never have said, for instance, that they were against the *Soviet regime*: hence requests for clemency were rational.

Thus the duality of the Party mystique, as it evolved from a 'band of brothers' fighting against heroic odds into a bureaucracy that 'handled' millions of people within the framework of a theological propaganda implemented by institutionalized brutality, created in the very nature of things a double system of values.

While the Stalin faction was consolidating itself, during the first half of the thirties, all those with doubts would sign any submission whatsoever with the tacit proviso that no attention would in fact be paid to it. This was doubtless the first major step in the transformation of the mystique of the band of brothers into the routine hypocrisy of the finished bureaucracy, in which ideology as such – that is, theoretical analysis – was totally extinct.

In its initial phase this breakdown of morality also implied the justification, in a practical sense, of the reigning bureaucrats for not believing in *any* promises made by Oppositionists who had been caught out. The sincerity of any such promise was inherently suspect. The very reason it had been given – the moral authority still retained by the Party – was also the reason it was insincere: how could it be credited?

This led to the attitude taken up at once by the Stalin group – total disbelief, in the circumstances quite justifiable.

Thus the foundations were laid quite early on for one of the most curious phenomena of the Deep Comb-out: an insistence on documentation known in advance to be false.

Kamenev was one of the most pathetic of the defendants in the first trial of the Leningrad Party people: he did his best, but failed to bring the others round to pleading guilty to the bogus charges. His failure excluded a Show Trial. It would have been ridiculous if half the accused contradicted the other half. The trial was held, accordingly, without admitting the public, even a rigged public.

On Stalin's orders Yezhov, in charge of the operation, demanded that the victims be killed, but this must have been a psychological contrivance of Stalin's designed to accustom the Soviet public to the possibility of killing even Old Bolsheviks on outrageous charges. It can be seen from the pace of development of the very idea of these trials that an elaborate build-up was required to escalate the manhandling of Party members from mere isolation to murder.

At the time of this first trial that was still out of the question. The prospect of the death penalty simply prompted a great many still influential Party members to send Stalin petitions; the Society of Old Bolsheviks, still functioning, collected signatures for a petition to the Politburo calling on it to heed Lenin's warning (in his 'Testament') against letting 'blood flow' between Bolsheviks.

In public Stalin himself advised against applying the supreme sentence. At this point he was doubtless satisfied with the mere airing of the possibility in public, and restricted Yezhov to a massive 'clean-up' of Party personnel.

Among Stalin's subordinates Lazar Kaganovich – his only Jewish associate – and Nikola Yezhov stood out. It was these two, in fact, who directed the intra-Party resistance to Kirov's policy of reconciliation. But it was Yezhov who was to give his name to the Deep Comb-out at its height (known in Russian as the *Yezhovshchina*).

Bukharin once described them: he thought Kaganovich the incarnation of duplicity; Yezhov looked to him like a wicked street urchin, tying a piece of paper to a cat's tail and gleefully setting it on fire.[9]

Yezhov was forty years old in September 1936; he had been doing Party work in the provinces until Stalin had taken him on in his secretariat a decade before. A job he was given on a purge commission set up in early 1933 to winnow through the Party membership made him privy to information on all personnel; it also tempered him for the Deep Comb-out that was to bear his name. In 1934 he was elected to the Central Committee at the Seventeenth Party Congress; a year later (February 1935) he was put in charge of the Party Control Commission.[10]

With Stalin's patronage he had gravitated to the very nerve centre of what Stalin himself considered the key function of all political structures – the control of personnel. Stalin not only put him on the Politburo, but gave him Kirov's work: he was in fact at the head of all those sections of the apparatus that had been thought of as Kirov's assignments. The result was that what was still thought of even by insiders like Bukharin[11] – as a balance of forces within the Politburo now seemed to shift decisively away from any reconciliation with Oppositionists.

Granted a free hand, Yezhov proceeded against the entire Party apparatus, beginning circumspectly with the extinction of innocuous organizations such as the Society of Former Political Exiles (political prisoners under Tsarism) and the Society of Old Bolsheviks, referred to by the group on top as 'ageing carpers' incapable of understanding the 'needs of the times'. The Communist Academy, a nest of 'theoreticians' – bookworms unfit for Stalinist construction – was also shut down.

The second Kamenev trial, held in the spring of 1935, put some members of the Kremlin guard in the dock. Kamenev, who could have had nothing to do with the charges, which revolved around an actual conspiracy against Stalin's person,[12] was also involved once again, obviously in order to push forward the vilification of the Oppositionists in preparation for their eventual fate.

Gorky was put in a curious position by the results of the second Kamenev trial. Like everyone else, he had been completely taken in by the official smoke-screen Stalin had thrown up around the assassination of Kirov: Gorky was innocent enough to be indignant at the 'terrorists' whose complicity was blared forth by the Party hacks. Gorky had insisted that measures be taken against them, but when he was convinced that the assassination was being used for political purposes – he did not even begin to suspect, apparently, that it was itself a political purpose – and in a direction opposed to Gorky's own aim of a Party reunion, he did his best to restrain Stalin's 'vengefulness'.

It is hard to disentangle Gorky's reasoning: if the terrorists were not in fact terrorists, why would Stalin want to revenge himself on them? If they were, why defend them?

By the time of the second Kamenev trial Gorky was more upset than ever; by then Stalin had realized that Gorky was simply not going to write a glamorous biography for him – Gorky had been tactfully though tenaciously evading the constantly repeated suggestion that he write a life of Stalin, which by now could be no more than a hypocritical blurb – and dropped the pretence of paying Gorky friendly visits. An ominous reminder that even Gorky was not beyond the power of the Soviet propaganda machine appeared in the form of an article against him in *Pravda*.

This was all part of the internal Party build-up that was to lead to the Great Charades. The general public could not realize what was going on; the terrorism that had become conventional against Party people since the first Kamenev-Zinoviev trial was being carried on for the time being in secret.

About a year after Kirov's murder Stalin seems to have decided on the broad outlines of his unusual plan – the presentation of fabricated scenarios purporting to represent trials in a courtroom.

Even against the background of the many frame-ups presented to the Soviet public during the preceding decade the novelty of Stalin's plan is striking.

In the past, public trials had been given to Social-Revolutionaries, Mensheviks, and British engineers. These had at least had the rationale that those playing the role of defendants could reasonably be considered enemies.

If White Guards were massacred, for instance, the massacre was taken to be justified if you supported the Soviet regime. If you were a White Guard yourself, you accepted such a massacre as another defeat at the hands of a detested enemy – war was war. The hypocrisy of dressing up a massacre by giving it the form of a trial was a mere embellishment, also part of warfare.

Though these proto-Charades had been no more convincing than the Great Charades of 1936–8 themselves, they had been presented, on the other hand, with no fanfare and had involved no Bolsheviks. Hence the scruples even in Stalin's entourage about the killing of the Riutin coterie in 1932 had never been extended to the earlier victims at all.

More especially, the charges in these proto-Charades were merely false, not impossible, while the Great Charades themselves were dependent on a quite demonic view of reality, actually part of the polarization of the universe characteristic of Soviet orthodoxy.

One of these proto-Charades, the Shakhty affair of 1927, may shed some light on Stalin's early technique of securing control over the Political Police and of the methodology underlying the Charades.

Yevdokimov, a Political Police official stationed in the North Caucasus, had cooked up a case against some engineers in a place called Shakhty. Since the case rested on nothing but his own assertions, his chief, Menzhinsky, the head of the Political Police, had demanded some evidence.

When Yevdokimov brought back some 'evidence' in the form of ordinary private letters, Menzhinsky had been even more sceptical: when Yevdokimov said the letters were coded, Menzhinsky asked whether they had been decoded; learning that they had not, since the code was in the possession of the addressees (who were to be arrested anyhow), Menzhinsky lost patience: he insisted that either a code was to be discovered within a fortnight or that Yevdokimov and his agents themselves be put on trial for sabotage.

Facing disgrace, Yevdokimov went to Stalin, at this time representing the Central Committee on the Board of the Political Police. Stalin told him to disregard Menzhinsky: he was to return to the Caucasus and handle the 'subversive' engineers while keeping in direct contact with Stalin. Two days after Yevdokimov's arrival in Rostov (capital of the Shakhty district) all the leading engineers in Shakhty were seized as a body.

This was a direct challenge to Moscow, particularly to Menzhinsky, chairman of the Political Police Board, Rykov, chairman of the Council of the People's Commissars (a successor of Lenin in this office, and later to figure as a 'defendant' in a Charade), and to Kuibyshev, chairman of the Council of National Economy.

At a special session of the Politburo, when Stalin was confronted by a temporary coalition between Rykov, Kuibyshev and Menzhinsky and told he had gone beyond his authority, he displayed a wire from Yevdokimov reporting 'counter-revolutionary' operations in Shakhty that seemed to 'lead' to Moscow. Kuibyshev backed down completely; Rykov was dumbfounded.

Stalin and Yevdokimov were now in effect allies: Stalin, having accepted the moral responsibility for the Shakhty affair, took charge of it. Yevdokimov was told to get 'sincere' confessions by any means from the accused engineers, and to treat the case as a matter of State consequence.

'Any means' meant torture; the procedure was worked out by two of Yevdokimov's aides. These men created the first paradigm of the Great Charades. The accused engineers confessed to monstrous and wildly improbable crimes that at the time were considered perfectly feasible.

The only ones who knew the genesis of this pure frame-up were Stalin himself and Yevdokimov's personal staff in Rostov. Stalin took the credit for having exposed all this subversion over the heads of Rykov and Menzhinsky, head of the Political Police.

By the time the possibility cropped up of extending this technique of accusing 'bourgeois' engineers and scholars of subversion – in the case of the Industrial Party and Professor Ramzin (1930) – no resistance was possible.

There was a curious slip in the preparations for the trial of the Industrial Party: the moment the official report was published it turned out that two capitalists who were supposed to have instructed the chief victim, Ramzin, had been dead for years.

The idea of scapegoats was of course no novelty, either in the Great Charades or for that matter in human history: it is an obvious device of rule.

In Stalin's career, what is of interest is the change in the species of the scapegoat; in 1928 and 1930, at the trials of the Shakhty Wreckers and the Industrial Party, the usual charges were made that eminent engineers and professors had been sabotaging Soviet industry on orders from exiled upper-class Russians (bankers, industrialists, capitalists), i.e. the people on whom Stalin had for years blamed the hardships of Soviet life – the 'remnants of the Russian bourgeoisie'.

Up to 1937 Stalin did not think it prudent to blame the Oppositionists for the various errors, blunders, crises, and shortages in the wake of his collectivization programme, but after the first Great Charade, with the killing of Zinoviev and Kamenev, he determined to blame the Old Bolsheviks for economic and social calamities as well as for terrorism, espionage, etc. This involved a complete shift of the General Line in propaganda. The Soviet government had been denying for years that there had been any trouble at all with the crash programmes of industrialization and collectivization, and Party agents had put out a euphoric line that was, on the whole, remarkably successful.

Now the decision to blame all the notorious disasters of the initial planning era on the Bolsheviks naturally involved an acknowledgement of their existence; this alone entailed a shift in propaganda.

Just as Stalin would never have bothered pretending to the Soviet people that the initial planning era was blissful, so, in the middle of the thirties, the converse implied that he considered it essential to apologize to the people for what they had been through: his apology took an organic political form, as it were, by blaming it on all his rivals within the Communist movement.

Though neither the Shakhty nor the Industrial Party trial was given the immense publicity that accompanied the Great Charades, and did not add to Stalin's personal prestige, they are of cardinal consequence from a technical point of view. They provided Stalin with a mechanism for the extortion of 'sincere' confessions. Once the technique was worked out it could be used anywhere at any time: it was of no importance whatever whether the confession accepted as sincere was also *true*.

Thus the theatrical procedures worked out under Stalin included a foolproof device. Enveloped by the propaganda whose manipulation had long since been systematized by the regime, it enabled Stalin to launch both the Great Charades and the Deep Comb-out without misgivings. By early 1936 he began issuing businesslike instructions to the Political Police.[13]

He had a conference called of about forty executive officers. These were informed by the head of the Secret Political Department, Molchanov, that a far-flung conspiracy headed by Trotsky, Zinoviev, and Kamenev had just been exposed. The organization had already, he said, been functioning for several years, with the aim of assassinating Stalin and the Politburo and taking power. The officers were then told that under orders from Yagoda, the People's Commissar, most of them were now attached to Molchanov's department to carry on an investigation of the whole plot, under the personal supervision of Stalin with the assistance of Yezhov, at the time Secretary of the Central Committee.

The officers were told that the information against the plotters was completely reliable; it was the starting-point for the investigators, whose further tasks would be, accordingly, simply to get full confessions from the accused, or rather the parties whose guilt was now established. Though some of them were known to have been incarcerated during the period when they were supposed to be functioning it was known, Molchanov said, that they had managed to direct the terrorists' activity even from prison.

After explaining the details of their future assignments, Molchanov showed them a secret circular signed by Yagoda, warning them against using illegal means against the prisoners, i.e., violence, threats, or for that matter promises.

The executives were very impressed. Two points, however, seemed especially baffling. How could *they* not have known about such a ramified conspiracy? And, if they hadn't known, why were they not being punished for negligence?

Stalin's scheme at this point was to bring a few hundred of the best known former Oppositionists to Moscow and 'break them down' by inquisitorial methods. He calculated that about 20 per cent would crack under the psychological pressure, and those 20 per cent, i.e. about fifty to sixty men, could then be used to testify that they had been following the instructions of Trotsky, Zinoviev and Kamenev. Their testimony could then be used against Zinoviev and Kamenev directly.

Thus the Political Police began with a small fund of material to be used in preparing an official case against the former Opposition.

To lubricate the procedure it was decided to use some stool-pigeons as decoys, both during the preliminary breakdown techniques and later on in court.

It was difficult to depend completely on the public performance of the victims; many who had signed confessions were discarded as the material was whipped into shape for the public show. It was important to avoid a scene in court that would embarrass the regime. Hence, of the sixteen prisoners in the first Great Charade – reduced from Stalin's original plan of at least fifty – five were working for the Political Police directly (Olberg, Reingold, Pickel, Fritz David and Berman-Yurin).

Valentine Olberg was a Latvian who had come to the Soviet Union on a passport bought in Czechoslovakia. A former agent of the Political Police, he had been an informer against Trotskyites in Berlin; he had once tried to get a job working directly for Trotsky, exiled at the time in Turkey. In 1935 he had been recalled to the Soviet Union and given a job in a teachers' institute where he was supposed to monitor Trotskyite tendencies among the youth.

Olberg was utterly docile. He regarded himself simply as an agent of the Political Police and thought it perfectly in line with his duties to help it against 'Trotskyism'. He signed everything put before him, objecting, futilely, only against signing depositions naming as his accomplices old Party comrades and even childhood friends.

The second witness used against Trotsky, Zinoviev and Kamenev was totally different: Isak Reingold, a big, powerful, high-spirited Party man, was a relative of the Finance Commissar Sokolnikov and had been acquainted with many Party people, including Kamenev. Reingold was useful since he knew Kamenev and Sokolnikov.

After weeks of constant interrogation for forty-eight hours at a time while he was kept hungry and sleepless, after threats directed at his family and relatives, nothing worked. Finally Yezhov thought up a trick. After being left alone for a few days to recuperate, Reingold was brought to Molchanov at night, shown a paper with the Political Police seal on it sentencing him to death at once and exiling his family to Siberia. He was then advised by Molchanov – actually an old acquaintance – to petition Yezhov directly to have the sentence suspended and his case reviewed.

The next night he was told that Yezhov had said the sentence would be rescinded only if Reingold agreed to help the investigation. Reingold was stubborn; he refused to sign anything at all unless some member of the Central Committee told him personally he was known to be innocent and was simply helping the Party.

Yezhov intervened personally. He told Reingold 'in the name of the Central Committee' what he wanted to hear; from then on Reingold cooperated with the Political Police. His depositions were painstakingly edited: Yagoda took them to Stalin, who returned them the following day with Molotov's name removed from the list of leaders whose assassination Zinoviev was supposed to be insisting on. The startled Political Police agents saw at once that Molotov's position had slumped.

Some other insertions of Stalin's cast some light on his mentality: they were made in his own hand. He put the following sentence into Reingold's mouth: 'Zinoviev said,' (Reingold said) ' "It is not enough to fell the oak; all the young oaks growing around it must be felled, too".' Likewise, Kamenev: 'Stalin's leadership is made up of too hard a granite to expect that it would split of itself. Therefore, the leadership will have to be split'.

Richard Pickel, the third of the Political Police stooges used in the first Charade, was not an Old Bolshevik either, but a rather sentimental fellow who had been a lyric poet in youth. He was on very friendly terms with all sorts of Political Policemen. He, too, yielded to pressure from some of these friends he used to sit around drinking with, but he refused to do more than keep to the promise forced from him in the very beginning – to provide depositions against himself and Zinoviev, whose chief of secretariat he had once been: he refused to inculpate any others unless they had already confessed or been denounced, in which cases he would provide confirmation.

After knuckling under, Pickel grew more and more dedicated. His old friends were ordered to treat him as they had in the good old days: he was given a better cell and visited by his former friends in the Political Police, who brought playing cards, snacks, soft drinks, and sat around with him into the small hours. This cheered Pickel up, though now and then he would relapse and remember where he was.

But Olberg, Reingold and Pickel were not enough; since Stalin had to show the comprehensiveness of the network, he had to have it spread all over the country. For this a large number of former Oppositionists were brought to Moscow to be worked over for their role as the terrorists' army; but the ordinary investigators could make no headway

at all, since the prisoners all had an alibi that could hardly be challenged
– they had been incarcerated for years, generally in obscure corners of
the country.

The investigators themselves hardly knew the degree to which the
whole plan was a fabrication; they were honestly perplexed. They
approached Molchanov with the complaint that they had no lever to
use against such prisoners, who simply referred to their alibi. They said
Yagoda's secret circular forbidding violence, threats, promises tied their
hands.

Molchanov pretended to be amazed: how could they, experienced
Political Police officers, not realize what was permissible and what was
not? They had to be politicians, he told them, as well as investigators.

When one of them pointed out that Yagoda himself had signed the
secret circular and asked how they could know they had to disregard it,
Molchanov gave the tersest of explanations: 'Now I am telling you
officially: Go back to your prisoners and give them the works – mount
them and don't dismount till they have given you the testimony!'

This phrase had been celebrated since a proto-Charade of March
1931. One of the chiefs of the Political Police, having failed to get a
false confession from Sukhanov, the famous memoirist of the 1917
period, that the Mensheviks had been plotting with the general staffs
of various foreign countries, was given by Stalin the simple formula
that was to become the guideline of the Great Charades and the Deep
Comb-out – 'Mount, and don't dismount!'

Nevertheless many prisoners simply did not crack. Even Yezhov's
threat – that the interrogators could always resign if they didn't feel up
to scratch – did not work: it implied a protest they would be instantly
accountable for.

The interrogators had a few successes during the week after the
breaking-in of the three stooges. Each confession was the result of a
deal in which the prisoner's innocence was expressly acknowledged
and the confession duly treated as a service to the Party. But when
Molchanov found out this group of investigators had been making such
deals, he called a special conference. He specifically forbade deals on
principle: thus he forced the investigators to extract their confessions
by taking the charges seriously and simply requiring an admission from
the prisoners. Deals were exceptions that could be authorized only in
special cases by Yezhov himself.

The Political Police, at this stage, really believed Stalin when he
gave his promise to spare the lives and families of the Old Bolsheviks.
They were horrified at the prospect of actually killing so many respected
old Party members; after all, the threat of death was quite different

from carrying it out. The veterans of the Political Police were shocked to learn that the death penalties were *for real*. Only the non-ideological younger careerists, who had entered the Party relatively late, preserved their *esprit de corps*. These were now to be seen strutting about with the atmosphere of a noble duty proudly performed. The others, the many who had been more or less loyal Bolsheviks, felt unmanned.

By the end of the same month, August, they were all told that a new trial was in the offing, also of a whole batch of former notables headed by Radek, Serebryakov, and Sokolnikov, all old-line partisans of Lenin. The Political Police were by now well aware that what Stalin had done to his former associates in the Party summits was to murder them *via* a juridicial form; but Stalin now seemed about to apply a systematic scheme of destruction.

On 1 September 1936, just after the Political Police were informed of the forthcoming second Great Charade, Stalin told Yagoda and Yezhov to pick out 5,000 of the most activist former Oppositionists, gaoled in various concentration camps or in exile, and have them secretly shot out of hand.

This was, in a way, even more startling, though of course less dramatic than the Great Charades themselves. Never before, even in the Soviet Union, had Communists simply been destroyed without even going through the formality of any accusation whatever. Stalin repeated the same order, with the same figure, in the following summer (1937), and perhaps many more times, presumably to eliminate the whole of the former Opposition. By that time, those being killed specifically as Oppositionists were one drop in the torrent of arrests, executions, gaolings and banishments that hailed down on the Soviet Union for more than two-and-a-half years.

The breaking down of prisoners was to become much easier after the first Great Charade, which showed that Stalin would stop at nothing. If he could openly arrange the killing of the former Party leaders, mere bravery was no help. After the results of the first Charade were known, holding out on the Political Police beyond a certain point was certain suicide, and possible torture or death for one's family.

When Zinoviev and Kamenev, finally reduced by exhaustion and constant threats to themselves and their families, agreed to surrender, they were still naïve enough to make a condition – that Stalin confirm his promises to spare their lives and those of their families and of former Oppositionists.

Stalin was delighted by the news of their surrender: he 'grinned and kept stroking his right moustache'.[14] When the two men were brought to him, with only one other member of the Politburo present, they pleaded with Stalin: How could he destroy the Leninist Old Guard? And could they believe in promises that had been broken so often in the past?

After accusing the shattered men of not thinking 'dialectically', Stalin began pacing the floor, speaking in a grave, moving voice. He called on them to remember: one, the trial was directed not against them but against Trotsky, the 'principal enemy of our Party'; two, 'if we did not shoot you when you fought against the Central Committee, why should we shoot you after you have helped the Central Committee in its struggle against Trotsky?'; three, 'the Comrades (he actually said 'comrades') forget that we are also Bolsheviks, disciples of Lenin, and that we don't want to shed the blood of Old Bolsheviks, no matter how grave were their past sins against the Party.'

Kamenev then got to his feet to announce that both he and Zinoviev would be put on public trial if they were promised that the Old Bolsheviks' lives would be spared, as well as those of their families and of former Oppositionists.

'That,' said Stalin with a straight face, 'goes without saying.'

Stalin's behaviour with respect to Zinoviev and Kamenev was quite strange. There was, perhaps, never any reason for them to *like* each other, yet the hatred Stalin had stored up against old colleagues surely had something morbid about it. Even those who knew him well were astonished by the ferocity of his hatred for Old Bolsheviks; when told that they were refusing to sign this or that, he was reported to turn quite green with rage and shout hoarsely, with an 'unusually strong Georgian accent': 'Tell them, that no matter what [Zinoviev and Kamenev] do, they won't be able to stop the march of history. The only thing that they still can do is – either die or save their hides. Give them the works until they come crawling to you on their bellies with confessions in their teeth!'[15]

The first Great Charade had been based on charges of terrorism only: psychologically, this was not wholly implausible. It did not, to be sure, fit the actual histories and characters of the Bolsheviks who appeared at the trial, yet inherently it was rather attractive: what could be more natural, after all, than wanting to kill Stalin? In the Soviet Union he was well known to have been personally responsible for incalculable numbers of victims in the wake of the great plans for socio-economic development; he had become the head of a government institutionally based on coercion. Thus the idea of killing him had a sort of common sense about it; Party members might be forced to admit the possibility that Old Bolsheviks too might waver in their Marxist devotion to non-terrorist methods – Stalin, too, was a Marxist, after all – and fly off the handle, while non-Communists, hating all Communists alike, must have nodded understandingly.

Nor was the linking of the terrorist charges to a struggle for power wildly unlikely: simply as a motivation – if the charges were accepted *in general* – it might easily appeal to the simple-minded, who would then merely have to be helped over the obstacle that even though fabulous plots were being incessantly hatched by a vast network of plotters whose leaders had personal access to Stalin every day not a hair of Stalin's head had been touched. But simple-minded people could swallow that easily.

Stalin launched the second Great Charade on the same basis as the first: having devised a 'Reserve Centre' consisting of the cast of the second Charade that was meant to take over wherever the Trotskyite-Zinovievite Terrorist Centre had left off, the Political Police began preparing their prisoners for the same kind of show. They got over the depressing effect of the execution of all the victims in the first show by claiming that those in the second would be safe since *their* terrorist centre was, after all, only in reserve.

But after only a few weeks they were told to stop and wait for further orders. When it came, the new directive flabbergasted the interrogators: Molchanov, in Yezhov's presence – vital to produce belief – told them they would have to get confessions to a plot with the German and Japanese General Staffs and Intelligence Services to seize power for the purpose of restoring capitalism.

This was not merely idiotic in substance: as a technical matter it complicated the functioning relationship between each interrogator and his prisoner. The latter difficulty to be sure, was circumvented quite easily simply by changing the prisoners around; each interrogator could start afresh with some semblance of psychological plausibility.

What had happened was, in a way, simple enough: Stalin had been disappointed by some slight reluctance in the foreign press to swallow the Charades as real trials, and by the reaction of the Soviet public.

Yagoda's intelligence reports had been unequivocal: the scribblings on the walls of a number of Moscow factories – 'Down with the murderer of the leaders of the October revolution'. 'What a shame they didn't kill the Georgian reptile!' – echoed a very widespread feeling that, had the prisoners in the first show been doing what they were accused of, more power to them!

This meant quite simply that terrorism might once more become as attractive to Soviet youth as it had been to a broad segment of revolutionary youth under Tsarism; the old fight of Marxism against terrorism might, in a word, be said to have been lost under the pressure of Stalin's

personal dictatorship. If even Old Bolsheviks could find no way out
from under Stalin except by terrorism, why, that might be the best
thing after all. The former leaders of the Party were, in short, taken for
martyrs. Stalin found it necessary to lunge ahead still more violently.

The handling of Party people, both before and during the Deep Comb-
out, was carried out against a background of shared ideology. It has
the interest of a study in the ikonization of ideas, in this case the
sanctification of the Party.

Alive, Lenin had been the leader of the Bolsheviks: that was never a
legal situation codified by law, but had arisen through his spiritual
authority. But in the mid-twenties, after Stalin came to dominate the
Party, the same authority was attributed to him, though it was still not
embodied in law and there was no question of his radiating the personal
authority of Lenin. Stalin had *power*.

Yet the Oppositionists did not admit that: they kowtowed to the
power, but semi-consciously rationalized it into an acknowledgement of
Stalin as Party leader like Lenin.

When, in the wake of Kirov's murder, the whole operation began and
Zinoviev and Kamenev – not knowing, to be sure, of Stalin's role – were
persuaded to accept the moral responsibility for the murder and thus
sacrifice themselves for the Party by unifying it against what might
have seemed to be a new wave of terrorism, they could scarcely have
accepted the reasoning: how, after all, could such preposterous lies help
the Party?

They had no choice. And this lack of choice was simply presented to
them in this particular formula, a ritualistic expression that in that
context compelled acquiescence, at least formally.

It was a chess-game, on the part of Stalin, played out against a background of innocent people – Party idealists and dupes, the naïve masses,
etc. – who naturally could not see the game. Once Zinoviev and
Kamenev said yes, as they had to, they were of course lost: but they
were lost anyhow: just then there was nothing else they could do.
Besides, at that moment they were not *quite* dead – who could tell what
might happen? Stalin was by this time directing the game: *he* knew it
was chess.

The universally accepted ikonization of the Party had some effect on
the spiritual working-over of the victims prior to the Charades. It was
an attitude that the gaolers could appeal to in the hope of extracting
from the prisoners a certain style for the scenario. It was an interrogator's approach. The idea might be expressed a little crudely: 'If you
are as devoted to the Revolution as you claim, you'll have to help the
Party. And helping the Party – at this stage of world history, etc. –

'means confessing to certain things the Party wants you to confess to'.

In the case of prisoners with a known Oppositional past that meant turning their past into Charade material by slanting it; in the case of non-Oppositionists it meant no more than underwriting something dictated by the Party.

The notion of personal honour, or of abstract desiderata like truthfulness, could not, of course, even theoretically prevail against a Party demand, however grotesque. Indeed, the whole notion of innocence was peculiarly irrelevant, really preposterous: it was obvious to both interrogators and prisoners that utility to the Party transcended all criteria.

This general criterion was relevant only to the *form* of the confession: Stalin wanted the confessions to be more or less plausible: the 'more or less' was inherently elastic. After all, the nonsensicality of the Great Charades was instantly apparent to many the moment the newspaper accounts appeared: it was evident that whatever might have happened it was not what the prisoners were confessing to.

Consequently it was only a question of creating a general impression. Within that general impression some pains were taken to put over a plausible story; some of the prisoners, once they had been tamed, had an interest in conveying some nuance of self-justification or narcissistic self revelation.

A statement made by Bukharin in his Charade, in speaking of the 'black vacuity' that overwhelmed people excluded from the Party, has a certain poignancy. For people whose sole purpose in life had been summed up by the sacrosanct institution of the Party, it was bitter to be cast outside, as it was to realize that the Party was no more. To the extent that the Party might be held to be not extinct – after all, it embodied the 'conquests' of the October Revolution – but merely afflicted, the chance of helping it might rescue a lifelong Bolshevik from that 'black vacuity', that horrible burden of the Russian intelligentsia – the answer to the question: 'What have I lived for?' It was this, perhaps, that enabled Bukharin to put into his final plea some psychological touches that may have been genuine.

The scenarists had, of course, a dual purpose in constructing the mock-dialogue between the prisoners and the 'prosecution' – to wipe out the Opposition spiritually, as a part of their physical extirpation, and at the same time to glorify Stalin. This dual aim had to be embodied in confessions, accordingly, that had a certain plausibility. This was a little difficult: why, after all, should hardened monsters, criminals and scum of the worst type, suddenly turn tail?

This attempt to construct a framework of psychological plausibility gives a further insight into the true nature of the Charades.

The scenarios were contrived to resemble a form of trial, but it was not a form defined by the *penal* code; it was not an instance of a forensic procedure, even of a forensic frame-up. It was like the penitential trials of the Medieval Church: the information had been gathered by officers of the Inquisition and a decision had been made as to what was to be done to the culprit; the stage was then set for a trial. What the culprit was supposed to do was simply to confess his sin, repent, and humbly return to the Church, which, of course, then forgave his soul (whatever might happen to his body).

One is bound to wonder whether Stalin had not absorbed far more canon law as a seminary student than he has been given credit for!

Consequently the problem of why hardened monsters should change so abruptly, and beat their breasts in a public display of penitence, cannot be viewed as an attempt at psychological plausibility. It was simply an instance of the penitential posture required as the final stage in an inquisitorial procedure.

Looked at as a medieval judicial exercise, the specific concept of the scenarios had this unmistakably theological background. The basic device in use throughout was the tacit presumption of a sweeping moral conversion – the notion of becoming a 'new man' and then, after seeing the light as a 'new man', becoming blissfully reunited with the Party once again.

It had the small hitch, to be sure, that it did not save your life – another medieval echo!

In the case of Zinoviev and Kamenev particularly, since they had often repented and recanted long before the Great Charades, the similarity between their confessions and those of medieval heretics is striking. A relapsed heretic was called upon to display penitence even though in such cases his death was a foregone conclusion.

A trivial detail has some interest: however persuasive – theatrically, psychologically or ritually – this duplication of an ecclesiastical form might have been to Stalin, shaped in youth by a Greek Orthodox seminary, one cannot see how at least the Jewish Marxists he had outwitted and humiliated could find anything salutary in such a public display. They had long since lost all hope!

This theory of conversion was itself rooted in the Bolshevik posture of total identification with the Party; hence the momentary lapse into a vile heterodoxy could be and was felt as a lapse from Grace; the return to the Party was presented as a return to Grace, even though the return was *en route* to the grave.

The praise accorded Stalin's wisdom, leadership, genius and so on was incorporated in this confessional technique, since Stalin's virtues were all immanent in the theory of Grace: it was through the insight into *his* wisdom, *his* leadership, that the erring sinner was finally restored to the bosom of the Party at the very moment that the Party's executioners were about to pull the trigger.

Theoretically, of course, the sincerity of the conversion might have been thought a sufficient warrant for complete salvation: if one is back in the Party's Grace, why not in the Party's good graces? If the context were as authentic, in fact, as its theological structure, if it were a real return to a real Church, that might have been a perfectly good question.

But of course it was not. In the scenario the prisoners were performing their roles only with a view to their histrionic and propagandistic effect. The mock-theological conversion was simply a device to bridge the gap between the dementia or falseness of the actual charges, and the performances of the men in the dock. The plausibility did not have to be based either on genuine politics or on genuine psychology – merely on genuine theatre.

Since the prisoners naturally expressed themselves in the jargon of Bolshevism, it was equally natural for the psychological interplay that was bound to take place between the interrogators and the prisoners to be facilitated if the interrogators could present themselves as Party people, too. The interrogator could indicate that he too had a distinguished record within the Party, as in the handling of Mrachkovsky, who stopped resisting when his interrogator showed him that he, too, had a splendid war record.[16] In many cases, especially before the Combout had assumed a mass character and begun to take in countless numbers of ordinary people, the interrogators and the prisoners had known each other or about each other for a long time.

This intimate byplay between interrogator and prisoner was naturally very variable: it might sometimes work the other way, when the shame felt by the interrogator led him to show too much sympathy, or take too much time in breaking down the prisoner. Thus it could not be depended on, if only because many interrogators, too, after all, were perfectly capable of realizing what madness it all was. Hence for them to be effective, humanly speaking, it would have been necessary initially to convert the interrogator to a wholehearted conviction of the moral necessity for the whole procedure.

It was obviously better to dehumanize the proceedings altogether, except in some cases, and apply the routine pressure without wasting too much time on sentimentality. This possibility of such intimacy was forestalled by having some second interrogator, without such a past, present without saying a word. This made any footing of intimacy impossible.

Later on, as the Deep Comb-out expanded, it became obvious that everyone was likely to be affected; this created another bond between prisoners and interrogators; both realized that it was only a question of luck which was which. Those Political Police groups that had provided the interrogators were themselves gaoled and interrogated in their turn. By the end of the first year of the Deep Comb-out – 1936 – it was an overwhelming likelihood that everyone who had been involved in any Charade was standing in the way of a snowballing process.

At the outset of this process the admissions and confessions were supposed to be extracted. Yet the phoniness of the charges, tacitly accepted by both prisoners and interrogators, ultimately produced a deal. It didn't matter whether the interrogators thought the charges bogus or not: apparently, at least in the beginning, some were not much less naïve than the public. Even in such cases the recalcitrance of the prisoners, their passionate indignation, outrage, etc. – at first – made it necessary, *de facto*, to work out the details of something that could be agreed to as the relentless pressure began to undermine the prisoners.

This method of working out a deal had all the aspects of a negotiation; functionally it did not matter whether the interrogator did or did not believe the charges. In the case of the relationship between the Political Police interrogator, Slutsky, and Mrachkovsky and Smirnov, for instance, Slutsky's attitude was tragic: 'We are all in this together, we know it's madness, but we must act', etc. This was not at all typical; characteristically the interrogators would simply outline the specific charges and expect the prisoner to create the endless bridges necessary between his own past, whatever it was, and whatever he was being called upon to confess to. Once the prisoner had been broken and had indicated that he was, *in principle*, prepared to sign false confessions, the actual details would be negotiated. Though prisoners might be willing to destroy themselves by confessions, they would balk at individual admissions: since their compliance was needed the interrogator would perforce make a bargain.

In the case of Bukharin, from Stalin's point of view a prize witness, a form of negotiation was reached despite the extreme pressure applied.

At the age of forty-five Bukharin had fallen in love with a beautiful young girl; in spite of his age, his pudginess, his general absence of panache, he managed to take her away from her fiancé (Sokolnikov's son), a very attractive young man. They had a child: Bukharin was mad with joy. Like other prisoners with children or wives, Bukharin was told that if he did what the Politburo wanted he would be spared – merely

gaoled. Radek was shown to him alive, a sample beneficiary of a bona-
fide promise of Stalin's to some of the prisoners in the second Charade.
Radek even seemed a little humane; at their confrontation he refused to
confirm some of the worst accusations contrived against Bukharin.

Stalin was determined, apparently, to destroy Bukharin's attachment
to Lenin, perhaps out of spite. In any case, he instructed the Political
Police to force Bukharin to sign a confession that as far back as 1918 he
had been conspiring to kill Lenin. As part of the general breaking-down
of Bukharin, Stalin had a number of old dissidents (Left Communists
and Left SRs) pretend at their interrogations that Bukharin had in fact
been plotting along those lines as far back as 1918, and that when Dora
Kaplan tried to kill Lenin in 1918 Bukharin had known all about it and
approved.

Finally Bukharin was broken down; at first he signed such a confession, but when he actually saw it typed out, two days later, he got so
hysterical he retracted everything. He had to be processed all over
again.

Since Stalin needed Bukharin he was, curiously, compelled to yield:
Bukharin refused to agree that he had wanted to kill Lenin or that he
himself had ever been a spy for Germany, or had been an accomplice in
the killing of Kirov and Gorky.

Because of this the script outlining Bukharin's intention of killing
Lenin had to be modified: it was negotiated down to a plan to 'arrest'
Lenin for twenty-four hours. Finally, the arrest of Stalin was supposed
to be part of it; by now Stalin's re-write school had established the
legend of Stalin as Lenin's right-hand man from the very beginning.
(In this third Charade, Stalin, preoccupied with the magnification of
his own past, had a minor witness, Mantsev, say that Trotsky had
wanted to arrest Stalin at one point so that 'Lenin and the Central
Committee would capitulate'.)

In the building up of the incriminatory material for use in the
Charades an organic way of exploiting the momentum of the interrogation would be a fantastic exaggeration of what might have been a
reality: for instance, a harmless interchange of sneers at the leadership
in a café conversation would be agreed to by the prisoner as laying the
groundwork for what might conceivably be turned into an actual
intention to kill the leadership: that intention would be transformed
into a plot, and that plot into an actual organization.

At each stage of this chain of development, a dossier could be built,
but the original point of departure — the harmless café conversation —
would be in only the first dossier, which would then be dropped by the
time, say, of the third stage, at which point the interrogator would be

able to start a new interrogation by saying: 'You have already admitted that you were one of the members of a subversive organization; now, who were your accomplices?'

By this stage, with the vanishing of the harmless café conversation, the fantasy, in reality made up out of whole cloth, would almost seem to be as well documented as anything could be.

Hence the articulation of these fables would have its own rationale: it might even seem persuasive to the individuals involved, since in the atmosphere of violence, hypocrisy and dementia the articulation of such fantasies and fairy-tales was the only element of reality. By accepting this technique of progressive transmutation both gaolers and prisoners might feel themselves to be anchored in reality relatively firmly.

This general development was facilitated by a Bolshevik trait that is derived both from a Russian characteristic and also, no doubt, from an element of Marxism that itself was perhaps taken over with such ease into the thinking of the Russian intelligentsia because it was inherently attractive. It is a form of dogmatism masked by pseudo-logic.

The desire, let us say, is to be consistent: a seemingly hardheaded, no-nonsense accepter of objective reality. The form of a statement exemplifying this would be:

If you really thought so-and-so, it would have been logical, i.e. consistent, for you to have done so-and-so; therefore, if you should have done so-and-so, you might have done so-and-so, and if you might have, you did. Right?

This was all part of formal Marxism, in the sense in which Marxism as such might be thought to constitute a system, and not merely a way of looking at things, advocating certain reforms and so on. To the extent that Marx (and Engels even more so) had imposed Hegel's logic on what *seemed* to be studies of empirical data – history, politics, sociology, economics – to that extent it was taken for granted that certain things simply had to happen in such and such a way. Even if the people involved knew what was going to happen – had, let us say, read Marx – they simply could not prevent a process embedded in reality from happening. This was one of the 'iron laws' that gave Marx and his followers pleasure.

This point of view, a little primitive, perhaps, even in so able a mind as Marx's, was made still more primitive in its Bolshevik version, which loathed any form of in-between position at all. Anyone occupying a position that was not an extreme, let us say, an intermediate position, could be dismissed by the formula: Whatever he thinks, he is *objectively* at the other extreme. More colloquially, he who is not with us is against us – objectively.

Thus a basic criticism of opponents, however close they might seem to be to the Bolsheviks, might be that if they really understood, in a logical way, what they were doing they would be out-and-out enemies; ultimately, this would lead to the statement that if they were *consistent* they would kill us.

This type of consequential thinking was turned against the prisoners, both in the Great Charades and in the depositions that preceded the gaoling and killing of millions of ordinary Soviet citizens.

The 'kernel of truth' idea was far from indispensable. It was at most a rhetorical convenience. As numbers began to swell in the wake of the Kirov murder – from December 1934 on – the rhetorical assistance afforded by building up a case on the progressive exaggeration of an innocuous remark into an actual combat organization was replaced by something far simpler, emotionally and perhaps logically more satisfying, and much more efficient as a procedural mechanism: wholesale fabrication, functionally identical with exaggeration, but cleaner, quicker and handier.

Nor was it necessary to make much use of any refinements of Bolshevik logic after sizeable numbers of people began to be processed. The psychological background of the confessions was simply prison life – solitude, misery, anguish, despair, especially solitude, which would so depress the prisoners that they would often cling to the interrogators as the only human beings accessible, as at least an area of warmth in a frigid wilderness. The prisoner's relationship to his tormentor would become his principal human concern. His feelings could thus be played upon: the interrogator would interrupt the sessions, leaving the prisoner wondering, or would alternate a long-drawn-out period of interrogation with a long period of solitude, until the prisoner, out of boredom, longed to be questioned again.

Sometimes the interrogation would seem to be broken off altogether; this also led to a yearning for a restoration of human contact, even in the form of the interrogation. Or the interrogators, in accordance with standard police methods, would alternate between the 'heavy' and the 'soft guy', who says 'no, no' and seems to be defending the prisoner. Part of standard procedure, also, would be the practice of showing the prisoner someone else's confession.

One of Stalin's intentions in ordering the scenarios seems to have been to make the prisoners, especially some of the more 'Leftist' ones, eat their own words by forcing them to take the blame for faults they had once attributed to him.

Just as the Leftist prisoners had once predicted, for instance, that Stalin's policies would lead to a restoration of capitalism, so they were now obliged to say that it was they who had been aiming at such a restoration all along; just as they had accused Stalin in the past of vengefulness and a lust for power, so they now used these personal qualities as an explanation for their own subversion.

This may also have been an element in their admitting, rather preposterously, to total passivity *vis à vis* Trotsky, towards whom most of them had always had at best a nuanced attitude and whom in fact none had ever followed blindly even before his exile.

In general Stalin, in the midst of all his fabrications and murders, displayed a sinuous sense of thrift. It was sensible for him to hit as many birds as possible with one stone; as stage-manager he found this easy. The case of the medical murders that played such a role in the third Great Charade illustrates this predilection of his.

One of the most obvious, quite common-sense criticisms of the Charades as a whole, as far as the chief charge, terrorism, was concerned, was: with all those preparations, why so few results? After all, there was a network taking in many thousands of people, directed by dozens of perfectly able men with a great deal of experience as men of action specializing in conspiracy and agitation, yet all Stalin had to show was the assassination of Kirov. It would thus have been convenient to lay a few more assassinations at their door; yet there had been no assassinations for two decades, except for the public action of Dora Kaplan when she wounded Lenin and the assassination of Uritsky.

A few people had died, of whom the best known, with an international reputation to boot, was Gorky. His son Peshkov had also died, as well as two other important figures: Kuibyshev, who had been on the Politburo and Menzhinsky, chairman of the Political Police. Stalin used these four figures to swell the number of alleged victims of the vast ring of terrorists and showed that Gorky's murder had been necessary just because he was such a great friend of Stalin's, looking up to him, admiring him, sponsoring his politics.

At the third Charade Yagoda was given the following lines, as an explanation of why Gorky had to go: '[Gorky] is a man who is very . . . devoted to the policy . . . now being carried out in the country, very devoted personally to Joseph Stalin.' While Vyshinsky, in his own speech, used the lines: 'It was not without good reason that [Gorky] bound up his life with the great Lenin and the great Stalin, as one of their best and closest friends.'

The difficulty was that all four of these men, including Gorky, had died apparently natural deaths, attended only by their physicians. In addition they were so prominent that since they had been ill for years the newspapers had often published progress reports on their health: Gorky had been tubercular even as a youth, and was sixty-eight when he died; it turned out that for years he had had no more than a third of his lungs.

Kuibyshev and Menzhinsky had had heart trouble for years, and finally died of it; all this had appeared in some detail in the Soviet press. The only way out for the fabrication of charges lay in the inculpation of the physicians, linking them somehow to the 'terrorist network'.

It turned out to be extremely simple, in the sense that the action of a lever is simple. In the case of the three celebrated physicians who had treated Gorky, Kuibyshev and Menzhinsky the lever was simply blackmail – the threat of torturing hostages.

Dr Levin, a man of about seventy, had a number of sons and a great many grandchildren; for all practical purposes these were hostages. Even though Levin was very close to the Politburo, and for that matter had treated Stalin himself and his daughter Svetlana, it was no use. He was obliged to testify that he had been Yagoda's principal assistant, together with Drs Pletnev and Kazakov, in the murder of the three invalids by medical means. The theory behind this, no thinner than the other testimony, turned on the claim that Yagoda had given them instructions to perform these medical murders on behalf of the terrorist plotters and that they had obeyed out of simple fear.

In this way three apolitical persons – including Pletnev, until then one of the adornments of Soviet medicine – were undone for the purely technical purpose of increasing the number of victims of the fictitious conspiracy.

There was a slightly corny element in the way Pletnev was broken down: it was a variant of the swindle known in English as the badger game, in which a young woman entices a respectable man (husband, father, celebrity) and arranges, for blackmail purposes, to be found with him in a compromising position by an alleged husband.

The Political Police sent Pletnev as a patient an attractive young woman. She saw him once or twice, then went to see the State Prosecutor with an hysterical story to the effect that Pletnev, a man of sixty-six with a very long, distinguished and unblemished record, had lost control of himself, pounced on her and had even gone so far as to bite her breast.

Pletnev, of course, had no idea what was happening, since he could not know who was giving the young woman instructions; he wrote to everyone he could – all the high officials he had been treating, the mothers of children he had helped, etc. The case went to court: he was found guilty and given a stiff term in gaol. The Soviet press, generally indifferent to cases unconnected with politics, devoted a lot of space to the 'brutality of sadist Pletnev', a 'dishonour to Soviet medicine'; the theme was taken up and repeated in June 1937 by the medical associations of a variety of cities who passed resolutions, often signed by Pletnev's close friends, ex-students, and so on, condemning the sadist. He was totally crushed and in the appropriate condition, accordingly, for the third Charade.

Whenever Stalin wanted to camouflage the arrest of a well-known and outstanding Soviet chief, he would do so by giving him some sort of interim job in an undistinguished commissariat, and he would disappear from *there*, i.e. from a place that was already somewhat obscure. Thus Yagoda, before being prepared for the third Charade, was first demoted to the Posts and Telegraph Commissariat, staying there a couple of months and then popping up in the dock in the last Charade.

Thus too with Krestinsky, who had been hoping that as long as he was at the Commissariat for Foreign Affairs, and thus in a position to be known in person to a number of European statesmen, he might not be molested by Stalin; hence, when (27 March 1937) he was made commissar for justice in one of the Soviet republics he knew he was on the way out.

An aspect of the Great Charades that has exercised many people was the mere fact of the confessions. Why, after all, should all these experienced men, many of them determined idealists of strong will and extensive experience, have confessed to such monstrous charges?

Perhaps the first thing that should be done is to invert the elements in the question: it was not that everyone in the Charades confessed, but the other way round: only those who would confess were allowed to perform.

Khrushchev's Secret Speech to the Twentieth Congress gave the names of some men who were simply shot out of hand because they refused to confess; there were countless others – among them, for instance, all the army officers.

Two theories often put forward as an explanation of the extraordinary confessions are mutually exclusive.

The chief and most plausible theory is the simple one – prisoners were forced to confess, not necessarily by physical torture alone, but by extreme discomfort combined with threats of torture and death directed at their families, especially children and wives. The other, which for many years has been a favourite of fashionable popularizers, is based on a sort of jesuitical conception of the magnetism of the Communist Party: the idea underlying this theory is that the Old Bolsheviks, at least, confessed in the conviction that they were performing a final service for the Party that gave their lives meaning.

It seems to be true that many individuals did provide their tormentors with confessions out of feelings of Party piety – but these were not the stars of the Great Charades, but medium-ranking members of the *élite*, essentially simple-minded idealists who, on the theory that an omelette requires broken eggs, would carry out the Party's last orders in the interests of what they still conceived of as socialism. Simpletons like these would duly appear in court and then be killed immediately afterwards, as would, for that matter, those who might have confessed on the basis of torture.

No more than a few score people were brought to the Charades while those who were simply shot out of hand, without appearing beforehand at any trial at all, amounted to hundreds of thousands. Countless people were killed who had never belonged to any opposition group at all; the ones who made their appearance at the much-publicized Show Trials were Old Bolsheviks and Central Committee members who were known to have at one time or another opposed Stalin.

As Khrushchev said in 1956: 'Out of 139 full and alternate members of the Party Central Committee elected at the Seventeenth Congress, 98 individuals, or 70 per cent, were arrested and shot (mostly in 1937–8). But of these only about ten were brought to trial, the others were shot either after secret trial, or with no trial at all. . . .'[17]

Still, a genuine question seems to remain: why did so many prisoners not only confess to the most extravagant charges but usually debase and humiliate themselves in public?

Many people have maintained that the prisoners might have made deals with the Political Police to stop being tortured, yet it seems unlikely that torture was applied to the prisoners in the Great Charades themselves, though there is not much doubt that torture was routine procedure against the countless prisoners of the Political Police when it was a question of getting confessions to build dossiers on. To the extent that torture was needed to extract a confession from someone at a Charade there was an obvious danger that it might be retracted in public, though there was never, to be sure, any real danger of a scene since the courtroom, rather small to begin with, was packed with servants of the Political Police and constituted a genuine public only in the eyes of innocent foreign journalists.

Yet there is no longer any puzzle about the technique of securing confessions to the fabrications of the Great Charades. It is enough to mention the Soviet practice of keeping hostages.

A decree of Stalin's that perplexed many observers at the time was published on 7 April 1935: it made children from the age of twelve subject to criminal charges and to adult treatment, including the death penalty.

At the time it was widely interpreted as another piece of social repression, along the same lines as the restoration of the splendid titles and decorations in the army (September 1935), the restoration of the Cossack Corps as an arm of the regime (December 1935) and so on.

The problem of handling the vast bands of homeless children that were one of the legacies of Stalin's slaughter of the peasantry had already been solved, apparently efficiently, by the summer of 1934: as early as 1932 Stalin seems to have given orders to shoot *en masse* the starving children who had come to cities for food, and also children with venereal diseases.

Hence the particular need for a *special* law seemed incomprehensible, particularly since it was a great shock to foreign public opinion and very embarrassing for the liberals who were being wooed at the time. Also, and even more strangely, the publicity that was allowed to attend the publication of this decree was peculiarly non-Stalin-like.

The reason is disclosed when the machinery of the Great Charades is examined: the use of children, wives and parents, as a method of breaking down the morale of prisoners and compelling them to confess at public shows proved to be vital. There was, in fact, no other way of ensuring both a pliable confession and reliable public behaviour than the threat of torturing the children of the prisoners. Most of the Old Bolsheviks were, after all, normal men psychologically, if anything exceptionally fond of their children and grandchildren.

During the preparations for the preliminary, pre-Charade trial of Zinoviev and Kamenev in January 1935, former Oppositionists had already been threatened with the killing of their children. Yet they did not, apparently, believe Stalin would go that far. The Bolsheviks had first to be shown a copy of the newspaper giving the government decree before they could be brought to believe that in fact he could, and that all their children and grandchildren as well were now in danger.

It was this decree, and the general threat of the torture and killing of the children of prisoners that accounted in very large measure for their pliability in the face of the fantasies they were obliged to subscribe to.

Yezhov, Stalin's principal agent for the Great Charades, ordered every Political Police investigator to keep on his desk a copy of the law providing for the treatment of criminal children on the same basis as adults. This was why those victims of Stalin who had no children did not appear in Charades. By the time the third Great Charade was presented there was no longer the smallest doubt in the minds of the cast that the lives of their dependents were worth nothing. Until then there had been some slight hesitation, even after the enactment of the decree subjecting children from the age of twelve to adult penalties; now a general atmosphere of dread prevailed throughout the summits of the apparatus.

That atmosphere was concentrated, in the case of the cast of defendants at the third Great Charade, by the Political-Police device of planting its stool-pigeons, in the guise of ex-Oppositionists, in the cells together with the real prisoners and spreading stories about how young boys and girls were taken off together with their parents to be killed. With torture, denunciations, betrayal and suicides now commonplace, these stories were eminently believable. Small children were kept in prison and treated the same way as adults, and even, according to a Soviet newspaper account in February 1939, made to confess to crimes.

There were differences in style between the various confessions. The words of Pyatakov and Rykov, for instance, give the reader a feeling of total resignation: as though the prisoners were merely putting behind them as expeditiously as possible a wearisome task: no resistance is shown; there was hardly any need for Vyshinsky to remind them of cues.

Some others – especially Radek – performed like really enthusiastic ham actors squeezing the last drop of juice out of a role. Radek may have been under less of a strain than the others. He seems to have made a deal that in his case was kept; he was not killed, though his ultimate fate remains mysterious.

A famous wit, Radek had always been thought of as altogether irresponsible. He was celebrated for frivolity and garrulousness. Lenin had once summed up a general feeling: '. . . Here I must observe that (Radek) has accidentally made a serious remark.'[18]

After making the usual humiliating – and politically destructive – sycophantic recantations of his Oppositional past, Radek had not only devoted his gifted pen to the construction of peculiar, almost lyrically venomous diatribes against Trotsky, but had done something to please Stalin personally. In 1933 he had composed a sort of science-fiction fantasy – *The Architect of Socialist Society* – revolving around the figure that Stalin would cut for posterity; written with immense verve, in the form of a lecture given by a historian at the end of the twentieth century, it gave a picture of Stalin as a total genius who had transformed mankind.

This book seems to have gratified Stalin enormously. If only from Stalin's systematic rewriting of history Radek had guessed at his morbid vanity; he played on it with great success. Stalin found it a welcome relief from the monotony of the usual Soviet stereotypes; he had an immense number of copies circulated, and ordered it to be painstakingly studied throughout the country in every Party cell.

For some reason Stalin turned against him. It is easy, of course, to see just why Stalin would have detested him more or less automatically: clever, articulate, witty, Jewish, cosmopolitan – almost every adjective refers to something Stalin found loathsome.

At first Radek was furiously indignant. Finally, after simply refusing to do anything whatever for the Police, he insisted on seeing Stalin to get a personal reassurance; only then would he testify. Stalin, who wanted him to play an important role, evidently needed him enough to give him in Yezhov's presence the reassurances he wanted. Radek flung himself into the preparations for his Charade with zest.

His co-prisoners generally spoke in a totally lifeless tone of voice, as though reciting something more or less from memory about something dead to begin with, but Radek would not merely accept cues from Vyshinsky – he would embroider on them with such lyrical inventiveness, such personal vim, such hardhittingly bogus conviction that considered purely as a display of virtuosity it was utterly convincing.

Radek threw himself into the role so energetically, while at the same time giving expression to his personal need to be clever, that he almost ran the risk of damaging, by an excess of wit, the presentation required of him. He said, for instance, that: 'all the testimony of the other accused rests on our [Pyatakov's and his] testimony. If you are dealing with mere criminals and spies, on what can you base your conviction that what we have said is the truth, the firm truth?' This reinforced another remark he had made, that the prosecution had learned about the whole affair 'only' from him – which carried the obvious implication that there was no evidence.

Radek kept to his part of the bargain well enough, while at the same time slipping past Vyshinsky, and perhaps even Stalin, various loaded remarks. The net effect was what counted: while Stalin might be vexed by slip-ups in the preparation of the Charades, he was doubtless indifferent to the results that a subtle analysis of the flood of bogus testimony might reveal. Stalin kept his word; Radek was given only a sentence of ten years. An eye-witness reports that his face actually lighted up, then composed into a guilty smile after he shrugged his shoulders at his fellow-prisoners as though puzzled. He then gave his audience the same look.

Some witnesses may have been persuaded that they were doing the Party a final service: at least this is reported of Mrachkovsky, an Old Bolshevik since 1905, practically the beginning, and one of Trotsky's coterie during the twenties. He was a heroic, emotional but not very astute man, who was persuaded by the interrogator to confess after having withstood all blandishments, including a promise from Stalin not to kill him. In the words of Mrachkovsky's interrogator:

I brought him to the point where he began to weep. I wept with him when we arrived at the conclusion that all was lost, that there was nothing left in the way of hope or faith, that the only thing to do was to make a desperate effort to forestall a future struggle on the part of the discontented masses. For this the government must have public confessions by the Opposition leader.[19]

This theory of the confessions has had a certain vogue, especially among intellectuals.

Stalin, though hostile to Pyatakov as to all former Oppositionists, was exceptionally lenient with him because of his urgent need for his services: his administrative ability would have been impossible to replace. He did his best to draw Pyatakov to him on a quasi-personal basis, but could not succeed: Pyatakov adhered to a rigidly formal relationship.

Pyatakov had abandoned his Opposition attachments in 1927; he was put on the Supreme Economic Council and made deputy to Ordzhonikidze. He had unbending will-power and limitless energy; in ten years he had laid down the industrial organization of the entire country. He knew every single factory and workshop; he personally inspected every important order. He drafted the plans for the development of Soviet industry, handled investment allocations, and even found time to study the novel techniques developed in German and American industry. He also supervised the implementation of the production plans and the import of modern machinery from Europe and America.

He was celebrated as an ascetic too; he ate properly scarcely more than a few times a week. His clothing was ill-fitting and cheap; excessively emaciated and sallow, he gave the impression, with his rusty vandyke, of a Russian Don Quixote. His wife, a Communist, was also a drunkard; they had a child who at the time of his Charade was about ten.

It was a sort of principle of Stalin's to make a point of using the testimony of intimates as a way of breaking down the prisoners. First of all, as a sort of student of psychology, it was his technical opinion that this was most effective, and then, in the case of people where his personal vindictiveness played a role, it also gave him special pleasure: he would instruct his agents in the Political Police to get a wife to testify against a husband, son against father, brother against brother.

Stalin waited for seven years, until the autumn of 1936 – after the country had been substantially industrialized and new specialists and executives had been trained – before having Pyatakov arrested.

Like most of the other prisoners, Pyatakov was broken by first breaking down his wife and his best friend, then using their depositions to break down Pyatakov himself. He was promised that his wife and his own life would be spared. His chief, Ordzhonikidze, a great friend of Stalin's, swore to him that all would be well.

But Ordzhonikidze proved powerless: the aftermath of Pyatakov's confession and death was that Ordzhonikidze, the only one left in the Kremlin with whom Stalin could talk in native tongue, was hounded to death in his turn.

He was killed – of a 'heart attack' – at the age of fifty, a few weeks after Pyatakov was executed. Stalin went through the appropriate motions: an observer saw him standing on top of Lenin's mausoleum, wan and with his head bowed, and was struck by 'the sorrow, the suffering, the unbearable pain depicted on the face of that great actor, Comrade Stalin'.[20]

Pyatakov's constructive career after he acquiesced in Stalin's ascendancy illustrates both the positive side of the Soviet regime, which has secured the allegiance of many enthusiastic idealists, and the *élan* generated in such idealists by the exercise of power.

Pyatakov was sent to Paris with a trade-mission after his capitulation. There he met a former friend, Valentinov, a Menshevik. Pyatakov called Valentinov a coward for abandoning the Soviet regime: Valentinov called him another for his capitulation to Stalin (the story had just appeared in *Pravda*[21]). Pyatakov retorted with a passionate speech to the following effect:[22]

The New Economic Policy did not represent the true Lenin, merely a Lenin ailing and enfeebled. The true Lenin was the one who had been brave enough to make a proletarian revolution *before* the prerequisites for such a revolution were there, and to create those prerequisites *after* the revolution.

How could a mere Menshevik like Valentinov even begin to understand what a miraculous party the Bolsheviks were? Miraculous just because they represented the human will, just because they accepted no laws, just because they regarded nothing as impossible.

Just as such a party could accomplish anything, so such a party could allow itself anything. For such a party a true Bolshevik would do anything!

A true Bolshevik, after all, will lose his identity and merge himself altogether and utterly with the Party; he will give up all his opinions, indeed, have none of his own, believe black is white and *vice versa*. There could, in fact, be no life for him outside such a party.

This was, to be sure, far from novel as an affirmation of faith: Trotsky, too, had said the same thing, characteristically, for instance, on his re-affirmation of the 'unity of the Party' after defeat in 1924, when he had said: 'My party – right or wrong . . . I know one cannot be right against the Party . . . for history has created no other way for the realization of what is right.'[23]

A curious sidelight on Stalin's life that came out in the Charades was his relationship with the chief of the Kremlin guard, Pauker, a Hungarian who had been captured by the Russians in 1916 and stayed on in Russia after the putsch. At home Pauker had been a barber and valet; he had a weakness for play-acting, and was a first-class mimic, raconteur and clown. With no political training or education to speak of, he made his way up through the backstairs of the Political Police because of his abilities as a valet. Ultimately he became responsible for Stalin's own safety as well as for that of the Politburo.

In contrast to Lenin, whose bodyguard had been two men and later – after Dora Kaplan's attack on him – four men, Stalin had a secret body-guard of several thousands, in addition to special units always on the alert. This huge bodyguard came under the control of Pauker, who was always in a general's uniform sitting beside Stalin in his car.

Pauker's inside track with Stalin gave him, of course, great material power; he got the Politburo food, clothing, country places. He would cater to their tastes completely, ordering for their wives and families Paris dresses and scents, radio sets, motor cars, pedigreed dogs He became a favourite of the Politburo members' families. Inevitably he became privy to the private lives of them all: mistresses, lovers, family squabbles, graft, corruption, foibles, peccadilloes.

Stalin apparently liked to have him around, perhaps just because there was no question whatever of his having any political interests, or indeed any interests at all beyond furthering his career. But he was most indispensable to Stalin as an entertainer. He not merely made a point of studying Stalin's tastes in food and drink, arranging to get him all kinds of delicacies, but would use his talent as a raconteur to get Stalin laughing at coarse and especially anti-Semitic jokes.

He realized that Stalin – puny and undersized – was very vain. At first Pauker put pads into his shoes, then invented some special shoes with elevator heels ingeniously concealed. Stalin even requested Pauker to put a little wooden stand on Lenin's mausoleum, giving him another two inches in addition to the one and a half from the heels; he also created the idea of the extra-long greatcoat associated with Stalin's personal appearances. The ensemble made Stalin look massive as well as tall.

Until he came across Pauker, Stalin, mistrusting even his barbers, used to shave himself, leaving his pockmarks even more obvious because of the difficulty of shaving cleanly over them. Pauker was the first person Stalin allowed to handle a sharp razor over his throat. He was also used by Stalin to buy, very secretly, obscene drawings abroad, which Stalin began arranging for in quantity at the beginning of the thirties.[24]

A few months after the first Charade Pauker gave one of his most memorable impersonations, reported in an odd anecdote[25] told in the summer of 1937, by an old friend of Pauker's.

Towards the end of December Stalin gave a little banquet for some Political Police chiefs, including Yezhov. They all got rather tight; Pauker put on a little skit in imitation of Zinoviev's behaviour on his way to be killed: writhing about, dragging his feet, rolling his eyes, Pauker-Zinoviev kept crying out piteously: 'Call up Stalin, Comrade, for God's sake, please!'

Stalin and the others roared so helplessly Pauker had to repeat the skit; this time he added another note, he lifted his arms and cried out: 'Hear O Israel, the Lord our God is One God!' Stalin lost control of himself: unable to contain his laughter, he begged Pauker to stop.

By the summer of 1937 most of these Political Police chiefs had already been eliminated. In July 1937 Pauker was dismissed; he was next mentioned in March 1938, in the third Charade, when Yagoda said he had been a spy for the Germans. Pauker was finished.

4
Out in Front

With negotiations finished and the material in hand, an artistic problem presented itself: how were these unusual fabrications to be presented? How could plausibility be established? Technically, how could details be harmonized, transitions installed, discrepancies eliminated?

These problems all bore on the cohesiveness of the whole production. Yet though never solved they turned out, in a curious way, to be unimportant.

From the point of view of publicity alone, for instance, it might have been thought that the best courtroom would simply be the biggest. Yet Stalin took special pains about this: after several meetings with advisers he finally settled on the small courtroom that became notorious; its size was not even noticed. The hall was carefully filled with menial employees, clerks, typists, etc., who would be given half-day passes. The audience, in civilian clothes, attended the performances in shifts, for the proper number of hours specified on each pass. The in-people at the very apex of the Party and government hierarchy, who were used to getting passes from the Political Police for all sorts of special occasions, were denied admission in favour of the typists and clerks.

Despite all these precautions the fear was very strong that some prisoner – many of them were, after all, men of immense temperament and will-power – might recuperate from his psychological breaking down and make a scene in public. It was countered by careful preparations: there were, in addition to the hand-picked attendants in the courtroom, special groups of *élite* Political Party officials, alerted to leap to their feet shouting at the first sign of any insubordination from a prisoner; the presiding magistrate would then simply have had to clear the room.

The Charade was unlike a real show in that it was put on for the benefit, so to speak, of the staff of the producing company; it was a show in camera. This is, of course, a contradiction in terms: indeed, just as the form of the trial was essentially a theatrical form, so the theatrical form

79

itself was in its nature a departmental, household skit, *reported* as though it had been both a show and a trial simultaneously.

The courtroom had formerly been the small ballroom in the old Nobles' Club. It had light-blue walls, with white columns, a high ceiling and an old-fashioned candelabra that at night gave a somewhat eerie light. It seated about 200 people.

The presiding judge was obese and jowly, with tiny eyes and a naked, pointed skull. The prosecutor, Andrei Vyshinsky, was tidily dressed in a white collar and dark suit, with a grey moustache and trimmed hair.

The judges and the court secretary sat at the back of the courtroom facing the hand-picked audience; there was no jury. Along the wall to the right, at a right-angle to the audience, there were four rows of chairs for the prisoners, barred off from the rest of the courtroom by a low wooden bar. Three robust soldiers, with rifles and fixed bayonets, escorted sixteen prisoners to their seats there. Along the opposite wall there was a small table for Vyshinsky.

A rather sumptuous buffet was arranged in a narrow passage leading from a small door behind the prisoners' rows, in a corner where Yagoda and his assistants could listen to everything on a special amplification system. The other rooms off the passageway were occupied by the guards and the prisoners, who could thus be kept under observation and fed.

The prisoners in the first Charade, though physically much improved since the preliminary investigations, still looked rather sallow, with rings under their eyes and a generally nervous, exhausted, grim look. This was in marked contrast with the Political Police stooges, who looked healthy and insouciant, except for Pickel, who looked depressed and listless.

Zinoviev looked worst of all: formerly plump, he now looked emaciated, worn, listless. His face was puffy, his eyes baggy, his skin doughy-grey. His famous voice, slightly shrill but musical, had sunk to a feeble whisper. Kamenev had a little white imperial and snow-white hair. Both men were fifty-four years old.

Just before the opening both Yagoda and Yezhov gave the prisoners their final instructions: first a reassurance that all promises given would be kept, and their lives and those of their families spared, then a warning against any treachery – any attempt to deviate from the script, for which, they were told, they would all be held collectively responsible.

The first Charade restricted its charges against Trotsky to terrorist activity, with only a suggestion of a connexion with the Gestapo. But since the reaction was not so enthusiastic as Stalin might have hoped, he thought it necessary to buttress its shortcomings with a second

Charade by creating an actual alliance between Trotsky, Hitler and the Mikado. But the victims who might have suited this enlarged role of Trotsky's – Zinoviev, Kamenev and the others – had meanwhile been shot; this put Stalin in the position of having to prepare another batch of victims who had been broken enough to testify to Trotsky's new role as outright agent and ally of Hitler and the Mikado.

It was because the details of the second Charade had not been foreseen that the major performers in the first Charade – all those with genuine Party pasts like Zinoviev, Kamenev, and Smirnov – completely denied any charges of involvement with the Nazi police; at the time of the first Charade no point was made of this with respect to any of the victims except for the four obvious stooges. At that time the scenarios had not evolved far enough.

Stalin's demands for the first Charade were rather meagre – a small matter of terrorism! The Political Police, after working over Zinoviev to the point where he was willing to confess to terrorism, doubtless asked him to go further, and say something to link both himself and Trotsky to the Nazis. At that point he must have baulked, and since that, too, was felt to be inessential in that phase of the evolving hoax he was not broken further. Even in the extreme situation of Zinoviev, Kamenev and the other Bolsheviks there was a limit.

The stooges, on the other hand, would admit anything; they were merely reciting lines that were dictated, not negotiated. Hence it is easier to see the general tendency of the developing Charades through the lines dictated to the stooges, confessing to different stages of alleged conspiracies merely in order to round out the record. They were really connecting up the testimony of the real targets of the Charades.

Thus the stooges in the first Charade were used simply to drop in the first mention of the Gestapo – what in a play is called a 'plant', a theme to be picked up later on and elaborated. Had Zinoviev, Trotsky's 'henchman', known of Trotsky's connexion with the Gestapo, there would, of course, have been no reason for him to hide that in a general confession on the basis of which he was, after all, killed.

The failure to involve the stars of the first Charade in the later charges against Trotsky as Hitler's ally simply means that Stalin's plan at that time had not gone so far. Similarly, the notion of the 'parallel centre' that came out in the second Charade – Radek, Pyatakov – is understandable only as a way of explaining just this ignorance on the part of the victims in the second Charade, in which Trotsky was linked up directly with Hitler. Had Stalin decided on that beforehand he could just as well have said so during the first Charade.

Theoretically, since Zinoviev and Kamenev were alive and members of the 'reserve centre' mentioned in the second Charade, they would have known about the parallel centre in the first Charade, and have exposed it. Yet the first Charade does not mention the parallel centre at all; this was specifically created *ad hoc* by the testimony of a Political Police witness in the second Charade (Romm, whom Trotsky had never met), who testified that as far back as 1932 the parallel centre had been contrived without Zinoviev and Kamenev hearing about it.

It is evident that just as the first Charade foreshadowed later show trials, which indeed took place, so the second Charade foreshadowed the third.

From a propagandistic point of view the main charges in the first Charade – a terrorist conspiracy against the Party leadership – could not be depended on to arouse any mass emotions. The second Charade had the advantage of aiming at plain patriotism. Incredible as the charges might seem to the politically minded Party members, it might at least be hoped that the Soviet man in the street, perhaps hating Communists already, might consider it plausible for them to be willing to dismember the country as a whole – and if so why not for Hitler and the Mikado? What seemed incredible to politically minded people might seem wholly plausible to Russian peasants, and also, of course, to Western correspondents.

The inclusion in the second Charade of Pyatakov, former Vice-Commissar of Heavy Industry, had the charm of finding a scapegoat for the incalculable wreckage caused by the breakneck industrialization; if Pyatakov's guilt in such a matter could be swallowed anything could.

The second Charade implicated the chief figures in the third, Bukharin and Rykov, despite the fact that in the interim – perhaps because of some hitch in the preparation of the Charades as a unit – both of them, in an official article, had been exonerated by a full 'investigation'.[1]

The sparing of Radek (with three others) may have been an agreed payment to him for a job well-done; the sparing of Sokolnikov might have been due to his acquaintance with the celebrated British Fabian couple, Sidney and Beatrice Webb, who had published a remarkable eulogy of Stalin's regime as befitting a country that was fundamentally both free and democratic. Stalin may have thought it helpful not to kill Sokolnikov, though the Webbs, to be sure, were capable of swallowing anything.

The third of the Great Charades, which put Bukharin and others in the dock, including the former head of the Political Police, Yagoda, was no more than a continuation of the expansion outlined in the second Charade.

Trotsky was still the head of this limitlessly ramified conspiracy,

which aimed to get rid of Stalin and his closest associates, to spy for
Germany and Japan and to dismember the Soviet Union on their
behalf. The heads of the army killed in June 1937 (Tukhachevsky and
others) were also stitched into the libretto of the second Charade. There
were a number of fresh traits: Yagoda was accused of having killed
Gorky and some others by poisoning, and some well-known physicians
were cast as defendants; Bukharin was allotted an additional accusation of also having conspired, together with the left-wing Socialist-
Revolutionaries, to kill Lenin, Stalin and Sverdlov as far back as 1918.

As before, the evidence consisted wholly of confessions, except for
Bukharin's reaction to the charge of having plotted against Lenin,
which he never admitted. There were some other subsidiary snags
struck during the testimony of some of the victims; Krestinsky, for
instance, retracted a confession he was said to have made, and then
retracted his retraction the next day, while another witness (Boris
Kamkov, a former Socialist-Revolutionary terrorist) kept denying that
there had been any plot against Lenin in 1918 at all.

Aside from these major strategic shifts in development, there
remained countless minor discrepancies of presentation.

Under Stalin's supervision, and sometimes with his direct literary
intervention, the craftsmen in the Political Police had to cope with a
problem that had three facets.

The main facet has already been indicated – the broad outlines of
the charges themselves as reflected in the characters of the victims
against a naturalistic background.

Not much could be done about this, of course, since the charges were
flatly contradicted by all reality itself; but granted the decision to go
ahead with the project there were then internal, technical problems of
detail to solve: how to tailor each particular passage to the effect
desired in the whole?

At this point the scripts can be assessed purely as scripts: the
technical problems of their composition may shed some light on the
literary creativity of the Political Police. It might have been thought
that with so much public attention great pains would have been taken;
nevertheless there were countless hitches. From a purely technical
point of view the scenarios for the Charades were sadly defective.

It was only natural, to be sure, to make slips in devising fictional
scenarios purporting to cover the complex activities of many individuals
over a long period of time and with countless ramifications. The manipulation of a reality that depends on the concatenation of thousands of
people, myriads of facts, incidents, dates, documents, interests, is
beyond the ability of any organization. It would have been difficult to

make so many data dovetail even from an avowedly fictional point of view, such as the composition, let us say, of a panoramic novel: when they had to conform with external reality as well it was obviously too much. That is why so many subordinate stooges were given roles as defendants.

The libretti for the Charades show a consistent disregard of the function of time and of the role of minor individuals. A witness in the first Charade (M. Lurye), for instance, said that he had been given Trotsky's instructions *via* German Oppositionists in March 1933; he passed them on to Zinoviev in August 1934.[2]

This is just the sort of error that is made in motion-pictures. All sorts of different scenes are shot in different sequences, at different times: someone must check on continuity; if a character is wearing a dinner-jacket in one part of the scene he must have it on when the next part is shot.

It is obvious that the continuity of the Great Charades was deplorably sketchy; had they been taken *seriously* as trials this alone would have exploded them.

In the same Charade a 'witness' (Olberg) said that the alliance between the Trotskyites and the Gestapo had begun early in 1933; two years later the Trotskyites were 'now standing before the dilemma'[3] of dissolving or uniting with the Gestapo.

Again in the same Charade, two 'conspirators' (Kundt, Matorin) are each mentioned once and then dropped, though the second, supposed to have been a secretary of Zinoviev's, had testified that he had been instructed by Zinoviev to kill Kirov.

This omission is all the more singular with respect to Kirov, since though his assassination and the suicide of Bogdan (another secretary of Zinoviev's) were the only terrorist successes that could be pointed to, not much was made even of these. The explanation was doubtless that Stalin's plans for his victims grew progressively so much more comprehensive and took in so much more ground – both geographically and politically – that the assassination of even a high functionary like Kirov was overshadowed.

This was one of the overriding factors that aggravated the general problem of how to present the image of the victims.

The dilemma was obvious: in psychological warfare opponents must be presented in two different ways at the same time, on the one hand as being devilishly ruthless, unscrupulous and efficient, and on the other as being fundamentally no more than a gang of contemptible flubbers, slobs and *shlemiels*.

In the first trial, Vyshinsky is concerned with showing up Zinoviev and Kamenev as monsters of duplicity and guile who have completely outstripped in cunning their model and source of inspiration, Machiavelli. Thus, 'Machiavelli was a puppy and a yokel compared with them'.[4] On the other hand, they were also – as he said about their use of Marx's formula that 'insurrection is an art' – 'unskilled masters' of the art[5] in addition to being, like the defendants in general, 'clowns, insignificant pygmies, little dogs snarling at an elephant'.[6]

The two themes, evidently contradictory in terms of common sense, could even be fused together, without apparent discomfort, in the prosecution's claim that the prisoners were simultaneously of a calibre to be taken seriously by foreign governments, which would gladly enter into actual treaty relations with them, and at the same time were miserable worms who could be hired as mere agents of various intelligence services. In the verdict given in the third Charade Vyshinsky in the same speech calls the prisoners people who had 'concluded an . . . agreement' with foreign states, and were, at the same time, the 'direct agents' of the intelligence services of these same states.[7]

The *leitmotif* of the prosecution was, of course, that the prisoners were not really an Opposition at all, but mere gangsters. Thus, in Vyshinsky's questioning of Rakovsky in the third Charade, Rakovsky, perhaps inadvertently, used the word 'Opposition' instead of the conventional designation, the 'Bloc of Rights and Trotskyites', the fiction devised for the Charade. Vyshinsky did not let him get away with it:

Vyshinsky: But what kind of an opposition are they? They are a bandit gang of counter-revolutionaries . . . [you forget] that you are being tried here as a counter-revolutionary, bandit . . . organization of traitors.[8]

The problem of the prosecution was difficult: in the three Charades dozens of people, theoretically directing a vast spy-ring under the orders of far-away Trotsky, were supposed to have been incessantly busy for decades – organizing various kinds of subversion, wrecking, treason, and so on. Yet nothing could be pointed to as a result of all this activity, with the exception of wrecking as an explanation of the myriad mishaps of Soviet life.

How could this unfortunate impression be overcome in the scenario purporting to set forth their confessions? Their criminal activity was generally supposed to have been carried on right up to the very moment of their arrest: they presented a picture of absolutely monomaniacal unflagging zeal – unfortunately with no results!

This gap between the scripts and reality was bridged by a proliferation of verbiage – curiously empty, abstract, tentative words and phrases that while 'padding' the syntax of the scenarios give a strangely blurred impression: 'forming a bloc', 'forming a centre', 'setting to work to organize', 'leading a group', 'directing activities', 'conducting negotiations', 'coming to an agreement' (with enemies), 'uniting forces', 'getting in touch' or 'establishing contact', 'giving' or 'receiving instructions', 'holding secret conferences', 'drawing up a platform', 'making preparations', 'entrusting' someone with 'the practical direction' of some action, 'deciding to expedite', 'checking up' on the situation or on the 'progress of preparation' somewhere.

It sounds like a caricature of bureaucracy in general, and especially so of the top-heavy Soviet bureaucracy, where the necessary division of labour and its management are distorted by inefficiency into the replacement of real activity by mere organization for organization's sake. In the Charades this kind of hypertrophy was ramified still further through the replacement of organization for organization's sake by meaningless verbiage that in its abstraction from reality sounds like double-talk.

All these empty 'activities' had been going on, according to the prosecution, for years. As Vyshinsky said in the third Charade, the 'whole bloc systematically . . . devoted itself to terrorism'[9] – yet nothing ever happened.

Aware of this chasm between intent and achievement, Vyshinsky bridged it with the inevitable rhetoric: in the second Charade, for instance, he calls it an argument drawn from scepticism: 'Of course, one may say . . . the many [terror] groups . . . have not much to show', but then rebuts this obvious criticism by saying that the chief prisoners, who were on 'fairly intimate' terms with the leaders of the Soviet government, didn't want to do the work themselves, or let it be known that Trotsky was behind it. As Vyshinsky said: 'That is our good fortune.'[10]

By the time of the third Charade, however, the script-writers thought it sensible to adjust this by making a defendant (Rosengoltz) confess that he had personally decided to commit a terrorist act against none other than Stalin; in order to do so he set about it with remarkable single-mindedness: 'He repeatedly tried to secure an interview with him.'[11]

The Political Police ran into the ineluctable dilemma of all false descriptions of reality: not involving Trotsky or his son directly – by concrete evidence or at the very least testimony – obviously made their case hopeless. Involving him on the basis of direct testimony, on the other hand, meant that some check could be made, that Trotsky might have had an alibi and so on. This was what happened. There were two instances where the prosecution attempted to introduce evidence aside from the confessions.

In the first Charade a prisoner, Holtzman, testified that in 1932 he had met Trotsky's son at the Hotel Bristol in Copenhagen, from where they had both gone to see Trotsky.

This one material fact, amidst the aridity of the overwhelming bulk of the evidence, was instantly contradicted, not only by Trotsky, but by an official statement from the Danish government, on 1 September 1936 (almost a week after the prisoners had all been executed) to the effect that the Hotel Bristol had been pulled down in 1917.

Apparently,[12] while Yezhov was working out a script for Holtzman to memorize, it became clear that he had to have had some place actually to meet Trotsky's son: Yezhov thought a hotel ideal, and had the head of the Secret Political Department of the Political Police get the name of one. The chief, Molchanov, thought it indiscreet to ask the Foreign Department directly for some such hotel in Copenhagen, since the name would soon be made much of in the press and it would look a little fishy. He cautiously had his secretary ring up the Foreign Department and simply ask for recommendations of a number of hotels in both Oslo and Copenhagen, on the pretext of needing them for some comrade on his way to Scandinavia. The secretary transposed the lists for the two cities: there *was* a Hotel Bristol in Oslo.

Similarly, a detail in Pyatakov's script caused a great deal of trouble. It had been suggested by Stalin, who thought it would sound better to say that Pyatakov's contact with Trotsky had not been by mail but face-to-face. Accordingly, Stalin had ordered Slutsky to work out the details of such a trip.[13]

Since the encounter with Trotsky was supposed to have taken place while Pyatakov was at a meeting in Berlin in December 1935, the train schedules of the time would have obliged Pyatakov to remain out of sight for a couple of days. This was too easily checked in a capital beyond Stalin's control; it was also common knowledge that Pyatakov had been constantly seeing all sorts of German businessmen and signing contracts.

When Stalin was told this he suggested a private aeroplane; he apparently believed some of his own myth, since he told Slutsky that the Nazis would be delighted to provide an aeroplane for 'such a job' – plotting with Trotsky to help the Nazis break up the Soviet Union in order to allow the Trotskyites to take power!

It was thus in conformity with Stalin's plot-line that Pyatakov testified that he had secretly gone from Berlin to Oslo in the middle of December 1935 in order to have a long chat with Trotsky. Since all the

Political Police script-writers had been made wary of circumstantial detail because of the unfortunate reaction when the Hotel Bristol detail of the testimony in the first Charade had blown up in their faces, this time they left out all detail, so that Pyatakov's story actually sounded peculiarly vague except, unfortunately, for the circumstance of the trip itself: Pyatakov had not been given the name he was supposed to have used in Norway, nor was anything said about a visa.

It seemed simultaneously just circumstantial enough and at the same time just vague enough to carry conviction; why should a plane not make the Berlin–Oslo flight and back overnight? Yet this detail was also *too* detailed: it blew up at once. The Norwegian press instantly proved that during the month of December 1935 no civil aeroplane *at all* had landed at that particular Oslo airport.

The Soviet authorities were stuck; Vyshinsky had to get a statement – from, of all people, the Soviet Foreign Affairs Department in Moscow! – that the Oslo airport 'receives all the year round aeroplanes of other countries . . . and the arrival and departure of aeroplanes is possible also in winter months'.

This did not work either, since another Norwegian newspaper immediately reported an interview with the director of the airport to the effect that not only had no foreign plane of any kind landed in that month, but that for eight whole months – from September to May – not a *single* plane had landed there.

It was mere common sense to avoid such pitfalls. Whenever letters were referred to in courtroom dialogue it invariably turned out that they had been lost, destroyed, mislaid, etc. Vyshinsky's general explanation of this as a consequence of plotters' caution took an extravagant form: in contrasting a conspiratorial with a legal organization, he said that in the case of the latter one would, naturally, find 'rules, minutes, a seal . . . decisions, membership cards',[14] which, of course, one had no right to expect from secretive criminals.

The same seemingly plausible point was made by the American historian Charles Beard to Trotsky himself, who replied, with a little more plausibility, that though conspirators would doubtless not leave around much material evidence, neither would they write long explicit letters to each other in the 'least prudent way. I would not . . . reveal the most secret plans to young people unknown to me, nor entrust them, at our first meeting, with serious terrorist missions . . . (In) the "confessions" I am presented as . . . primarily concerned with furnishing the greatest possible number of witnesses against myself for the future prosecutor.'[15]

During all these public Charades it may be of some significance that Trotsky's own archives were stolen on 7 November 1936, evidently by the Soviet Political Police; since none of them was ever published it seems likely that they may have been used in the negative sense – to prevent the scenario-writers in the Political Police from making needless boobooes in addition to the ones they had already made in the first two Charades.

The general picture of the conspiracy that emerges is one of almost clinical lethargy and carelessness that would be quite striking in the case of real people and particularly so in the case of the major prisoners, who were without exception men of unusual energy and intelligence. This impression, which would be genuine if it reflected a real state of mind or if the testimony itself had been genuine, does not arise from the psychology of these men, but from the highly artificial conditions under which the scenarios were being composed, and more especially because there was really no need for the Political Police to do more than Stalin had in fact required them to do, which was to prepare something that would stand up *more or less*.

For it was not only Europe, after all, that was to 'swallow it' as Stalin said, in the sense that the public proved gullible. It was 'swallowed' by highly professional students of affairs. Indeed, the gullibility here of liberals and dupes of the Communists staggers belief.

This very inefficiency of the prisoners, of course, was then used in its turn to build up rhetorical material for the scenarios; it enabled the script-writers to give the prisoners something else to do – to complain about how inefficient everything was.

Kamenev 'expressed dissatisfaction with the slowness [in] the work of preparing terrorist acts';[16] Pyatakov, in the second Charade, says that Trotsky's son 'expressed extreme dissatisfaction . . . with the fact that things were moving very slowly';[17] Pyatakov also 'expressed dissatisfaction over the fact that our terrorist struggle was still being confined to general talk'.[18]

This last, of course, is priceless, since it sums up the totality of the terrorists' alleged activity, which was *nothing* but talk – the talk in the literary seminars of the Political Police.

One of the consequences of building up the dossiers against the prisoners in the Charades – and to a large extent in the ordinary Political Police dossiers used in the Deep Comb-out as a whole – on the basis of no actual evidence was to create a peculiar conception of the nature of a conspiracy.

The fact that the demonstration of the conspiracy could be based on nothing *but* confession – since the bogus charges could not be supported by any documented *action* – was to be pregnant with both psychological and political consequences. There was no way, aside from the confession, of knowing about the conspiracy. The conspiracy could be claimed to be anywhere, at any time, and to involve anybody whatsoever – *regardless of mere appearances*. The fact that a given individual could refer to decades of work, extravagant diligence, devotion, and zeal was structurally, as it were, quite meaningless. Since the charge did not have to be based on evidence, but on mere affirmation, there was simply no way of countering it by evidence, which by definition was bound to be merely negative, hence irrelevant.

Insofar as this conception of conspiracy gave a quasi-theoretical background to the procedures of the Political Police in processing the population of the Soviet Union, it was of course an immense boon; it enabled them to make the grinding work of extracting confessions more normal, as far as their own psychology and that of their prisoners were concerned, by creating the semblance of an authentic judicial framework.

This represented, of course, the institutionalization of a kind of paranoia, since the method of claiming that anyone might be guilty despite all appearances entailed the conception of everyone wearing a mask *behind which anything might be taking place.*

Paranoid suspicion, after all, never goes against logic *as such*; it is always *possible* to have enemies everywhere; it is simply rather improbable.

In the context of the Soviet Charades, accordingly, it was always possible for people to be plotting their heads off. Why not? There was plainly a great deal to plot about. Thus the translation of that logical possibility into a factual accusation had a sort of emotional appeal; while it might be far-fetched to trace that paranoid disposition up to Stalin it would seem not to be excluded. It was he, after all, who was the source of it.

Thus what might have been the individual paranoia of Stalin, or at least a hyper-mistrustfulness that might be called that, was incorporated in the procedure of composing the scenarios: it was essential not only because of the absence of evidence, but, perhaps more significantly, because of what must have been felt to be the inherent unsuitability of the victims from a characterological point of view.

In devising the scenarios, for instance, the question must have constantly been asked: Isn't this a *little* strong? Will they go for this, do you think?

To counter arguments based on plausibility, of both an evidential and a characterological kind – the script had to take them into account and then explain them away: this would be done by indicating that all instances in which the people had publicly done the opposite of what they were accused of doing were simply evidence of duplicity. Vyshinsky, for instance, gave this attitude lapidary expression in the first Charade when he said that 'Zinoviev carried this perfidy to such lengths that after the murder of . . . Kirov he sent an obituary notice to *Pravda*'.[19]

Even activity on the part of the prisoners that seemed to be aimed at the exposure of other conspiracies was also no more than a form of duplicity, designed to divert attention from their own conspiratorial activity. A prisoner might have confessed to some duplicity in order to go on with other, still greater duplicity. Zinoviev, for instance, after Kirov's murder, had been forced to admit to his ideological complicity (in the preliminary trial of 15–16 January 1935).

To make *that* plausible he had confessed to duplicity; later, in his Charade in August 1936, he was accused by Vyshinsky of practising *still more* duplicity!

Vyshinsky (to Zinoviev): 'you . . . spoke about (your own) duplicity, but you spoke about it in such a way as to conceal the fact that even at that moment you were continuing the policy of duplicity.'[20]

Duplicity would, of course, have been natural to plotters: hence the accusation of duplicity is *as such* perfectly rational; which is just why, when there is no other evidence, it must be linked to a paranoid frame of mind.

The macabre note here is that the duplicity was obviously on the part of Stalin, whose policy at this time may be said to have been a master-piece of duplicity *vis-à-vis* Hitler, since both his foreign policy (People's Fronts and so on) and his domestic policy (Trials, purges, massacres of Party people, socialist oppositions, and so on) can be interpreted as a cover for his real aim – revealed much later – of arranging an entente with Hitler.

Thus the rhetorical formula put into Kamenev's mouth in his Charade might have been put there by Stalin himself with characteristically cynical humour: (Kamenev) 'We assumed that in these negotiations [with the Party leaders and the government after a successful campaign of terrorism] myself and Zinoviev would occupy the leading positions . . . while our participation . . . in the terroristic acts would remain secret from the Party and the country.'[21]

This notion – of the leaders of a large-scale terrorist campaign being able to keep it completely secret – was concentrated still further in the testimony involving Trotsky.

Thus Stalin (in a speech made to the Central Committee plenum on 3 March 1937)[22] found it perfectly reasonable to say that Trotsky had forbidden both Radek and Pyatakov to tell even a tiny handful of Trotskyites just what the real platform of the Opposition was: even the people who were supposed to be engaged in the actual labour of the 'restoration of capitalism', the defeat and dismemberment of the Soviet Union at the hands of Hitler and the Mikado, were supposed to hide this platform, Stalin said, 'not only from the working-class . . . or the Trotskyite rank-and-file as well . . . but even from the upper Trotskyite leadership'.

A curious portrait of a conspiracy emerges from this assumption that the bulk of terrorist conspiratorial activities will consist of deceiving not only the enemy but one's own colleagues; Stalin, aware of this, specifically condemned as 'rotten' the theory that someone 'who is not always engaged in wrecking . . . cannot be a wrecker'.[23] Essentially Stalin's remark, while sounding rational, has a merely incantational value: Since you're a plotter, you plot! And since you are a plotter you hide your plotting!

Another kind of slip has philosophical implications. Marxists, of course, make a fetish of determinism; it is a Marxist cliché, with a special vogue among Bolsheviks, to say, 'It is no accident that . . .' on the assumption that everything is predetermined and that there is a complex web of causality for the universe whose fabric can be penetrated by Bolsheviks, and by them alone.

Yet a remarkable quality of casualness was introduced into the scenarios obviously because there would often be no other way of stitching things together. One can visualize the Political Police seminar in creative composition, painstakingly arranging fictitious conspiracies, crimes, and so on, and throwing questions at each other as they fill in the outlines of their handiwork:

'Now, how does so-and-so get in touch with so-and-so?'

'Well, his sister had once been engaged to a tractor engineer . . .'

'No, that won't do; we killed him off years ago.'

'Well . . .'

When a hitch cropped up it could be coped with by means of the contrivance used, for instance, in the first Charade, when one of the conspirators (Holtzman) said that his sinister career had begun upon his 'accidentally' running into one of the other prisoners in the street.[24] This sort of explanation for involvement is very common; it evidently points to a lack of energy in the scenarists, since it is always possible, after all, to create logical or pseudo-logical links in a composition. Data involving numerous individuals, of course, heighten the risk of carelessness.

Yagoda said, at the end of one of the principal sections of his confession: 'this is the information I consider it necessary to place before the court.'[25] Another witness, in the first Charade, when asked whether something about a conspiratorial meeting was true, said, 'As it now appears, yes.'[26]

Sometimes a major development is treated with blithe nonchalance and a vagueness that the prosecution simply disregards. A witness in the second Charade, discussing his collaboration with another in wrecking, says: '. . . he drew up the plan and this elaborated plan was accepted; we reached an agreement and all that sort of thing.'[27] The last phrase seems to highlight the sheer fatigue in the construction of fictions that overcame both the witness and the prosecutor.

The literary effect is displayed with peculiar obviousness in this multiplication of trivia: thus, in the midst of completely vague or self-contradictory projects on the part of the conspirators, one would mention someone picking up a pencil to illustrate some point, or putting a letter in his pocket, giving the salutation of a letter – 'Dear Friend' – and so on, in an effort, evidently, to give, in Pooh-Bah's words in *The Mikado*, 'an appearance of artistic verisimilitude to an otherwise bald and unconvincing narrative'. And indeed, if the Great Charades could be set to music who would come to mind more fittingly than Gilbert and Sullivan!

There was, in fact, a sort of hypertrophy of imbecile detail that probably bespeaks exhaustion on the part of talentless script-writers in assembling the vast mass of non-existent relations and pseudo-facts. The plethora of silly minutiae seems to have begun with the second Charade; it really cast in high relief the hopeless task that – from the point of view of credibility – the Political Police had set itself.

In the second Charade, Muralov among his other remarkable crimes confessed to having used Shestov, another prisoner, in order to recruit still another prisoner, Arnold, a chauffeur, to kill Molotov; Arnold had decided to do so by driving a car with Molotov in it over a cliff at a dangerous point in the road.

Arnold, an ordinary professional criminal, calmly confessed in this Charade to being perfectly ready to sacrifice his life for the sake of the Opposition, and to have done so in instructions received from one unknown person *via* another. Muralov could, of course, have dropped in on Molotov in Moscow and shot him on the spot without going to the trouble of taking an unknown professional criminal into his confidence. For that matter, Pyatakov could just as easily have shot Stalin.

The building up of senseless detail was necessary as Stalin's horizons broadened with the second and third Charades, and also, no doubt, with the fanning out of the Deep Comb-out, the general terror that went by the name of the Great Purge and that, though it was to become and to remain an element of Soviet life, was always officially denied.

In the first Great Charade, after all, based on charges of mere terrorism, there might have been, to the minds of many Soviet citizens and even of Party people, a tiny kernel of truth, buried, to be sure, beneath a mountain of fantasy, but still there.

Even intelligent Soviet patriots, for instance, were taken in to some extent by the first Charade, on the basis of a sort of common sense.

Stalin had undeniably brought about the slaughter of millions of peasants during the starvation years of 1932–3; he had blanketed the country with terror, and had created a nauseating cult of his own semi-divinity. It was, in a way, not too extravagant to expect that some Old Bolsheviks might have flown off the handle. As an idea, at least, it was not impossible, though simply as an idea. There were, of course, yawning fissures in the first Charade too: why not kill Stalin instead of Kirov? And if they had embarked on terror for reasons of *principle*, why not say so? Terrorism is senseless unless it is proclaimed as such.

This last point illustrates a sentimental hangover of many intelligent Soviet patriots – until the full scope of the Great Charade and the Deep Comb-out stood forth revealed such patriots were still full of naïve idealism. The idea of a trial being used as a political device cast in the form of a medieval penitential display, of being stitched together out of whole cloth, of being, in fact, an actual invention disguised by traditional forms, took a long time to penetrate the minds of intelligent people; it was still harder to swallow than to grasp.

One of the reasons so many knowledgeable people in the Soviet Union still actually wavered before the second Charade, was partly an objection based on a sort of old-fashioned principle: if the Old Bolsheviks had had the courage to take to a course of terrorism, wouldn't they have blazoned their motives forth to the world? Made the dock a tribune for their principles, as revolutionaries had done under Tsarism?

Even intelligent men do not seem to have asked themselves: would Stalin have allowed it? Was Stalin the Tsar – a mere gentleman? Instead of perceiving that the very fact of their having confessed to such nonsense implied that they had been put on stage *in order to do just that*, hence that the actual conception of the Charade had been sinister, such knowledgeable insiders, evidently with an infantile belief in the probity of institutions, found the prisoners' behaviour inconsistent *after* they appeared in Stalin's dock instead of before.

Some of the hitches were trivial, in a way, though inexplicable if the Great Charades had not been a hoax.

In the penitential structure of the Charades, the guilt of the defendants was made much of. It had nothing to do with the content of the Charades, but was simply incorporated in their style – the rhetorical jargon that seemed natural for the Political Police and Stalin to use against the prisoners in public and that was also, perhaps, a natural style for the prisoners' own confessions.

This may explain the wording of one of the indictments, which, in the first Charade (Zinoviev and others), reads: [the leaders of the] 'centre figured that having been "forgiven" [by the Party for avowed deviations] they could, after killing Comrade Stalin, utilize this "forgiveness" to come into power.'[28]

This is obviously nonsense. If they had killed Stalin they would simply have killed him, explained their motives in Marxist terms, and either succeeded in holding on to power or failed. In a realistically conceived event, they would not have needed these theological categories of forgiveness for sins, etc. But with the Party background of hypocritical affirmation of loyalty the concomitant sinfulness in the feelings of people aware of the deception involved might well be, and in fact were, expressed in this theological idiom.

The same Charade had another hitch.

The prisoners had said in their last pleas that they were not even thinking of asking for mercy – they were much too contemptible for that – and the death sentences were duly announced (at 2.30 a.m., 24 August 1936). Nevertheless, on the evening of that same day another official statement was issued to the effect that the prisoners' appeal for mercy had been rejected; they had all been shot.

This minor hitch, which has nothing to do, of course, with guilt or innocence, was an artless revelation of a naïve bureaucratic blunder: it indicates that a scenario was prepared behind the Charade and that the hitch was in that scenario and not in the Charade itself.

On one occasion, Vyshinsky, doubtless the finest actor of the whole courtroom troupe, expressed with characteristic sincerity an unusual idea. In his closing speech in the second Charade he points out that 'every judge, every procurator, and every counsel for defence . . . knows when an accused is speaking the truth and when he departs from [it]. . . .'[29]

This was a particularly strange thing for him to say since in both the initial trial of Zinoviev and Kamenev for inspirational responsibility for the Kirov killing, and in the first Charade where the two appeared with the others, Vyshinsky had failed to detect that they departed from the truth since they were now charged with actually organizing the Kirov assassination.

By the time of the second Charade it was evident, also, that they had departed from it still further by not revealing the existence of the parallel centre and for that matter not discussing its connexion with the Nazis and the Japanese militarists or their programme to restore capitalism. In the second Charade, in fact, Vyshinsky went out of his way to denounce the performers in the first for blanket mendacity.

Yet poor Vyshinsky was debarred from pointing this out, since in the first Charade the contents of the second had not yet been decided on; it would have been absurd for him to accuse Zinoviev and Kamenev of any *particular* lie since he must have known that their entire testimony was a tissue of lies stitched together by the Political Police, doubtless with his own assistance.

One of the most grotesque of these slips was the curious fact that many of the major prisoners had been given an alibi that might have been thought perfect, and in detective stories, at least, recurrently crops up as such, namely, being in prison.

During a large part of the times under discussion the prisoners were in exile or in gaol. When one thinks of Vyshinsky's claim of the whole bloc's 'systematic devotion' to terrorism the incoherence really becomes outstanding; it was coped with in the Charades by simply soft-pedalling this quite destructive fact. It was, to be sure, immediately assessed at its proper value by those who rejected the Charades out of hand, but those who chose to believe in them were not shaken at all: they could, after all, be waved aside as mere details, as could, indeed, any discrepancy, however substantive.

The inventiveness of the script-writers in the Political Police did not need, perhaps, to be of a very high order; the essential function of the Charades was merely to create a certain atmosphere *in general*. Because of this a plainly silly fabrication on the part of the prisoner might slip into the scenario; it would then have to be supported by a sort of supplementary rectification made in Vyshinsky's speech for the prosecution. Thus, in the third Charade a prisoner gives an account of being jostled in a German bus, after having had secret conversations with Theodor Dan, the Menshevik; he says he was rushed to the police station, where he was recruited into the German intelligence service after being threatened with exposure on account of some pictures that had been taken of him and Dan. It had become 'obvious' to him that he had simply been trapped and had to work for them. Vyshinsky supports this infantile story by some clichés about how intelligence agents are recruited in general: 'We know . . . that they are caught in a dance . . . card games . . . a bottle of brandy.'

This imputation of blackmail to the putative conspirators may reflect in its own way an element of Soviet life. The Political Police were well known to recruit agents by blackmail; it was natural to project this element into the lines assigned the prisoners.

So many pains were taken to concoct the Charades and at the same time so much sloppiness went unnoticed that it is often pleasurable to become aware of contrivance in the very texture of the prose. The celebrated interchange between Vyshinsky and Kamenev in the first Charade is a priceless instance:

Vyshinsky: What appraisal should be given of the articles and statements you wrote in 1933, in which you expressed loyalty to the Party? Deception?
Kamenev: No, worse than deception.
Vyshinsky: Perfidy?
Kamenev: Worse.
Vyshinsky: Worse than deception, worse than perfidy – find the word. Treason?
Kamenev: You have found it.[30]

The same literary impression is given by a brief interchange in the third Charade: Vyshinsky again asks for a definition:

Vyshinsky: How would you qualify this . . . in the language of the Criminal Code?
Bessonov: (no reply)
Vyshinsky: Perhaps I can help you?
Bessonov: I think you can do it better than I. What coming from me just now may sound insincere and unconvincing will sound real if it comes from you.[31]

High comedy again! Even if it is not true that Bessonov is 'resisting' tacitly by his pretended acquiescence in the farce, still, saying with a straight face that Vyshinsky's statements will sound real is surely a form of dramatic irony!

A nightmarish quality often emerges from the tacit contempt demonstrated by both Vyshinsky and the prisoners for all details of the charges. In Radek's Charade, for instance:

Vyshinsky: And the fact that Pyatakov brought you the directives, was that treason, too, against the country?
Radek: A very indefinite term. That was also treason against the country. What's the difference, perhaps it was treason against the country, perhaps it was not.[32]

This has an irresistibly comic effect; the implication seems to be: just get on with the script, forget the details!

In the third Charade Bessonov had referred to sources of financial aid among 'Polish, Rumanian and Yugoslav circles'. Vyshinsky says: '(The organization was) maintained by . . . bourgeois circles – Polish, Rumanian and Bulgarian?' Bessonov simply replies, 'Yes'.[33]

Bulgaria and Yugoslavia are all one in such a script.

The Bolshevik style of hardheaded, down-to-earth 'objectivity' created a paradigm, as it were, for the confessional style of the Charades, too.

Nothing is more sentimental, in the eyes of a real Bolshevik, than excusing political mistakes by a plea of sincerity. Bernard Shaw's remark about the road to hell being paved with good intentions fits the Bolsheviks like a glove. Their hell is the hell of error, heresy and hetero-doxy that lies in wait for those who have fumbled the Great Key.

When the Great Key is in the hands of the Right Thinker it opens all doors. When a substitute is used, as it must be when in the hands of the Wrong Thinker, iniquities must follow.

Whether the culprit desires such iniquities or not is a matter of utter indifference to the march of the Dialectic. The most important matter is not at all what the individual may long for, or for that matter says he longs for, but what in fact happens – what his actions lead to regardless of his desires. By misunderstanding the tasks of the moment, for whatever reasons, the Party man or Party group put themselves objectively in the service of the countless enemies of the Party. There is simply no way out.

In their turn moral evaluations flow from this alleged insight into reality. Just as one's own side, which has the Right Key, is to be approved of, the other side, with the Wrong Key, is to be condemned.

Since Bolshevik clichés pretended to base all political decisions on expediency alone – making any discussion of a choice, as between moderate and extreme means, quite out of place – and since the Party was the sole repository of criteria, the Party's view of what was expedient was the only legitimate, or even conceivable touchstone for Bolsheviks.

In the case of opponents, however, while the same kind of 'objective' and 'consistent' logic was taken for granted as governing the Opposi-tion's behaviour, its moral evaluation was reversed. Thus the Opposition would be driven by the 'logic of its own position' to committing the most extravagant crimes – heinous, of course, since they represented a principle of evil – and the plausibility of the crimes would be brought home to the audience – conceived of, naturally, as Bolshevik itself – by indicating the rigorous train of logic – Bolshevik logic, to boot! – that had landed them in the soup.

When the Japanese, according to a prisoner at the second Charade, requested that 'undermining work' be done and 'data' provided, it was approved of because it 'resulted from the logic of the struggle of the Trotskyite organization.'[34]

This was, of course, comprehensible in the context of the Charades.

Since the prisoners had been compelled to confess to objectives that in their nature were extreme, it was only natural for them to strive for these extreme objectives by means that were also extreme.

In this way the logic and consistency enshrined in Bolshevik tradition were applied in reverse, with a 'minus sign', as the Bolsheviks say, and turned into a would-be plausible account of the depravity of the Oppositionists.

The Great Key itself, of course – evidently a gimmick for narcissistic self-congratulation – is the product of an attitude that as a subjective phenomenon is part of the bedrock of Marxism (also, curiously enough, of Freudianism, Hegelianism, indeed of anthropology, too, in all forms).

Its essence is the assumption that the holder of the Secret Key understands what you are doing better than you do yourself: you *think* you are promoting something or other, but *in reality* – a reality you can't grasp, since you lack the Secret Key – you are promoting something utterly different. As Lenin said: 'History loves irony ... You were going to a certain room, and you got into another.'[35] Or in Stalin's version: 'They knock on one door and open another'.[36]

Just as a psychoanalytically-minded person need never answer an argument, but can merely nod sagely to show he understands the *source* of the argument, or an anthropologist, listening to a primitive person explain some ceremony, will nod sagely as he grasps the *real* meaning of the ceremony, so the Bolshevik will grasp the real impact of a political position and disregard protestations about its purely subjective motivation, the pious wishes that may attend it.

He must, of course, be the Right Bolshevik with the Right Key, or at any rate the Right Political Police.

Vyshinsky, interrogating Radek, for instance, asked him whether he was 'for the defeat or for the victory of the USSR'.

Radek: All my actions these years testify to the fact that I aided defeat.
Vyshinsky: These actions of yours were deliberate?
Radek: Apart from sleeping, I have never in my life committed any undeliberate actions.[37]

The word 'deliberate' serves two purposes: on the one hand Radek agrees that he 'aided defeat', thus by-passing, in effect, the whole question of his subjective intentions as quite irrelevant, since objectively, as Radek points out, all his actions testify to it. On the other hand, there is a crevice through which a punishment is felt to be morally justified – in the event of the frame-up's success – just because, in spite of everything, his action was 'deliberate'. Thus, psychological requirements too could be satisfied: if a prisoner used the Bolshevik criterion of expediency it would sound cynical, and make a 'shocking' impression.

In the first Charade, for instance, a prisoner says matter-of-factly that it was natural for Trotskyites to use the Gestapo: it was part of the logic of the situation.[38]

In the second Charade Trotsky's son, Sedov, is ascribed a matter-of-fact acceptance of the role of spy for the Nazi intelligence service: 'It is absurd to use words like that. In a fight it is unreasonable to be as squeamish as that. If you accept terrorism, if you accept destructive undermining activity in industry, I absolutely fail to understand why you cannot agree with this.'[39]

With respect to the charges of terrorism levelled at lifelong Marxists, the audience might have been perplexed as to how veterans of an ideology that denounces personal terrorism should have suddenly gone overboard for the programme of pure, though meaningless terrorism. In keeping with his general style of formulating unspoken, though obvious objections on the part of some ideal audience, Vyshinsky asks the question flatly:

And how did these gentlemen [the prisoners] reconcile their alleged Marxism with . . . terroristic activity? In no wise! And yet these people called themselves Marxists at one time! Probably . . . Zinoviev still considers himself a Marxist. He said here that Marxism could not be reconciled with terrorism . . .

During this trial . . . Reingold . . . said: 'In 1932, Zinoviev . . . argued in favour of resorting to terror as follows: "although terror is incompatible with Marxism, at the present moment these considerations must be abandoned".'[40]

In short, because of the literary nature of the scenarios, when a gap must be jumped over it is simply jumped, by saying, in effect: 'Well, we decided to jump it.'

Similarly, in the Charade for Pyatakov, with respect to the Bolshevik belief that the senselessness of 'individual terror' naturally applies to specific acts of violence, too, he says that his own point of view was merely 'criminal', as in his statement that 'such isolated actions' – the murder of Beria – 'would be senseless'.[41]

This harmonizes with the general theme according to which the prisoners are denatured altogether and simply stigmatized as gangsters and bandits, while at the same time they give perfectly intelligible though of course false and often incoherent accounts of highly sophisticated political reasoning.

The authority attributed to Trotsky is breath-taking: with no funds, no organization, and no power, indeed, of any kind whatever, he is charged with being able to control the actions of people thousands of miles away from him who had never shown him any devotion in the

past. Even those who might at one time have been genuine Trotskyites
– however the word was defined when it was coined by Stalin – never
accepted Trotsky's authority unreservedly, yet when their lives are at
stake, they embark on a campaign of criminal subversion merely on
Trotsky's say-so. Thus in the third Charade, concerning a discussion he
was supposed to have had with two of the prisoners in 1937, after
Pyatakov had been executed, Krestinsky says:

'When we saw that this business [of terrorism] . . . was left unattended
in our Trotskyite ranks after [Pyatakov] was shot, and at the same time
. . . Trotsky had written that terrorist acts were necessary, the three of
us met to discuss what was to be done.'[42]

Vyshinsky, aware, perhaps, in his capacity both as a primary script-
writer and as an editor, that even from a literary point of view there
might be something extravagant about the whole formulation, meets a
conceivable criticism head-on: 'Perhaps this is all an invention? Perhaps
[some witnesses] just gave rein to their fantasy? Perhaps this is all a
pack of lies, an invention, the irresponsible chatter of the accused who
are trying to say as much as they can against the others in order to miti-
gate their own ultimate fate? No! No! This is not an invention, not
fantasy! It is the truth!'[43]

Sometimes this habit of the prisoners of blandly making over-all admissions and then becoming vague, self-contradictory or downright
negative with respect to the specific components of the admissions,
would be countered by Vyshinsky directly. Thus, to a witness who has
just said: 'I think I have replied to everything, and have spoken clearly,
I do not deny things', Vyshinsky replied: 'This "everything" does not
satisfy me. I do not want "everything". I want each one separately.
"Everything" will be said by the court in its verdict. At present –
"everything" is not enough for me.'[44]

The extravagance of the charges, assented to with a straight face,
would often sound so absurd if placed in a realistic context that the
impression is bound to be created of a script that is being handled
irresponsibly just because it is a script and is no longer taken seriously
even within the make-believe atmosphere of the courtroom.

Thus one of the prisoners in the third Charade, after making the usual
generalized admissions to the most improbable wrecking activity, makes
specifications that are manifestly preposterous: 'To give some idea of
the extent of this wrecking work [in the retail trade, to boot!] I may
mention that of 12,135,000 shops that were inspected by the Co-
operative Trade Inspectorate, cases of overcharging and defrauding
purchasers were established in 13,000 shops. The actual number was
considerably larger.'[45]

This implies the presence of many more than at least 13,000 accomplices in a conspiratorial network. It sounds, of course, like a big joke.

Now, it is obvious that the prisoner could hardly have invented such a story out of a whole cloth; it must have been given to him. But why wasn't it seen to be a piece of nonsense, like indeed the overwhelming majority of the detailed instances of 'conspiratorial' wrecking throughout the Soviet economy?

The scenarios were not improvised in the courtroom; they took many months to prepare, as is plain from the length of the interrogations that finally broke the will of the prisoners. By the time all reality was excluded from consideration the librettists were simply preoccupied by *belles-lettres*; from that point of view the question was merely one of plausibility conceived within a framework capacious enough to dwarf discrepancies.

It is known that Radek, in whose case the likelihood of a deal with Stalin was very high, since he was merely exiled, was extremely helpful in the preparation of his script. He understood how to make it far more plausible than did his relatively primitive gaolers. There is no reason to think he was displaying covert resistance *via* veiled language. We can take it for granted that his composition of an acceptable scenario for the Charades was at least conscientious.

Yet even Radek's sense of humour, or contrariness occasionally ran away with him. The following remark he made in the second Charade is characteristically cynical – blandly frank – when understood. Referring to the proofs of Trotsky's criminal activity Radek says: 'In support of this fact there was the evidence of two people – the testimony of myself, who received the directives and the letters from Trotsky (which, unfortunately, I burned), and the testimony of Pyatakov, who spoke to Trotsky.'

What indifference, even contempt, this extraordinary remark implies for the reactions of any human intelligence! The 'Prosecutor' has been consistently treating Radek and his 'accomplices' as unscrupulous crooks, in fact, monsters; now by keeping complete silence in the face of this blanket acceptance of total responsibility for the testimony, he indicates that the whole thing is simply woven out of whole cloth!

This seems to have been a little exceptional; Radek's zest for analysis was generally deployed in a more general way. The lines he largely wrote for himself are valuable indications of the principles underlying the composition of the libretti as a whole. Here is a sample of his political prose. He is discussing the 'line' attributed to Trotsky in 1935:

We were to fight in order that foreign capital might rule, which would put us completely under its control before it allowed us to come to power. What did the directive to agree upon wrecking activities with foreign circles mean? For me [it] meant . . . that our organization was becoming the direct representative of foreign intelligence services. We ceased to be in the slightest degree the masters of our actions. . . .

This denoted in practice that if such men [Livshitz or Serebriakov], with decades of revolutionary work behind them, could descend to wrecking . . . their moral fibre would have to be utterly broken, and they would act on the instructions of the class enemy. Either they would lose their bearings, or they would become spies. If they lost their bearings, I could do nothing with them; if they became agents of foreign states, others would give them their orders. As a result, if foreign fascism came in, this fascism, far from letting Trotskyites get into power . . . would destroy the organization because it had no need to trouble itself with this crowd of anarchist intellectuals. So that even if my attitude to the country did not weigh with me, there was pure egotism.'[46]

Thus far, Radek's lines plainly refute the fundamental idea behind the scenarios, that is, behind the ostensible 'theory' created by Stalin. Anyone listening to it would scratch his head and say: 'Then how . . .' etc. It would be quite easy, in fact, to imagine this segment of Radek's testimony in the hands of the defence, if such a thing were possible, and being used to destroy the fundamental conception of the wrecking campaign as outlined in Vyshinsky's libretti.

But, of course, nothing of the sort happened; after going on a little longer with this kind of explanation of why the Oppositionists could not have gone in for the subversive actions they had been accused of, Radek suddenly but smoothly, with no transition, ends up with a final sentence that abruptly restores the whole point of the scenario: '. . . (thus) for the phantom of power, Trotsky was ready to sacrifice the last man capable of dying for him.'[47]

The basic question throughout the Charades was why anyone should have been willing to die for Trotsky to begin with: Radek has just shown they couldn't even get power, especially not from the fascists, yet within the context of the docile courtroom, the bemused foreign newspapermen and the totally controlled media, this blatant *non sequitur* is presented as though instead of destroying the official story it confirmed it.

A similar point was made by another distinguished revolutionary, Rakovsky, in the third Charade:

Vyshinsky: . . . for the sake of what did you Trotskyites wage this struggle against the Soviet state?

Rakovsky: For the sake of the seizure of power. . . . There was no ideological premise whatsoever. . . .

Vyshinsky: . . . And the object was a . . . struggle against the Socialist State
for the purpose of seizing power in . . . whose interests?

Rakovsky: Citizen Prosecutor, if I tell you that we wanted to seize power in
order to hand it over to the fascists, we would not only be the criminals we
are, but we would be fools. But . . . [dots in text].

Vyshinsky: But?

Rakovsky: But when we thought it possible to seize power and to hold it
without handing it over to the fascists, it was insanity, it was a utopia.

Vyshinsky: Consequently, if you had managed to seize power it would inevitably have fallen into the hands of the fascists?

Rakovsky: I share this estimate entirely.[48]

In the same style as Radek's 'analysis' cited just previously, Rakovsky
essentially destroys the logic of the behaviour imputed to the prisoners.
Vyshinsky, seemingly unaware that the rationale of his whole case has
been annihilated by a prisoner who is, after all, his witness, seizes on the
nub of 'fact' and then forces it on Rakovsky, who even after making the
admission sound wholly irrational admits it anyhow.

In a real trial, of course, such incoherence would be incomprehensible;
in a carefully arranged form of trial, too, it would be an indication of
some slip-up. Yet the fact that Vyshinsky – in real life highly intelligent
and an able lawyer – could pay no attention to such thematic contradic-
tions implies that in the tension of the public proceedings no energy was
left over for scrutinizing the effect of what was being said.

This concept of plotting seems never to have palled. When Trotsky
was finally killed by a Political Police assassin, the letter given the
assassin in case of capture was full of the same myth:

Having gone to Mexico to be close to Trotsky, 'the greatest leader of
the working-class', the assassin found that Trotsky was, in fact, a mere
criminal and counter-revolutionary who was instigating him to 'go to
Russia to organize there a series of attempts against various persons
and, in the first place, against Stalin'. He also discovered that Trotsky
was plotting away with 'certain leaders of capitalist countries' against
Mexico as well as the Soviet Union.

Trotsky's assassin, on a mission organized – at a rumoured cost of
about $1,000,000 – by the Soviet Political Police, had found that the
Charades were perfectly all right! With the addition, in view of the 1939
pact between Stalin and Hitler, that this time Trotsky was hinted at as
being in the service more exclusively of 'American Imperialism' rather
than simply of the Gestapo. This was in 1940 – two-and-a-half years
after the last Great Charade!

A paradox in the Great Charades was the presence of some factual
elements.

Scenarios had to be composed to demonstrate a fiction; since this is well-nigh impossible, there was often a need for real material. The more fantastic the aim of the script-writers the rarer the material was bound to be. Genuine, i.e., verifiable material is naturally more vulnerable to exposure than pure fiction. Nevertheless, perhaps for the sake of convenience, resort was sometimes had to actual truth. There are many perfectly accurate statements throughout the fictional dialogues.

The actual material used didn't particularly matter, since the purpose it could be made to serve remained wholly fictional anyhow; it merely had to be stitched into the fabric of the scenarios as a whole. In general, accurate statements about, say, the Marxist views of the Opposition could promote the purposes of the scenario if these were fitted out with an introduction and a conclusion to the effect that the prisoners were merely pretending to hold such views.

Nikolayev, the dupe selected for the initial operation – Kirov's murder – kept a diary clearly indicating that he was a solitary malcontent; this factual situation was then portrayed (in the hearing of Nikolayev and his 'associates' on 28–9 December 1933) as a mere device on the part of Nikolayev, 'with the object', as the indictment reads, 'of . . . concealing his accomplices and . . . masking the true motives for the murder of Comrade Kirov'.[49]

In the same way all statements reported as having been made by various Oppositionists indicating that Marxism had always been against the use of individual terror, were presented with introductions or conclusions indicating that they *said* that to mask their true purposes.

This device has, of course, a dual point: on the one hand it accommodates the obvious retort: 'But they are Marxists'; on the other hand, it tucks the prisoners into the scenario.

In the case of the suicide of Zinoviev's secretary (Bogdan), who left a note explaining it as due to the Party purge, the note itself was explained as a blind, intended to make people think just that.

All historic statements made by the Opposition at any time could be presented as camouflage; from the point of view of the Charades, intended to annihilate Trotsky morally as well as politically, it was enough for Stalin and his Police to be able to make their own positive accusations, based merely on affirmation, and treat all real evidence as being manufactured precisely to *seem* like evidence: thus the very fact that Trotsky spoke against fascism could be made – for those who accepted the Charades as trials – to look like part of the plot.

Within the overarching framework of the fiction whole chunks of factual material could be turned to use, fitted into the over-all design by the interpolation of rhetorical bridges between various sections of the material.

Thus a secret agreement between the Soviet Union and the German government after their rapprochement in 1922, concerning the collaboration between the Red Army and the Reichswehr, could be presented years later as instances where 'Trotskyites' had done some 'plotting' with the Reichswehr. This naturally disregarded the rationale of the operation as an agreement between the two governments and the obvious fact that the Weimar Republic was in any case not Nazi.

Taking for granted the element of constraint in the Great Charades, some have thought that the prisoners often contrived to indicate, at least to the percipient, that the whole show was nonsense.

On many occasions the prisoners seemed to be bickering with the prosecution on some minor points of the script; out of the many instances of resistance on small points a not implausible picture of masked but total resistance can be pieced together. This would not have affected the main outcome of the Charades – humiliation and death at the hands of Stalin – but in their own minds they might have got away with it, on the assumption that their own generation or at least posterity would understand what a concoction the whole thing had been. For history-obsessed men, like most Bolsheviks, especially ideologues like Bukharin, this might actually have meant something.

From the point of view of the prosecution, on the other hand, it is conceivable that these bargaining demands of the defendants might have been agreed to, on the theory that it didn't matter anyhow.

Thus an entire apparatus of admissions followed by denials of detail seems to have been made use of by many prisoners: something would be admitted in a general way, then retracted in a specific way. The prisoners might have assumed that the initiated would understand that any denial of anything whatever constituted a denial of the whole, since the starting point of the whole enterprise was one of confession to monstrous charges. It might have been conceived of as a 'word to the wise'.

In the first Charade, Smirnov, who was supposed to have denied everything in the pre-trial investigation – as they must all have done – finally comes to trial where, of course, he now admits everything. His total resistance is now, presumably, over with. Yet Smirnov carries it on nevertheless in this form:

Smirnov: I listened to those instructions [of Trotsky's] and communicated them to the [Trotskyite-Zinovievite] centre. The centre accepted them but I did not take part in its work.
Vyshinsky: So when did you leave the centre?

Smirnov: I did not intend to resign; there was nothing to resign from.
Vyshinsky: Did the centre exist?
Smirnov: What sort of centre?[50]

Then Vyshinsky has to backtrack by calling on Smirnov's co-defendants to confirm the existence of this same centre, so that the effect on the audience – had it been an audience! – was presumably, in Smirnov's mind, to indicate to them what nonsense it all was.

Even in Radek's testimony there are indications that he might have been tipping off the *cognoscenti* to the worthlessness of his testimony. In referring to the testimony of the witness who has just told a long story about having been a go-between for Trotsky and Radek, the latter mentions as a 'minor inexactitude' the witness's statement that he had given the actual names of Stalin and Voroshilov in the first of many letters, when in fact that would have been impossible since names were never mentioned except in a code and they had had as yet no code. This could be extended to mean that if the witness's testimony was wrong on such a basic, though seemingly minor point, everything he said was worthless. The reasoning runs as follows.

The witness indicates that he really didn't know the plotters' actual technique; that is, he was lying on this point (Radek had established this particular witness's first-class memory), and if he was lying, he had not been one of Trotsky's go-betweens, and if he had been lying about the fundamental point he was just lying in general.

This theory of veiled resistance has been applied most plausibly to Bukharin's testimony.[51] He is thought by some to have deviated subtly from the script in order to compromise the Charade and thus deal a final blow to the Stalin regime. By introducing silly discrepancies, by denying basic details, he meant to disclose the technique of Stalin's fabrication while at the same time showing the public what he meant by the programme of capitalist restoration attributed to him.

If he had simply chosen to deny his guilt altogether he would doubtless have been shot out of hand like countless others, and thus have been vilified after his death with no rebuttal possible.

Bukharin had also been subjected to brutal physical treatment, even torture, greater even than that of the others, but had withstood the treatment. Though it would have been simple to torture him to death, it suited Stalin to have him destroyed in public. For his part, Bukharin, having agreed to the macabre bargain of appearing in court and testifying to the prosecution's script, made in effect a pseudo-confession. By the mere fact of presenting the public with a riddle Bukharin was really providing the riddle with an answer. If a confession of such seriousness sounded enigmatic, there could be only one explanation of the enigma – that there was something fishy about the whole thing.

If a case for this veiled resistance theory can be made plausible, Bukharin would certainly have been a fitting exponent of such subtlety. He was the only performer in the Charades to contradict, by implication, Stalin's politics; moreover, his resistance to the charge of complicity in the 'plot' against Lenin was unyielding. Nor did he behave throughout his performance like a listless, broken man.

Not at all an organizer or administrator, Bukharin was almost wholly an intellectual. Small and slightly built, with a gentle manner and delicate features, he was very sensitive. He was a cosmopolitan who spoke foreign languages well (English and German), an amateur painter, a passionate butterfly collector. With all his intelligence he was often like a somewhat hysterical child, sobbing and sighing in all directions in any crisis.

His charm was unusual: beyond his rationalism he had a great deal of gaiety, artistic delicacy, and a sort of boyish expansiveness. His predilection for logic naturally led him to create symmetrical, abstract patterns of argumentation and thinking that like so many Marxists he mistook for reality. It was a quality that often led him to take up, in the jargon of Marxist dialectics, extreme positions. It was child's play for such a wordsmith to bounce from Left-wing to Right-wing Communism: those who liked argumentation for the sake of itself could follow him with pleasure.

Bukharin – referred to by Lenin as the 'darling of the whole Party' – had been famous as a theoretician even during his early thirties. After 1917 he was well-established as the Party's leading theoretician. The horrors he had seen under Bolshevik rule moved him back to what he himself conceived of as the 'humanism' he thought underlay the splendid intellectual edifice of Marxism; it was just here that his divergence from actual Bolshevik practice was bound to grow greater and end, doubtless inevitably, with his death.

In 1935 he was allowed to go to Western Europe to buy some archives, including the archive of Marx and Engels, for the Soviet government. During the trip he had a long conversation with the well-known Menshevik scholar, Boris Nicolaevsky, who has left a detailed record[52] (their conversation was stitched into the conspiracy Bukharin helped 'expose' in the last Charade).

In the beginning Bukharin, like all Bolsheviks, had been *against* humanism: 'Earlier,' he said, 'destructiveness was necessary and the struggle against humanism inevitable. But now we have entered a different period, when we are faced by tasks of construction. . . . Not only our Communism, but your Socialism [to Nicolaevsky] must become rooted in this humanist base, like the Communism of Marx.'

Bukharin had been appalled by the atrocities of the collectivization campaign. As he said: 'We were conducting a mass annihilation of completely defenceless men, together with their wives and children.' The campaign was so savage, so cruel, so gory that many seasoned Bolsheviks committed suicide; some lost their minds, others left the service altogether.

But what depressed Bukharin even more than the collectivization itself was the change in Bolshevik psychology: those men who participated in the ferocious campaign against ordinary men, women and children were themselves necessarily hardened beyond anything that any previous revolutionary experience could have indicated. Bolsheviks with the stamina, or callousness, to go ahead without losing their minds had to accommodate themselves to the sweeping changes.

'They are no longer human beings. . . . They are really cogs in some terrible machine. There is taking place a real dehumanization of the people working in the Soviet apparatus, a process of transforming human power into an empire of the "iron heel",' he said, quoting Jack London's celebrated, infantile indictment of what London conceived of as capitalism in his book, *The Iron Heel*, favourite of Continental socialists and to this day widely read in the Soviet Union.

Nicolaevsky records an episode from their trip that highlights the scholasticism of Marxist eggheads. On this trip Bukharin particularly wanted to take a look at Marx's original manuscripts: the actual manuscript of *Capital* was fished out of the archives. Painstakingly leafing through Marx's original notebooks, trying to decipher Marx's notoriously illegible handwriting, Bukharin was looking for the discussion of 'classes'.

Nicolaevsky, famous for total recall as well as for erudition, quickly found it; Bukharin, holding 'his head with both hands', began reading the famous lines. In this section Marx's handwriting was still more illegible; his pen seemed scarcely able to keep up with his thoughts. Very abruptly, in the middle of the passage, Marx's train of thought was broken off.

Bukharin, says Nicolaevsky, was 'clearly checking to see if the draft might not contain some clue to the omission that would throw new light on the course of Marx's thought . . . and he did not find it. He began to read the passage once again, but having satisfied himself that nothing new would be found, he broke off, sighing, "Ah Karlyusha, Karlyusha [Charlie, Charlie], why didn't you finish? It was difficult for you, but how you would have helped us!" '

Surely a scene of high comedy! The Bolshevik enterprise, based, after all, on the boldness derived from an absolute faith in the utter rightness and timeless applicability of Marx's 'method', had just taken hold of an enormous peasant country, quite contrary to Marx's own doctrines, but claiming them nevertheless as its sanction, and by 1936 had already been responsible for the deaths of untold millions of people. And now, at this crucial turn, with millions wallowing in their own blood, Bukharin went *back* – back to the source, back to Marx, who had landed them in such hot water in the first place!

It was Bukharin's scholasticism that made it easy for Stalin to undo him within the Party. After Stalin had utilized his verbal agility against the 'Left Opposition', he turned on him and undermined him even as a theoretician. At the April plenum (1929) where Bukharin had been routed, Stalin quoted Lenin's *Testament*:

'Bukharin is not only the most valuable and biggest theoretician of the Party, but also may legitimately be considered the favourite of the whole Party; yet his theoretical views can only with the very greatest doubt be regarded as fully Marxist, for there is something scholastic in him (he never has learned and I think never has fully understood the Dialectic).'

Stalin pronounced the last words here with great emphasis; he wound up with a small peroration of his own: 'So Bukharin is a scholastic theorist with no dialectics; but dialectics are the very soul of Marxism!'[53]

For Lenin to have been able to say that the greatest theoretician of the Party was unable to understand the Dialectic – the essence of Marxism, as well as its crown! – shows what pitfalls await the Marxist student of history. How, indeed, could the greatest Bolshevik theoretician not grasp the Dialectic!

Bukharin was responsible for the composition, even the wording of practically the whole of the 'Stalin Constitution' of 1936. He was proud of it, because though the Party had long since given up the semblance of responsibility even to its own membership, the Constitution established the equality of all citizens before the law, and even universal and equal suffrage.

This at the time when the Bolshevik leaders, answerable only to themselves, had slaughtered millions of people, when the Stalin cult had reached extravagant dimensions, and when it was perfectly obvious that the Constitution was merely a perfection of the hypocrisy that characterized Stalinism as a whole!

Bukharin's impulsive, warmblooded emotionalism found a way out, of course. Another metaphor! The difficulties, blunders and savageries of the Bolshevik regime were, of course, not so good. But he had *faith*, faith that the development – including the slaughter, including the callousing and the dehumanizing of the Party people – was somehow going 'forward' anyhow: if you have faith in that forward development you are 'saved'. 'It is like a stream running to the shore. If one leans out of the stream, one is ejected completely,' he told Nicolaevsky with a scissor-like gesture of his two fingers. 'The stream goes through the most difficult places. But it still goes forward in the direction in which it must.'

Alas for Bukharin! The scissor-like motion of his two fingers certainly indicated that he knew what was going to happen to him; he had no illusions about his own fate; on the other hand, he couldn't abandon his own handiwork, the only cause that gave his life meaning to himself. He might be done for, but he still believed in a better future for Russia under the Bolshevik regime.

The sheer physical terror that Stalin had begun, by 1928, to inspire in people near him, had grown to enormous proportions by the early thirties. During this same trip to Western Europe Bukharin left a record of his feelings about Stalin, in the course of a secret conversation he had with Theodor Dan and his wife Lydia, sister of the most famous Menshevik, Julius Martov. Lydia Dan has left an account of their conversation:[54]

Dan said: 'Of course I don't know Stalin as well as you do. . . .' Bukharin, very excited and the words tumbling out of his mouth, interrupted him: 'That's just it! You don't know him the way the rest of us do! I once said they could bring Marx's tomb to Moscow, yes, transport it and set up a statue over it – not a very big one – and next to it they would set up a bigger one of Stalin, say, reading *Capital.* . . . And Stalin would be holding a little pencil, to make notes, if necessary, or let's say corrections – corrections of Marx!

'You say you don't know him well, but we do. He is actually unhappy at not being able to convince everyone, including himself, that he is greater than everyone; this unhappiness of his may be his most human trait, indeed his only human trait, but what is no longer human, but something devilish, is that because of this unhappiness of his he can't help revenging himself on people, on everybody, but especially on those who are superior to him or better at something. If anyone speaks better than he does, he is doomed! Stalin will not let him live – since such a man would be an eternal reminder that Stalin is not supreme. If anyone writes better than he does, he's finished, because only Stalin, only *he* has the right to be the premier Russian writer.

'No, no, I tell you he's a small-minded, malicious man – no, not a man, but a devil. . . .'

I shall never forget the expression on Bukharin's face at that moment – fear and hatred had completely distorted his normally good-humoured face.

When Dan, quite upset, asked him how then, with such an opinion of Stalin, he, Bukharin, and the other Bolsheviks had blindly entrusted to this devil their own fate, the fate of the Party, and the fate of the country, Bukharin got very excited, changed about at once and said: 'You don't understand, that's something completely different. It wasn't entrusted to *him*, but to a man whom the Party had confidence in; it just so happens that he's – something like a symbol of the Party. The rank-and-file, the workers, the people all believe in him. It may be that it's our fault, but that's what's happened; that's why all of us have slid into his gullet, absolutely certain of his devouring us. And he knows that and simply picks the most suitable moment.'

Then I too couldn't restrain myself and broke into the conversation: 'Well, in that case, why are you sliding into his gullet now? Why go back to Moscow?'

I remember Bukharin's face, overcast by a look of naïve perplexity. He shrugged his shoulders as though annoyed, and said: 'How can I help going back? By becoming an *émigré*? No – living as you do, as *émigrés*, I could never do it. No, let come what may. And who knows? For that matter maybe nothing will happen.'

By that time the first of the Great Charades must have been well in train; it is more than likely, for that matter, that Stalin had allowed Bukharin to visit Western Europe to lend a touch of plausibility to the charge of conspiracy!

Whatever Bukharin might have said about Stalin's devilishness he was quite incapable of grasping its extent. By the time he appeared in the small Moscow courtroom, performing in Stalin's Charade, he must have been willing to try anything, one might think, to get through to an outside audience.

There are some individual instances in which such resistance has been surmised. In the first Charade, for instance, a prisoner (Yevdokimov) asks an evidently rhetorical question:

Who will believe a single word of ours? . . . Who will believe us, who played so detestable a comedy at the fresh grave of Kirov whom we had killed; who will believe us, who only by accident, not through any fault of our own, did not become the assassins of Stalin and other leaders of the people? Who will believe us, who are facing the court as a counter-revolutionary gang of bandits, as allies of fascism, of the Gestapo?[55]

Now, if we omit the phrase 'us, who' from the formula 'who will believe us, who . . .' replacing it with the shortened sentence to read: 'Who will believe', etc., we can see that the opposite is true – no one will believe it! Thus we have a statement that we can *now* see to be true even through the camouflage of the Charade.

The plainest evidence of such resistance is the intriguing incident of Krestinsky's conduct during the third Charade: he was the only prisoner to deny a major charge.

Krestinsky had once been a close assistant of Lenin's for organizational affairs, and secretary of the Central Committee of the Party. He was also Justice and Finance Commissar while Lenin was alive; besides this he had been a diplomat (an ambassador to Germany) for ten years and a deputy of Maxim Litvinov.

He was broken because of the hold over his fifteen-year-old daughter, who because of her age was subject to Stalin's decree (of 7 April 1935, subjecting children to the same treatment as adults). His denial of the charges made a curious impression just because it was unique, and also because of the over-night retraction, which led many observers to wonder what sinister treatment had been applied to him.

On the very first day Krestinsky said quite flatly: 'I plead not guilty. I am not a Trotskyite. I was never a member of the bloc of Rights and Trotskyites, of whose existence I was not aware. . . . In particular I plead not guilty to the charge of having had connexions with the German intelligence service.'

There was some speculation about whether a man might have appeared at last who was brave enough to reveal the machinations behind the confessions.

But the next day (3 March 1938) it was all over: that morning Vyshinsky scarcely looked at Krestinsky, who was sitting mutely behind the wooden bar. It was not until the evening that Krestinsky got to his foot with a statement:

Yesterday, under the influence of a momentary keen feeling of false shame, evoked by the atmosphere of the dock and the painful impression created by the public reading of the indictment, which was aggravated by my poor health, I could not bring myself to say that I am guilty. And instead of saying 'Yes, I am guilty', I almost mechanically answered: 'No, I am not guilty.'
Vyshinsky: Mechanically?
Krestinsky: In the face of world public opinion, I had not the strength to admit the truth.

The use of the word 'mechanical' here implies that the scenarios, worked out over a period of months or years and imposed on the prisoners over a period of at least many months, were somehow spontaneous bursts of soul-baring.

In any case, though essentially lifeless, like the script in general, this detail created a little dramatic interest. The idea summed up in the whispered phrase, 'But what did they *do* to him?' was bound to come to people's minds.

The general difficulty about the theory of veiled resistance, despite the plausibility of a few alleged illustrations of it, is the role of the Political Police: how could *they* have been deceived?

At the time, certainly, those who accepted the Charades as real trials noticed nothing! And it surely was obvious, with the total control Stalin could exert over the court and all the performers, that if something had looked strange it would have been noticed, if only by Vyshinsky, trembling for his own skin.

It is likely, since the prisoners agreed to acknowledge false charges publicly, that the instances of *apparent* resistance to *some* of the charges were themselves approved in advance by the Political Police as part of the general bargain. It is true that Bukharin gives the impression, almost systematically, of agreeing to the main burden of the charges, but then refusing to go as far as admitting extremist details. For instance: 'I categorically deny my complicity in the assassination of Kirov'[56] (and some others, including the writer Gorky). Vyshinsky, in his cross-examination, seemed to be trying to get Bukharin to make such an admission, but Bukharin, while agreeing to other charges, evidently equally fictitious, drew the line there.

This must have been agreed to in advance by the Political Police, otherwise the scenario would have been written differently. Its justification, from the theatrical point of view, was that Bukharin convinced them that it would make the whole performance stand up better if it was not so monotonously of a piece. Bukharin must first have persuaded his interrogators and the Political Police script-writers to agree with his assessment of the public's reaction.

Psychologically, of course, this was an inestimable balm to Bukharin; he could, in a way, be altogether sincere in the very midst of the imposture.

This conception of plausibility must have been a consideration in the minds of the Political Police from the beginning. It is the only explanation of the reluctance of a number of the prisoners to agree to literally everything: they often held a little back, i.e. the extremist acts their supposed views – criminal, bandit, etc. – might have been thought to lead them to. Thus Rykov also denied complicity in Kirov's murder[57] or in the five alleged medical murders, though he inculpated some other prisoners (the 'Trotskyites' in contra-distinction to the 'Rights').[58]

This must have been agreed to in advance as part of the bargain between Rykov and the choreographers of the Charades. From the point of view of the overall effect, after all, nothing would be changed, whereas it could be plausibly maintained that a tiny element of asymmetry would heighten the purely theatrical effect of plausibility.

It is a little unlikely that the Political Police and the prosecutor could have been persuaded by the prisoners that the over-all effect of plausibility would be heightened by minor denials; indeed, there was something convincing about Vyshinsky's recurrent irascibility; his occasional explosions of annoyance were quite different from his purely theatrical outbursts of streamlined, rhetorical, collective denunciation of the prisoners. It is hard to imagine him, as an actor, losing his temper in quite that way.

It is even less likely that the Political Police would not have perceived any real resistance instantly and nipped it in the bud. The hold they had over the prisoners was evidently omnipotent: they were forcing them, after all, to sacrifice their lives and above all their reputations in order to further Stalin's enterprise. That hold over them could surely have been depended on to extract from them the last little drop of resistance that might have been left, had it not been suitable to Stalin's purpose, too. Hence all the overt signs of resistance – the coy denials of detail when sweeping charges were confessed to, the specific denials of general admissions, the seeming retractions, the confusions of details, indeed the whole paraphernalia of the scenarios that on an even cursory examination discloses such gaping holes – must have been agreed to or gone unnoticed in the bargains made between the Political Police and the prisoners.

It is possible that, since the prisoners had not *memorised* their lines, there was some latitude in the tug-of-war between Vyshinsky and the victims. Even if the tug-of-war was itself merely a theatrical device, it might have had some elements of tension, personal hatred, irritation on both sides, and an over-all reluctance to go through with the whole thing that might have constituted crevices through which the prisoners might, conceivably, have hoped to smuggle through some elements of reality.

On the other hand, one of the most striking aspects of the Great Charades was the remarkable degree of conformity in the acceptance of the major charges. Three great Trials were held, ostensibly of vindictive, ruthless, unscrupulous and fanatical haters of the Soviet regime and its leaders, yet with only one exception (Krestinsky, pp. 112–13) all the prisoners took pains to kowtow to Stalin; they seemed to be making the dock not merely a platform for their own self-degradation but for the glorification of the regime.

Krestinsky's reversal must be regarded as a change made in the script as a response to criticism. Like some of the other episodes, it was devised to counter one of the main objections made about the first two Charades – the oddity of there being no denials at all. Krestinsky was chosen for this role because as an experienced lawyer he could tailor his behaviour more skilfully to the juridical setting of the Charade.

One of the reasons for the uniform behaviour of the prisoners was, precisely, that such uniformity was the criterion for their selection to begin with: many, many thousands were done to death quietly, either because their testimony was redundant or – more likely – they either refused to appear altogether and, without families to be tortured and killed, could not be made to, or because for the same reason they could not be depended on in court.

Hence, since the prisoners who actually gave performances were a hand-picked group, the points on which, while accepting both the major charges and the fundamental politics of the regime, they might appear to bicker with the prosecution about details, are of interest primarily as showing the technique applied to the composition of the scenarios.

It seems plain, for that matter, if the Charades are to be looked at for a moment from outside the context of Stalinist Bolshevism, that plausibility was not, after all, Stalin's cardinal preoccupation. Indeed, the growing extremism of the main charges seems to indicate a total unawareness of their unreality.

There is an amusing pendant to the Krestinsky incident. After Krestinsky had denied the charges, Vyshinsky called another prisoner (Bessonov) in order to show him up.

Bessonov starts explaining how Krestinsky had given him various criminal instructions; Vyshinsky tells him to cut it short, since he (Vyshinsky) is sure Krestinsky will be telling him all about it shortly.

Vyshinsky knows *in advance* that Krestinsky is not going to be troublesome.

Krestinsky's chief utility in the Charades was as the exponent of a specific charge against Trotsky that Stalin had thought of as a way of extending the parabola of his accusations into the past and thus of creating a symmetrical portrait of perfidy.

Over the decade and more that Stalin had been undermining Trotsky there had been an ascending spiral of denunciations, beginning with a deceptively naturalistic, political coloration, as it were – routine quasi-Marxist vituperative formulae (Trotsky's 'underestimation of the peasantry') – and gradually building up to the hysterical crescendo of the Great Charades.

In the first Charade Trotsky was accused of preparing terroristic acts; in the second it was terrorism plus espionage for the Nazis; in the third Krestinsky was used to accuse both himself and Trotsky of having been German agents all the way back in the past – as early as 1921!

By this time Stalin was entangled in patching up the fabric of the Charades, which as a whole had been sadly ramshackle; destructive criticism could be met only very haphazardly. In retrojecting Trotsky's perfidy into the far past, accordingly, Stalin made the same mistake of over-reaching himself as he had with the invention of the material evidence based on the Bristol Hotel in Copenhagen and Pyatakov's aeroplane flight to Oslo: while propping up Stalin's central idea at one point, it pulled it to pieces at another, since it destroyed the general motivation ascribed to Trotsky, namely, of selling out to the Nazis as part of a bargain for a return to power.

In 1921 Trotsky, at the absolute summit of his career, second only to Lenin, did not have *very* much reason for becoming a German agent: why should he become a spy?

In view of Stalin's early training in a Greek Orthodox seminary, it is refreshing to recall his poker-faced reference to Trotsky as 'Judas' in the interview he gave the German-Jewish novelist, Lion Feuchtwanger.[59]

Vyshinsky as prosecutor gave a remarkable performance, but he was no more than a technician. He had nothing to do with the conception of the Charades as a whole; he was useful because of his combination of utter pliability, technical competence, literary skill, and fine voice.

The only thing about the Charades that Vyshinsky could have known with any certainty was that the charges were all false. This was evident not only because of the absence of proofs, but also because in the preparation of the scripts the real movers behind the scenes occasionally had to consult with him in order to help him avoid any mistakes and to bridge over the countless defective joints in the articulation of the testimony.

The consultations were very superficial, since Vyshinsky could never be informed of the overriding directives emanating from Stalin, of the methods of breaking down the prisoners, or the actual personal negotiations between Stalin and some of the most famous victims. Vyshinsky did not even know what was going to happen to them when the show was over.

There was no reason why he should: there was no reason at all to use him beyond his technical services. A Menshevik until 1920, he was known to no one in the Party until sometime in the thirties, and seen in public only after Kirov's murder, which marked his sudden rise if not to importance at least to prominence.

He was in a particularly ticklish situation. In spite of the immense labour poured into the preparation of the performances, there were so many slip-ups possible for which he was likely to be blamed that he was in a state of tension throughout the whole period. His Political Police chiefs treated him with contempt, leaving him to make as good a public impression as possible with the remarkable concoctions they presented him with – he might even be charged with wrecking in his turn!

Yet even this element in Vyshinsky's pliability does not quite explain the frenetic zeal with which he discharged his obligations to the dictatorship: he abused the prisoners with such manifest delight, with such unfeigned sincerity, that it is impossible not to see in his excess of zeal an authentic human pleasure in the humiliation of an enemy.

Vyshinsky, like Mensheviks in general, had had normal differences long before with the Bolsheviks; afterwards, joining the Bolsheviks so tardily and with a compromised past, he was forced to humiliate himself in order to further his career. When a chance came to serve his Bolshevik boss by annihilating other Bolsheviks Vyshinsky found it easy to perform this task with blissful satisfaction.

It was precisely in the vilification of his former adversaries that Vyshinsky's linguistic resources served him best; the language he used against them sounds almost incredible today, as indeed it sounded at the time: 'Human garbage', 'beasts in human form', 'mad dogs', 'hideous scoundrels', 'dregs and scum', 'shoot the mad dogs!', 'crush that cursed reptile', etc.

Perhaps the strangest single element in the fabrications underlying the third Charade was the presence in the dock of Yagoda, the producer of the first Charade. That was bound to seem like a downright admission of the nonsensicality of the whole operation, yet it had a rationale derived not from Stalin's personality, but from the purely technical requirement of eliminating the traces of a fabrication.

Despite all his power Stalin had fallen foul of a conventional bureaucratic situation: the rumours of his involvement in the Kirov killing had spread too far, and, what is more, he was not kept abreast of this because he had been depending on one of his major accomplices in the Kirov affair – Yagoda, who ever since being called 'Bungler!' on the scene of the denouement with Nikolayev was naturally very chary of letting Stalin know how far such rumours had spread.

What had happened to make it obvious, within the Political Police apparatus at least, that Stalin had arranged Kirov's death, was his elimination of all the men in Kirov's personal apparatus in the wake of his assassination. Hundreds of topmost officials were suddenly summoned by the Political Police and given new assignments in remote areas. It was not the Party that reassigned these officials, but the Political Police itself, for the first time in Soviet history; since Stalin was known to be the real boss of the Political Police this was widely taken as one more sign that he had had a direct hand in Kirov's killing, especially when put together with the collateral information – the removal of Kirov's guards, the indulgence shown Nikolayev after his first capture.

From Stalin's point of view the only way out was to have it admitted that the Political Police had, in fact, been behind the killing – through Yagoda's criminality – while shunting suspicion away from himself. Since in the first two Charades Kirov's killing had been put in the lap of Zinoviev and Kamenev, it was only natural in the third Charade, since Yagoda was now being blamed for Kirov, to make him for the sake of consistency an accomplice of Zinoviev and Kamenev as well.

The result had a certain logical strictness: why should not Yagoda, who stage-managed the first Charade and was thus the executioner of Zinoviev and Kamenev, have been unmasked finally as their accomplice? It was precisely because they were his accomplices – according to this version – that Yagoda had got rid of Zinoviev and Kamenev.

His skill as Stalin's intimate and agent made him indispensable. Of Yagoda's countless services, big and small, the sweep, the efficiency, the ferocity and the cruelty with which he wiped out all of Stalin's former Party colleagues had endeared him to Stalin most of all. There could never be any reason to fear him; he could never have joined, say, a genuine Communist faction aimed against Stalin since there were already far too many corpses between Yagoda and any element of the Communist Party; similarly, Yagoda was also hated by everyone in the Politburo and the government, if only because the vast authority allowed him by Stalin was bound to exacerbate relationships, aside from the fact that one of his many activities was making use of thousands of stool-pigeons who kept the whole government in a state of constant tension.

Yagoda was thoroughly unprincipled, which made him even more useful to Stalin, who always preferred to be surrounded by men with hidden vices whom he could keep under the threat of exposure.[60]

He was incredibly inflated by what he took to be his unique position in Stalin's service and what he may have thought was esteem. While performing a unique service for Stalin in tormenting and killing Zinoviev and Kamenev he was completely puffed up, especially when Stalin, after giving him a specially designed uniform as a field marshal, gave him an apartment in the Kremlin. This was universally interpreted in the summits of the bureaucracy as a sure sign of real power. Yagoda used to talk with Stalin every single day, yet was apparently incapable of piercing his extraordinarily dense veil. There was a rumour that Stalin had promised him a seat on the Politburo in payment for his services in eliminating Zinoviev and Kamenev; it was all completely plausible.

Yagoda's inflated arrogance was accompanied by an endless vanity. This expressed itself in an obsession with trivialities – decorations, medals, insignias, uniforms, etiquette. He personally created designs for full-dress uniforms, laboured over restoring the pomp of changing the guard, tightened up to the point of preposterousness the regulations of behaviour between officers, the hierarchy of the government, and the Political Police.

When he finally turned up to perform in his own Charade he made a confession that sounded like all the others. He confessed that he had implemented a plan to assassinate Kirov and also to poison his own former chief Menzhinsky, and Kuibyshev, a cabinet member, as well as Maxim Gorky and the latter's son Maxim Peshkov. This operation did have a certain rationale: what had been unbelievable about the infantile fantasies ascribed *en bloc* to Trotsky, Zinoviev, Kamenev, Bukharin and so on was quite plausible to ascribe not so much to Yagoda, as to Stalin, the sole beneficiary of the crime.

Some of these facts constitute a progressive revelation, only slightly veiled, of what may have been the real course of Stalin's preparation of the Kirov killing:

Yevdokimov (Stalin's accomplice in the 'Shakhty affair', now a performer in the first Charade), refers to another prisoner (Bakayev) who had 'stated that the terrorist . . . enjoyed the confidence of a number of leading Party workers and officials of the Soviet organization in Leningrad. This insured them every possibility of pursuing their preparations for a terroristic act against Kirov.'[61]

In the third Charade some further information is given: '. . . . the accused Yagoda . . . gave special instructions to the accomplices working in the [Leningrad section of the Political Police] not to hinder the perpetration of the crime.'[62]

We are already fairly close to Stalin in this third, progressive breaking down (in the scenarios) of elements evidently drawn directly from some historical situation. For either Yagoda, Stalin's creature at the time, got instructions straight from Stalin himself – since he would scarcely have engineered Kirov's killing on his own account – or else Stalin had purposely kept Yagoda in the dark, either on a general principle of distrust or in order to keep it handy for Yagoda's undoing later on. There is some evidence that the second variant was a little more likely.[63]

Yagoda, in his own lines in the third Charade, seems to have gone out of his way to make the point that he was not an accomplice in, still less an organizer of the Kirov assassination.[64] If Stalin did all this over Yagoda's head the explanation may be that he simply gave orders to Medved (head of the Leningrad Political Police) telling the latter to get out of Nikolayev's way, in order to let him, as the dupe of the Political Police, act out Stalin's own intent.

There is evidence that Stalin, who left Moscow for Leningrad the same evening as Yagoda, kept Yagoda from carrying on an enquiry, reserving this for himself; there was also a curious 'accident that befell Yagoda while Stalin was still in Leningrad. While being driven in his automobile at night . . . a truck crashed . . . into Yagoda's car . . . but [he] came out alive.'[65] Thus it may well be that Yagoda, too, had been duped, at least up to a point. When Vyshinsky explained Yagoda's behaviour as that of a 'murderer with a guarantee that he would not be found out' the irony implicit in all the Charades stands out in high relief. For whatever Yagoda's personal role was, the guarantee was genuine – it came straight from Stalin!

Some developments can be seen quite clearly only now, with the evidence accumulated long after the Charades.

In connexion with Stalin's plans concerning Gorky, for instance, Yagoda's lines in the third Charade are of interest. Yagoda is explaining the defendants' decision to have Gorky killed:

Yenukidze explained to me that the Bloc of Rights and Trotskyites, considering that the overthrow of the Soviet government was a prospect of the near future, regarded Gorky as a dangerous figure. Gorky was a staunch supporter of Stalin's leadership, and in case the conspiracy was carried into effect, he would undoubtedly raise his voice in protest against us, the conspirators. Considering Gorky's immense prestige within the country and abroad, the centre, according to Yenukidze, had adopted a categorical decision about Gorky being physically put out of the way.[66]

The content of this, in its articulation of what actually seems to have happened, seems accurate: it is simply the operative personnel who have to be changed. If Yenukidze (one of Stalin's old friends, undone by him) is replaced by Stalin, the sequence becomes clear; the morsel of dialogue is assigned its proper place as genuine history – masked.

If we simply read, for instance, that it was *Stalin* who was explaining the necessity of wiping out the former Oppositionists, we can see the purely literary transposition – Stalin had the interest in Gorky's elimination put in the mouth of the bogus conspirators in the third Great Charade.

Properly understood, this passage explains the transition of Stalin's pretended deference and coddling of Gorky in 1930 to his feeling in 1936 that there was nothing left to be done but get rid of him.

According to Bukharin, when Stalin's attitude towards Kamenev hardened in the course of 1935, Gorky, who had been interceding for the former Oppositionists as best he could, also declined in favour.[67] Gorky had been completely taken in by Stalin's elimination of Kirov: convinced that bona-fide terrorists were involved, he demanded harsh measures. It was not until after he saw that Stalin was exploiting

Nikolayev's role for his own political aims that he tried to prevent Stalin from taking his revenge.

Hence it was obvious from the moment Stalin decided, first on the killing of Kirov, and then on the broadening exploitation of the tactic to strike out at the Party and the population at large, that Gorky was at best a nuisance.

His prestige abroad, which was one of his chief attractions for the Stalin regime, was just what sealed his doom. It was his prestige with Western intellectuals, the inevitability that they would seek him out for information if they came to Russia, that made him more and more inconvenient. However naïve he had shown himself to be during the first part of the thirties, swallowing many of the myths of the regime, by 1935–6 he was definitely turning sour.

Around the time Gorky was refused a passport to go to Italy, to visit a writers' congress in Paris in 1935,[68] he had also begun writing more or less openly to some Western friends. Stalin became alarmed by his relations with Western writers. When Yagoda told Stalin at one point that some Western writer wanted to see Gorky, Stalin had at first thought of merely blocking such a meeting, but when Yagoda pointed out how suspicious that in itself would be, Stalin came to the conclusion that Gorky was simply not worth the trouble.

In any case the creative design of the libretti left more than enough room for these occasional pockets of real history.

Once Stalin is seen as puppeteer, pulling the strings of what, from his point of view, was a private show, it is amusing – in a way! – to see him manipulate his own show as a political device. It is instructive to see how each Charade could be used to lay the foundations, or the *possible* foundations, of another Charade.

Thus, if a man was mentioned in a libretto without being specifically pointed up as an actual target, it could be assumed that he was on some list or other and would soon be for the high jump himself. If he was mentioned as a target it meant he was still all right. In this way the Charades to some extent cross-referenced each other.

Tukhachevsky, for instance, the principal Soviet army marshal, who was tried in a closed session – i.e., not in a Charade – was merely mentioned by Radek in the second Charade; even though he was still at liberty and did not *seem* inculpated by Radek's testimony, he was killed a few months later. Contrariwise, a prominent figure put forth as a target of conspirators about to be sentenced to death might be thought to be on his way up the ladder; this happened to Beria, who was mentioned in the second Charade as a potential victim of some terrorist action in 1934; he became boss of the Political Police in 1938.

It must have been obvious to all prominent Soviet personalities, once the Charades and the Comb-out were in full spate and utterly baseless charges began to proliferate, that no one was out of danger. Since people were being killed on charges of trying to assassinate members of the government, if they left someone out, the obvious question was – why?

In the first Charade, the Trotskyite-Zinovievite 'terrorist centre' was supposed to be aiming not only at Kirov but at a whole list of other Party leaders, a handful of people that in this version did not include Molotov, who was not named once during the whole pre-investigation or the Charade itself. Molotov was the second person in the regime after Stalin, and indeed, titular head of the government.

This must have given Molotov some sleepless nights. Trotsky longing to kill everyone in the government but Molotov! What a nightmare! What was Stalin thinking of?!

During Trotsky's last years in the regime Molotov had been second only to Stalin in the leading group, whereas the others whose blood Trotsky was supposed to be after (Kaganovich, Kirov, Voroshilov, etc.), were quite secondary.

This impression was confirmed by Vyshinsky: when he asked Zinoviev whom they were all plotting to murder, and Zinoviev answered, laconically, 'the leaders', Vyshinsky himself says no more than: 'That is, Comrades Stalin, Voroshilov and Kaganovich!'

The 'that is' is, of course, priceless, both as an indication of the librettist busy at his typewriter, and of the danger in which Molotov now found himself – he had been specifically excluded by the prosecutor at a treason trial from the group of leaders. Vyshinsky repeated this in his summation, again excluding Molotov, three times, from the enumeration of leaders.

Molotov must have been having serious difficulties with Stalin; one of the tactics used against him was just this device of including or not including his name in the list of targets of the 'criminals'.

This is confirmed by a study of the rumours circulating during the middle thirties about friction between Stalin and Molotov, perhaps linked to the question of making the celebrated switch away from the Soviet analysis of the 'Third Period', which Stalin had thought of as another agony of capitalism that would do away with Hitler; this was on the eve of the switch to the policy of the Peoples' Fronts that lasted until Stalin's pact with Hitler.

During this period Molotov was never quoted, never praised, never photographed, and sometimes not even mentioned in the Soviet press. Thus his omission from the list of the targets of the terrorists was simply a confirmation – in the most sinister circumstances – of something already outlined in a more innocuous context.

The differences with Molotov did not last very long; just before the August 1936 Charade it seemed clear that there had been some sort of reconciliation with Stalin: Molotov's name once again began appearing with its previous aureole.

Stalin had in fact been playing with him all this time, dangling before him the possibility of a reconciliation. When Molotov went to the south for a vacation – often the prelude to an arrest, since Stalin liked to have his colleagues arrested off-duty – Stalin did not go to the railway station to say goodbye, as he generally did, but sent a wire saying he had merely missed the train. He let Molotov stew in the south for six weeks, then decided to stage a reconciliation, since Molotov could still be useful, if only through his unusual capacity for hard work (for years his nickname had been 'Rock Bottom').

But it had taken too long: it was now too late to go to the excessive trouble of rewriting all the voluminous records that had been fabricated for the Great Charades; besides, it did not hurt, perhaps, to keep Molotov in a state of permanent tension!

This became evident during the second Charade (Pyatakov, Radek and others), which was prepared after the reconciliation between Molotov and Stalin. Hence Radek casually mentions Molotov as one of those whom the terrorist acts were to be aimed at, and refers this all the way back to 1932, in direct contradiction, of course, to the evidence of the first Charade. Pyatakov naturally confirmed this. Thus, while the prisoners in the first Charade had spoken freely about terrorist acts instigated by Trotsky in 1932, Molotov's name had evidently slipped their minds, just as it slipped Vyshinsky's!

This curious form of exegesis enables us to perceive Stalin, a little obscurely, as a kind of artist: his literary contrivances certainly had a peculiar potency.

Internationally, the first Charade was not a complete success. It gave rise, in the main, to suspicion and embarrassment. Nor could these be dispelled by the notion of an honest mistake, if only because of the systematic nature of the Charade and its plainly laborious, though defective, preparation.

This implied no particular sympathy for the victims, who had no following of any kind. In the general working-class movement Trotsky's own following was well-delineated as a sectarian group. 'Bourgeois' opinion could have been summed up by the phrase, 'a plague on both your houses'.

This might have been thought surprising, since the first Charade was put on with extravagant publicity by a government that was esteemed by many quite uncommitted to its doctrines. If only because of the rise of Hitlerism the Soviet Union, quite apart from serving as a beacon for many dissident tendencies throughout the world, had become in the minds of reformists at large the symbol of a struggle against reaction. This attitude was buttressed by its convergence with old-fashioned patriotism and nationalism in a variety of countries that were frightened not of Nazism but of a resurgent Germany. Moreover, the to-do made by the Soviet government about its 'democratic constitution' guaranteed it a special veneration in the most articulate liberal circles in the West. Nevertheless the mistrust of many authoritative critics was not allayed.

Trotsky made the wry point that not even his most energetic political opponents in France, England or America referred to the Show Trials when his last major book, *The Revolution Betrayed*, appeared, some time after the accounts of the first Charade.[69] By that time his name had been blazoned all over the world as a vicious ally of the Nazis and of the Japanese militarists against France and the United States; the fact that this was not referred to even by reviewers who took issue with the book itself demonstrates the failure of the Soviet publicity campaign to make a dent on real opinion. This was so even in France, a country both with the greatest stake in the relations between Hitler and Stalin, and with the liveliest left-wing politics.

Yet though Stalin failed to impose the first Charade on Western public opinion as a whole, he was singularly successful with its liberal sector. Fundamentally, in fact, his tranquil assurance that 'Europe would swallow' the whole thing was borne out.

It was accomplished with astounding ease. Though the general atmosphere of the era, preoccupied with Hitlerism, makes the gullibility or moral blindness of so many prominent people psychologically understandable, the widespread combination of hypocrisy and obtuseness is bound to remain baffling.

Sir Bernard Pares, for instance, a lifelong student of Russian history, thought the sabotage of the prisoners had been 'proved up to the hilt', that the evidence as a whole was 'convincing'.[70] The novelist, Feuchtwanger, who was present at the second Charade, totally falsified it for Western readers: 'The whole thing was less like a criminal trial than a debate carried on in a conversational tone by educated men who were trying to get at the truth.'[71]

It would be hard to match such falseness: the clearest thing about the otherwise repulsively arid stenographic report of all the Charades is the systematic attempt to degrade their victims, to say nothing of the almost hysterical personal abuse that was indulged in with such gleeful ferocity by Vyshinsky.

The tension triggered by the first Charade swelled steadily with the second and third Charades, augmented by the execution of the Red Army generals in June 1937. The process as a whole continued to remain bafflingly mysterious, but whereas the bourgeois sector of public opinion never lost its indifference to the implications of the Charades – the extent of the Deep Comb-out was not suspected until very much later – its liberal sector became fervently committed to the official Soviet version; its fight against the small segment of opinion influenced by Trotsky's self-defence became more and more venomous.

Trotsky himself, established by the Great Charades as arch-fiend, was flabbergasted. Deported from the Soviet Union somewhat ambiguously in 1929, at a time when Stalin still had to keep up appearances, Trotsky had spent more than four years on a little island off the Turkish coast. Then, after a year or so of twilight existence in France, he had been deported again, this time to Norway, where he was hit by the news of the first Charade. Afraid of the Soviet Government, the Norwegians had interned him, and finally, when Trotsky was invited to Mexico by the socialist regime of Cardenas, shipped him off. He defended himself as best he could in Mexico – the last two Charades took place after his arrival – until his assassinations in 1940 by an agent of the Soviet Political Police.

For some years after his exile Trotsky seemed optimistic. Still with a revolutionary halo for many, against the background of a lively left-wing movement throughout Europe, he could hope for a resurgence of proletarian initiative that might restore his fortunes. Like other Marxists he took it for granted that capitalism was on its last legs. If there had been a resurgence of revolutionary elan; if a self-conscious Proletariat smashed the Bourgeoisie in Western Europe, it might also be expected to exert the most powerful influence on the Soviet Union, outweighing the peasant backwardness that had deflected, hampered and perverted the Revolution.

The rise of Hitlerism, and the crash programmes collectivizing, industrializing and terrorizing the people of the Soviet Union, frustrated all Trotsky's hopes. Trotsky's sympathizers failed to establish mass movements. With the Nazi accession to power, also, all Soviet partisans were in a box: just because of Stalin's lethal blunders the Soviet Union, more vulnerable than ever, had to be defended with still greater zeal.

Trotsky's idealism proved futile: as Stalinism took shape it could not be explained by the idiom of Marxism. Marxist platitudes could not explain a dictatorship that could destroy the summits of the Party, of the bureaucracy, of the government, and institute a reign of terror based on the adulation of an individual.

How could that be reconciled with the Soviet 'system', with the national ownership of the means of production, with the laying of the foundations of socialism, and for that matter with socialism itself?

The failure of the Revolution to extend itself and the consequent isolation of the Soviet Union were merely forerunners of a general decline in the working-class movement on the one hand, and, to the extent that it remained viable, of the systematic subordination of its Left-wing to the interests of the Kremlin. The movement Trotsky had hoped for so much from proved to be a passive instrument of the Soviet bureaucracy.

Though by the mid-thirties Trotsky's political career was well-nigh extinguished, the developments set in train by Stalin's vast intrigue gave his name an eerie lustre that he was altogether unprepared for.

In 1935–6, as the news of the terrorism within the Party began only very gradually to filter out to him, he was stunned. Despite the increasing harshness of his strictures on Stalin he had nevertheless underestimated the extent of the terror that followed Kirov's murder – the gigantic concentration camps throughout the Soviet Union, the brutality of the new treatment of the inmates, the torture and trickery of Political-Police procedures in extracting fantastic confessions. What *he* had called terror was as nothing compared with what happened in the middle thirties!

His normally powerful mind was altogether undone by the panoramic fabrications of the Great Charades. Stalin had outdistanced all historical imposture.

Trotsky's bafflement at the incredible content of the Great Charades, their sheer dementia, when considered rationalistically, is pointed up by the defence he found himself reduced to. He undertook to *disprove* the charges of the Charades – to establish an alibi showing that not one of these charges even *could* have been true.

This rational campaign encountered practically insuperable difficulties. Straitjacketed by his isolation in Norway, by his remoteness in Mexico, he had to back-track all his years of exile; to collect substantiation of his real activities from his vast, broken-up archives as well as from periodicals in many languages; to find witnesses, to gather information from former secretaries, bodyguards, and followers – many of them now enemies – as well as from government departments, from police headquarters, from acquaintances.

He and his tiny band went through endless torment in their struggle against the resources of a great state, with its armies of propagandists, agitators and intellectuals of all kinds. The exhausting labour took months and months; it consumed his strength and that of his followers.

He even wanted to bring together a counter-court that would decisively refute the charges in Stalin's theatre. He hoped at first to organize it in Switzerland, with the collaboration of the international working-class movement and the Second International.

He collided at once with the fact that the German and Austrian sections of the Second International and of the Trades-Unions International had been obliterated by Hitler; Léon Blum, head of the People's Front government in France, was completely dependent on Stalinist support.

Trotsky's followers then tried to get some well-known left-wing intellectuals to rally to his defence, even though he had spent a lot of time sneering at the endless numbers of 'Peace committees' and the like that were the favourite Stalinist device of the era. But the strategically favourable position of Stalin as chief defender on the Left against Hitler also made that difficult. In fact hardly any intellectuals to speak of came forward in Great Britain or France, while in the United States there were only a handful, though some of them were well-known.

In Russia itself, every intellectual who was not himself gaoled or killed joined the chorus led by Stalin: international names like Gorky, Ehrenburg, and Sholokhov were all integrated into the impostures in Moscow, while in the West endless numbers of representative intellectuals rallied with a self-righteous zeal never to be entirely gainsaid even long after the Great Charades.

These coteries of various shades of pink, red, and liberal supporters of the People's Front idea in America, for instance, boycotted the Commission of Enquiry that was finally set up under the sponsorship of Professor John Dewey. Numerous liberals and fellow-travellers – professors, artists, writers – in addition to the expected camp-followers of the Soviet regime, signed a manifesto (published March 1937) maintaining that 'all men of good will' must work against the Dewey Commission which was 'dealing a blow to the forces of progress' and also, naturally, helping fascism. Trotsky was to satisfy the Dewey Commission as to his innocence; to that extent his defence, within the tiny milieu that might read its Report, was effective. Yet the whole enterprise of 'refutation' was futile.

It was not so much that Trotsky could not establish his alibi for the two material charges – Pyatakov's aeroplane flight to Oslo, the rendez-vous at the non-existent hotel in Copenhagen – or for that matter make out a convincing case of his own against the Charades. It was easy, indeed, to pluck apart the fabrications of the Great Charades on the basis of mere analysis; Trotsky did this very handily merely by examining the transcripts in his study. Long before the third Charade, for that matter, he even predicted the involvement of its principals.

After all, since a scenario must have structure it is, at least partly, predictable!

The problem was simply too bulky for rationalism. For Trotsky it was doubtless insoluble. The very nature of the charges, their utter groundlessness, the mere fact that they depended on confessions and not on material evidence, entailed the pointlessness of a mere disproof.

The falsity of the Charades was instantly apparent: anyone not blinded by prejudice or sentimental commitment could see at once that they consisted of mere fiction and performances. Those who accepted them did so primarily as either an act of faith or for corrupt tactical reasons – neither category was interested in evidence to begin with. Trotsky's response was sadly beside the mark.

With the very first Charade it was plain that Stalin intended not to combat Trotskyism but to anathematize it. He was creating a different universe; Trotsky was no longer a mere opponent but an agent of the Devil; the Charades disclosed a corner of Hell; they were intended to shock the public into accepting a radical transformation of its worldview.

Trotsky's rebuttals, on a plane of rationalism long since transcended by the Stalin dictatorship, were no more than intelligent. Philosophically, they were merely obtuse. Trotsky was still waging political warfare, ineffectually; Stalin was creating a secular cult.

Trotsky was not to live long enough to learn the scope of the Deep Comb-out; that did not come out until after the Second World War. His explanations of Stalinist degeneration, inadequate during the thirties, were utterly irrelevant by the time the re-institutionalization of Soviet society, engendered by the massacre of the Deep Comb-out, could be assessed.

What Trotsky found indigestible, indeed, inconceivable, was his enforced transformation into an object. A fictitious person, coupled with a fictitious theory, was yoked to the service of an orthodoxy his doctrinaire Marxism prevented him from appreciating.

Lenin had once said no situation existed from which there was no way out. Trotsky's circumstances refute this: by the time the Great Charades were staged he was hopelessly nailed to his cleft stick.[72]

5
The Deep Comb-out: Techniques

Some five months after the second Charade (11 June 1937) a terse announcement appeared that Marshal Tukhachevsky and seven other top Red Army men had been arrested as spies and executed. With the Nazi regime arming to the teeth, the idea that the topmost figures of the Red Army had been executed was scarcely conceivable. It was if possible even more startling, more enigmatic, than the Great Charades themselves. It gave a special pitch to the increasingly ferocious tensions of the thirties.

One of Stalin's domestic successes had been the army. It was the support of the army that probably enabled the regime to sustain the shock of the crash programmes of collectivization and industrialization of the early thirties and for that matter the Deep Comb-out itself.

During the first Five-Year-Plan the Party substantially increased its hold over the army; by the end of the Plan all senior commanders and 93 per cent of the divisional commanders were on the Party rolls. Throughout this period there was no trace of army opposition to Stalin's projects.

This exemplary attitude may partly be ascribed to Stalin's coddling of the army. Soldiers who were collective farmers and their families were given all sorts of material concessions; officers were given great advantages not only in pay rises but in housing, supplies, and so on. A great deal of attention was paid to officers' prestige: the re-introduction of titles in 1935 seems to have stimulated an inundation of the military academies. The army was substantially increased in size around the same time; a capacious officers' corps was soon formed of youthful, recently trained officers, generally from the working class. By May 1937 some three-quarters of the officers' corps were made up of these youthful officers created by Stalin's fiat. The higher commands were largely occupied by veterans of the Civil War. This created the conventional friction revolving around the pressure of promotion, a friction that was complemented by the long-standing bad blood between the Civil War veterans and the relatively cultivated political officers who had survived the modified compromise system established in 1925. This compromise had been based on the retention but down-grading of the influence of the political commissars, installed *en masse* during the Civil War to monitor the numerous Tsarist officers who had to be retained for lack of trained Bolsheviks. In practice this meant that there were still a great many political officers who were more or less out of tune with the generally uneducated veterans of the Civil War.

Stalin exploited these two sources of friction when he dipped the army command into the bloodbath.

In retrospect it is plain that a premonition of the army's decapitation had been given early in 1937; not only had two army leaders been referred to chillingly in the second Charade (January 1937), by which time the blood was flowing freely in the wake of the first Charade (August 1936), but during the February–March Central Committee plenum Stalin himself, whose every word during this period carried exceptional weight, had hinted broadly at the dangers besetting an army when even a few spies were on its staff. By April of the same year Tukhachevsky was being snubbed in public.

The 11 June report of Tukhachevsky's execution also mentioned some of the most prominent district commanders; another officer (Gamarnik, head of the Political Directorate of the army) was reported as having committed suicide on 31 May when told he was under arrest.

These officers were not charged with anything specific; for that matter there is no good reason to think a trial was ever held. A flood of stereotyped accusations simply appeared in the press, all in harmony with the script of the second Charade, to the effect that they had been spying, plotting to dismember the country on behalf of Japan and Germany, and also to carry out a putsch in the service of the Trotskyite and Right-wing Oppositions. (These accusations were to reappear in the Bukharin Charade of March 1938.)

The army was now put through a thorough combing out, proportionately much more substantial in the higher command posts; it was very harsh with respect to the military and the political officers equally.

Lethal comb-outs were heralded by the resumption in May 1937 of the old dual system of political commissars, in contrast to the gradual whittling away of this system since 1925.

The decapitation of the Red Army cannot be discussed in the same way as the Great Charades. It is an integral part of the Deep Comb-out, the Great Purge, which, though it took place under the umbrella of the

Great Charades and the accompanying propaganda, was never publicized.

There has been some question, to be sure, of the possibility of a genuine conspiracy at least in the army; indeed, precisely the absence of a trial for the heads of the army might, in this case, make the notion of a plot seem plausible – why expose military secrets?

But there seems to be no collateral evidence against the Red Army generals; and what is most convincing is the fact that the conspiracy was not dealt with at all like a real conspiracy – which would have been simply nipped in the bud without warning – but in the usual political way characteristic of the Charades themselves, with one hint after another being dropped well in advance of action.

There is some indication[1] that Stalin might actually have been personally duped by the Gestapo in a successful ruse contrived precisely to destroy the Red Army high command.

The logic of this manoeuvre on the part of the Gestapo is certainly persuasive: knowing what was going on in Russia, what could have been more tempting than persuading Stalin to overreach himself and kill off his own army command?

According to this suggestion the Gestapo is supposed to have manufactured some evidence against Tukhachevsky and the others in conjunction with the Soviet Political Police; this bogus evidence was then filtered back into Russia via Czechoslovakia by means of Soviet agents in Paris.

The much later official Soviet version[2] of this, however, is an admission that the Comb-out of 1937–8 was not only cooked up but that it sapped the army's capabilities until new commanders were trained. In view of the scope of the Deep Comb-out, with its millions of victims, in view of the long-drawn-out preparations for the Great Charades themselves, with the simultaneous though clandestine massacres of uncounted thousands of dissidents in the concentration camps and elsewhere, the Tukhachevsky affair can be made intelligible only within a larger context. It will be seen, in fact, that the killing of so many officers was an integral part of the combing out of the population as a whole, and especially of the great 'apparatuses' of the Soviet Union. The decapitation of the army was the tip of an iceberg; it can be understood only in conjunction with the vast subterranean process of the Deep Comb-out, the process, triggered by Kirov's murder, that was both masked and 'justified' by the Great Charades. The only publicized element in the Deep Comb-out itself was the execution of the handful of army celebrities in June 1937; for some time the range of the Comb-out within the Red Army as a whole was not generally known.

Stalin had conducted a number of major purges before – the clean-up of Party cells in the cities and the universities (1925), in the countryside (1926), and the two general clean-ups (1929–30, 1933) – but the difference between these 'normal' purges and the Deep Comb-out was profound. Moreover it was a difference of *kind*. The Deep Comb-out itself was broken up into three segments, associated with the names of Stalin's successive executors respectively; the preparatory Comb-out of 1935–6 (Yagoda), the Deep Comb-out proper in 1936–8 (Yezhov), and the mopping-up stage in 1938–9 (Beria).

These segments correspond, a little roughly, with the momentum of the process as a whole. The heightening of the general terror came about with remarkable rapidity.

Despite the hysterical fanfare in the press, the era inaugurated by the Kirov killing arrived without much drama. The steps taken in the immediate wake of the murder did not impinge on very many people; for a while there was no feeling that the general process of social convalescence, after the ordeal of the early thirties, was being hampered.

During the month of the murder – December 1934 – a decree was enacted authorizing death sentences in a summary form, and also – more significantly, perhaps – authorizing the drastic punishment of the relatives of anyone accused without necessarily showing any connexion between them and the actual case. The same law also made it a duty to denounce one's closest relatives.

Yet at first the feeling of terror was not general. It was only in the beginning of 1935 that the Party purge, which had begun in a quiet way, without much publicity (it was called 'checking Party documents' or 'regularization of Party affairs'), began rapidly snowballing. Denunciations became legion. Indeed the number of denunciations and 'unmaskings' became in and for itself the criterion of a given person's political reliability – not in the old-fashioned sense of establishing *genuine* reliability, but by creating a picture of compliance with what was required by the authorities.

Each of the Great Charades, which took place within the space of one and a half years, was accompanied by an immense number of arrests, which were carried out during it and afterwards. Initially all those arrested belonged to practically every political segment of Soviet society, beginning with the members of all former Oppositions, notably with the sympathizers of Trotsky, Zinoviev and Bukharin, but fanning out to include all members of all other parties in general – the Mensheviks, then the Social-Revolutionaries (rivals of both Bolsheviks and Mensheviks), then the 'bourgeois' parties of the Constitutional Democrats (Kadets) and the Octobrists, then other parties (Anarchists and

Trudoviks), then the exponents of various nationalisms – the Armenian Dushnaks, the Georgian and Ukrainian Nationalists, Pan-Russian patriots, Zionists – in short the spokesmen for literally every expression of political opinion, long since proscribed, were now being energetically wiped out.

Left-wing groups were obliterated. These groups had all been quiescent for years; there had not been a trace of political activity, for instance, in any of the Bolshevik Oppositionist coteries for many years, nor had the Mensheviks, Social-Revolutionaries, Trudoviks, or Anarchists lifted a finger for a long time. Even for those who had had some record of an Oppositional past, it was a question only of long-dead activities, of youthful allegiances made at a time when no revolutionaries, whatever their differences, would ever have thought of destroying each other.

They had remained inactive generally after having surrendered to the dominant faction and thus regained their freedom. The politically-minded prisoners who began pouring into the gaols and concentration camps of the Soviet Union from 1936 and 1937 onwards had rehabilitated themselves, as they thought, long since: they had docilely registered approval of all twists in the 'General Line of the Party', even denounced former comrades who had in their turn fallen out of favour. Yet now they were gaoled again for having belonged to some heterodox group long before.

That was the least of it: at the beginning of 1937 the gaols began filling up with Bolsheviks, too, who had never been anything but loyal to the central faction, who had never supported any of the Oppositions even through sympathy. The shutting down of the Old Bolsheviks' Club seemed to be itself a reflection of a new offensive against Party members: the voluminous dossiers of the Political Police, going back for years, might contain anything.

Yet the arrests of the Bolsheviks seemed to be as completely indiscriminate as the arrests of all the others. It was not enough to take as a pretext, say, some critical remark and expand it by interpretation into evidence of an Oppositionist tendency or disloyalty: even if that were the specific *occasion* for an arrest, the arrest itself was evidently decided on quite independently of the presence or absence of such notes in dossiers. The movement against the Party membership was far too general to be understood as arising in response to the discovery of remarks that were either treasonable or wrongly thought to be so.

This later movement, against the people at large, never really sank into the public consciousness of Western countries: it might be said that too much attention was paid to the Great Charades, and since these

Charades, even though they took in large numbers of people, nevertheless dealt only with individuals, numbering, after all, only a handful,
it was always possible to regard the phenomenon as peripheral. Even
though informed people quickly learned of the extent of the bloodletting
embarked on by Stalin, it could never, just because of its scope, be made
to seem so spectacular as the Charades themselves.

Even after hundreds of thousands of revolutionaries of all kinds, including Bolsheviks, had been gaoled, it was still possible to think that it
was all taking place within the relatively narrow circle of politically
eminent or at least distinguishable people, of ideologically-minded persons who had fallen out somehow with the ruling faction and naturally
got into trouble.

Thus it could be regarded by the ordinary person, the person patron-
izingly called the average man, as a squabble at the top and no concern
of his.

But the movement that began in the second half of 1937 was fantastic
in all respects. Not only did the dimensions of the repression expand,
but it took in people who had never been members of a political party at
all. The winnowing process, which in the case of avowedly political
people had been pretty random to begin with, but still might have
claimed some sort of rationale, now, as it fanned out through the whole
of the population, became completely capricious, or seemed so.

For months the Political Police seemed to be working twenty-four
hours a day: carting ordinary citizens off in paddy-wagons in cities and
countryside alike, snatching people out of houses, workshops, labora-
tories, factories, universities, army barracks, and government bureaux.
Peasants, workers, functionaries, professionals, intellectuals, artists,
officers all wound up in the same cells.

Fifty republics and autonomous areas of the Soviet Union had separate governments with hundreds of People's Commissars: hardly one
survived; nor did a single one of the immense Soviet industrial enterprises retain its director or its chief engineers. Not only were they
snatched up in this universal dragnet, but for months afterwards their
replacements were also arrested, as were *their* replacements.

The officers' corps was ground to powder in June 1937, in the wake of
the first big smash-up of the topmost stratum headed by Tukhachevsky
and others – eight of the most famous generals in the Soviet Union.

The basic strategic units of the whole army system were the military
districts, each with a commander: every commander of such a military
district was arrested, as was his replacement only a few weeks later:
within only a few months some of these districts had had half-a-dozen
commanders in relays, until the supply of generals ran out altogether,

and their districts were taken over by colonels, then by majors, and finally by lieutenants.

The shake-out of the Party summits and of the labour unions was already finished. At the time, the Central Committee of the Communist Party consisted of seventy-one members and sixty-one deputies, completely docile Party members of many years' standing, whose lives had been gone over with a fine-tooth comb by all the Party's control organs and by the Political Police.

Three-quarters of these people were arrested as spies. The Politburo consisted of ten members and five deputies: a third were taken by the Political Police. The ramified apparatus of the Communist International was ferociously cleaned out.

A fine-tooth comb was also applied to the writings of the cowed and purchased intelligentsia: the search was for 'Trotskyite contraband'. There was not the smallest reason to consider any of the writers Trotskyites, yet the winnowing went on among them, too. To save themselves some writers would concentrate on stories of the remote past, others might write children's stories; most of them gave up any attempt to write from an independent point of view at all and simply mouthed more or less automatically whatever the watchword of the moment was; literature became a form of commentary on various decisions of the Party. It was this period that consummated the total unreadability of Soviet prose.

Science was the darling of the Soviet regime. Scientists were generally pampered in all respects as the regime strained every tendon in its effort to catch up with the West at least in science, which was, of course, just where it could be done, since it was not a question of transforming the lives of immense masses of people but of creating a favourable environment for relatively tiny handfuls.

Yet when the Deep Comb-out began in 1937 scientists were not spared: many eminent ones were arrested and others were so frightened that work was stopped on many original projects in favour of more routine chores where originality was not needed and hence could not be dangerous.

When Pyatakov, a principal actor in the second Charade and long-time chief of heavy industry, was arrested, his arrest seemed to be a signal for the winnowing of heavy industry throughout the Soviet Union; when the Vice-Commissar in charge of railways (Lifshits) was arrested the railway network began to be buffeted; an immense amount of labour was simply undone by the Political Police.

When the third Charade was being prepared the whole of the peasantry was involved; arrests among peasants became epidemic; millions were jammed into trains bound for the far north. So much had happened to them, so many blows had rained down on them from above since the October putsch, that it was quite impossible to understand Bolshevik politics. Except for some of the new type of peasants who had already been formed to some slight extent by the collectivization programmes hardly any of them even bothered to ask for an explanation.

The ethnic minorities were hit with peculiar ferocity. Russia had been a mosaic of peoples for centuries: not merely were there countless peoples speaking all sorts of different languages, but in the ebb and flow of Russian life small settlements of all major ethnic groups had long been scattered everywhere, in big towns as well as on the land, without losing their customs or being assimilated.

Many minorities had their roots outside the Soviet Union – Letts, Lithuanians, Finns, Greeks, Bulgarians, Poles, Persians, Chinese. Stalin obliterated many of these minorities: the men were gaoled and the women exiled to Asiatic Russia; the children were often carted off to orphanages run by the Political Police.

The Political Police applied to these minorities the formula they were using against the whole population – they were *all* spies! They divided up the espionage assignments by nationality: Germans, Poles and Letts were given the role of having spied for Hitler; the Far Easterners – Chinese, Koreans and Mongolians – were assigned to Japan; while the Middle-Easterners – Armenians, Assyrians, Persians, etc. – were assigned to the British Intelligence Service. The symmetry of this Political-Police decision was not accepted with equal docility everywhere: though the Armenians didn't protest against being enrolled in the service of Great Britain, some of the Chinese were deeply offended at being accused of serving Japan.

All these millions of ordinary people were of the sort that would be involved in politics only in moments of crisis. In gaol and in the concentration camps these throngs of unintelligibly associated people, drawn together only by the randomizing dragnets of the Political Police, were so bewildered they could not begin even to formulate questions to ask, let alone answer. They would look to the numerous intellectuals, also assembled by the Political Police randomizer, hoping for some explanation. But the intellectuals themselves were if possible still more baffled. Peasants found the enigma more endurable: the fatalism so often manifested in extreme situations spared them the need to speculate.

Intellectuals, naturally, *had* to find an answer. Yet they couldn't. The bulk of the time spent in prison by hundreds of thousands of such intellectuals was spent on just this shattering enigma: why?

What did it all mean? Why had the Monster Dictator gaoled his own supporters? Not merely his meek and docile followers, but his most unswerving, indeed fanatical partisans? Why were confessions that no one on either side could believe so necessary? Who needed them? For what?

The most grotesque stage in this whole pulverization process was reached when the combers-out were themselves combed out – when the Political Police began to arrest each other. People who had been interrogating prisoners for months, grinding out one preposterous confession after another, would suddenly find themselves in the same prison cells as those they had been processing. Examiners would become prisoners overnight – all on the same charges. Most significantly, the Political Police officials also failed to grasp what had been happening; the process was as impenetrable to them as to everyone else, but they were ruthlessly harrowed.

The Comb-out that was imposed on the very organization implementing it was even stranger than the obliteration of the Old Bolsheviks.

The Political Police, a characteristic Soviet institution that for complexity and importance must surely be unique, was extraordinarily ramified. It was organized along lines that ran closely parallel with the State and the Party; it had a general political department, an economic affairs department, military, transport, cultural departments and so on, that would correspond to the governmental departments of the same name. For instance, in control of every factory or industrial enterprise, every university, training college and scientific institution was a 'triangle' made up of the government representative, the Party secretary, and the chairman of the trades union organization concerned. (This last was a hangover of the fictional control of production by the workers that had been in vogue 'theoretically' during the early period of the Soviet Union.)

However, there was a fourth department head – the secret section in direct charge of the Political Police. The offices of this special section were clearly marked in every Soviet building by the iron sheeting over the door; a special entry pass was always needed.

The heads of these special sections in factories and institutions were responsible to the Political Police's corresponding local departments, all of these organized in regions, districts and so on throughout each Soviet republic, with the hierarchy leading up to the summit in Moscow. Like the Party itself the Political Police was rigidly centralized.

The Political Police also controlled the GULAG, the administration of the forced labour camps; this meant the control of whole branches of production and of big areas. There was also a secret statistical department.

The troops stationed along the borders of the Soviet Union came under the Political Police, not the Ministry of Defence. There were also detachments of these 'special Political Police forces' in the interior – they were used for exceptional situations like collectivization.

The Political Police also had a foreign department, responsible for a great deal of sabotage abroad. This department controlled all diplomatic and consular Soviet representatives abroad, all members of trade missions, in fact anyone with any official contact with foreigners.

For some time the kernel of the Political Police had been the Old Chekists, as they proudly called themselves (on the model of the Old Bolsheviks), taking their name from the initials of its first post-revolutionary incarnation ('Cheka' means 'Extraordinary Commission'). These were idealistic veterans who had been through the putsch and the Civil War. Most were proletarian; some were petty-bourgeois intellectuals.

Until the outset of the thirties a great deal of idealism was still available in the Soviet Union: large numbers of workers and intellectuals, still devoted to the professed ideals of the regime, worked for various Soviet organizations abroad at great risk and without reward. As idealists they looked down on espionage for gain with deep contempt: young people worked tirelessly for romantic reasons; their information was of great use to the Soviet government.

With the Comb-out, all motives based on idealism became suspect: all organizing abroad was restricted to the Political Police. The result of this political cynicism was the replacement of those who worked out of idealism with paid agents; compromise and blackmail were used instead of voluntary cooperation.

By the end of the twenties the Political Police recruited its personnel often through the Party or the Young Communist League: this was regarded as a great honour; refusal would have meant political extinction. Most of the Political Police staff were chosen from among the students, Young Communists who instead of studying did their 'social work' and devoted themselves to all sorts of administrative chores. Thus only those who were going into the technical or economic departments as a rule finished their university education.

The lower Political Police officials lived quite modestly, though much better than other officials of equivalent rank. But the top officials lived in the lap of luxury – high salaries, big apartments, cars, cheap goods at special prices in special shops; special leave in the Caucasus or the Crimea.

The Political Police, always an *élite* in the Soviet Union, rather resembles the traditional officers' corps in Prussia before the First World War. Bearing, deportment and dress are supposed to be distinguished, aristocratic. They are known for having the most attractive wives, often of the 'former people', the old aristocracy or wealthy classes. There is a special caste atmosphere about the Political Police: their children go to special schools, while low-echelon jobs in the organization are frequently filled by the younger members of the families of superior officials. It is such a privilege to be in the Political Police that top personalities throughout the government or Party apparatus intrigue to get their children into it. A network of family connexions gradually grew up in the Bolshevik summits.

An enormous number of 'confidential' people also work for the Political Police without being part of it; typists, messengers, charwomen, in fact everyone employed by it, no matter how menial their work, is confidential, and must have a more thorough screening than anyone else.

During the Comb-out the Political Police worked unbelievably hard, especially the examining magistrates and their superiors. Examiners regularly worked until 4 or 5 a.m. (night-time interrogation was more effective).

The work of breaking people psychologically was a strain on the examiners themselves. Prisoners would be subjected to special interrogation and all its suffering for only weeks or months, but the examiners had to do it for very long stretches, sometimes years, and then only with the aid of drugs. They were also vulnerable to the harassment of their superiors, the constant nagging for 'vigilance', the pressure for the unflagging disclosure of one senseless plot after another. They kept having nervous breakdowns.

An incident is related of an interrogator who used to nip away at a bottle of vodka, sometimes getting drunk. One day he was caught out by Yagoda himself on a surprise visit with a deputy; they found the interrogator weeping away at his desk, moaning: 'Today I'm interrogating you, tomorrow they'll be interrogating me. Alas, our life is worth no more than a kopek!' and the prisoner patting his shoulder consolingly.[3]

A prisoner being grilled by his examiner, a young lieutenant without much experience, suddenly stopped hearing the endlessly repeated question, 'Who recruited you?' Stupefied, he saw his examiner burst into a 'flood of tears'.[4]

Doubtless only the most simple-minded examiners believed wholly in the prisoners' guilt. The examiners had to go through all the motions of forcing the 'enemies of the people' to construct their own legends, fully aware, no doubt, that it was all nonsense, yet also, perhaps, with the feeling that there was no smoke without fire. Morally, this enabled them to carry on; as long as they had this strong though vague feeling that the people they were interrogating were morally in another camp they could perform their tasks with zeal, however the details might be fabricated. Their attitude, in short, stemmed from faith.

The Political Police officials lived in terror of the 'special department', which was a sort of police for the Political Police. This special department spread the same fear within the Political Police as they themselves did throughout the country. There were such special departments in every military unit from the battalion on up, and for that matter in every concentration camp.

What was perhaps the strangest thing about the naïveté – as it could later on be seen to be – of even such hardened men as the Political Police was their curious assurance that they would not be touched themselves.

Some of the interrogators were men who were still inspired by the idealism of the early period of the Soviet regime: they sincerely imagined themselves to be the guardians of revolutionary institutions that had arisen on the foundation of an ideal, and were so dismayed by what was now being required of them by Stalin that they committed suicide.

It never occurred to them that they, too, were in danger. This was all the stranger since Stalin's plan for a general sweep must have been matured by the time of the first Great Charade, in which he had ordered the insertion of a passage (into Reingold's script) that later on could be seen as significant: the appointment of a Political Police official is mentioned there in connexion with the 'possibility that the [Political Police] was in possession of the threads of the conspiracy against the State that was being prepared by [Zinoviev and Kamenev]'. This Political Police officer (Bakayev) was 'charged with the function of physically exterminating the persons who directly carried out terroristic acts against Stalin and Kirov, as well as those officers of the [Political Police] who might be in possession of the threads of the crimes committed.'

Stalin knew very well that the whole thing was a fabrication of his own, i.e. that nothing like that *could* have been in Zinoviev's and Kamenev's mind. Then whose mind could it have been in? Someone, after all, did contrive that sentence. And since that was Stalin, it might have seemed clear to the police chiefs, who by the time the sentence had been carried out against the prisoners in the first Charade must have been aware of the lengths that he was prepared to go to, that what he was describing was in fact the state of mind of a person wiping out witnesses to a crime.

Hence the sentence Stalin had inserted into the first Charade might have indicated to the police chiefs, had they been less trusting, that it would soon be their turn. Once they saw that he had not contrived a mere manoeuvre in blackening his rivals' reputations, but had actually, from their point of view shockingly, wiped them out, they should have realized that Stalin's logic called for their own extirpation. Strangely guileless, after all, and preoccupied by their zeal in carrying out their duties, the police chiefs, if unable to benefit from their quite unusual power, could at the very least have taken to their heels.

This plan to wipe out Political Police officers privy to the Charades had also been contrived with great technical care, in which, moreover, there was no need to risk the mistakes that marred the Charades.

In October 1936, a few months after the first Charade, Stalin replaced Yagoda with Yezhov as People's Commissar for the Interior. On the theory that the Political Police had to be expanded and improved, Yezhov brought along a few hundred new functionaries who were made assistants to Political Police department heads in the capital and the countryside. These men were to take the place of those marked by Stalin for death, and often had no real police training at all.

Yet in the two-and-a-half years he was in charge (1936–8) Yezhov implemented Stalin's orders on an unprecedented scale. For two decades the Political Police had been the indispensable arm of the Soviet dictatorship, beginning with Lenin, but the terror it had been spreading was as nothing compared with Yezhov's.

In his celebrated Secret Speech Khrushchev refers to the 'tenfold' increase in the 'number of arrests following charges of counter-revolutionary activity between 1936 and 1937'. This increase was followed between 1937 and 1938 by another increase, which became geometrical (Khrushchev omits this point).

This vast campaign against the population was camouflaged by the two final Charades (Radek, Pyatakov and others, and Bukharin, Rykov and others) and the decapitation of the army through the killing of Tukhachevsky and other outstanding generals. It was Yezhov's task to prepare the material for these events.

He moved very prudently.[5] After allowing his new officers to get the hang of things by working for a number of months alongside the older men they were to replace – primarily to get the second Great Charade off the ground – he set about implementing Stalin's idea of covering his traces.

He convened a conference of all those police officials who had been Yagoda's deputies and central department heads, telling them all they had been given assignments somewhere else in the Soviet Union to scrutinize the political conduct and character of the local Party committee heads; they were given apparently bona-fide documents and sent off (only four department heads were left out). The next day all these men set out quite unsuspectingly: each one was removed from his train at the first stop and taken back by car to a gaol near Moscow. The same procedure was followed two days later with all their aides.

This part of the operation was done so carefully that for some weeks no one even realized what had happened. Meanwhile Yezhov replaced all the guards and the officers commanding the Moscow Political Police with newcomers, very often from Georgia. He prevented flights abroad by taking over the functions of the passport office and replacing the commanders of the Political Police air-force.

To ensure his own safety he moved into a specially guarded wing of the Political Police building, with a very complicated access-way covered by special guards who checked every visitor's papers at a great many points. His own safety assured, Yezhov began to have all the interrogators for the Charades arrested one by one, as well as all the other officials who might be privy to any of the behind-the-scenes preparations. They were picked up in their offices during the day and in their homes at night.

By this time the Political Police officials were terrified: it became a fairly common sight to see one of them leaping from a window of their headquarters in the centre of Moscow; Political Police from other sections who came to France and Spain around this time had all sorts of stories to tell about armed guards cleaning out the Political Police blocks of flats to the accompaniment of pistol shots from suiciding officers whose turn had come. Terror pervaded the city.

In the case of the police officials there was no occasion for a charade at all; they were simply shot out of hand. The claim was then circulated that they had been executed because of Trotskyism plus espionage: the espionage charges were distributed among the various countries that a given officer might have had some connexion with: Poles were spying for Poland, Letts for Latvia, etc.: Russians were allocated to the intelligence services of France, Germany and Great Britain.

The split between public and private consciousness was now un-bridgeable. For years, to be sure, the Soviet Union had been grounded in institutionalized mendacity: conformist lying had dominated all aspects of public expression – the press, the school system, radio and films, and of course Party councils and factory mass-meetings.

Even before the Kirov killing no one really expected that anyone would take his public remarks seriously *in private*; it was understood that lying was merely a required tribute to appearances. This now changed radically. People abruptly grew timid even with their best friends; no one would speak openly with anyone. The most that might happen between people who did know each other well was that one might speak very carefully in highly veiled, oblique language; even that made people very nervous. As the terror began in earnest in the middle thirties the chasm between what anyone could in fact believe and what he was called upon to believe by the regime, now bristling with weapons in every cell of its being, yawned fantastically.

Thus the Political Police poisoned all relations. People would denounce friends to forestall being denounced themselves; brothers and wives were now put beyond the bounds of trust. During this whole period any expression of personal opinion *at all* would have implied an irreconcilable contradiction with all official expression, since the regime was wedded to a manifestly false and almost demented theory of political reality. The logical result was quite simple: *no* opinion could be expressed, since no sensible person, beginning at least with the second Charade, could be expected by those who knew him to believe any official version of anything.

The secret language that did develop to some extent between old friends did not do them much good – what is easier to decipher than a secret language? And this was all the easier for the Political Police since they too, of course, had exactly the same disbelieving attitude at heart as other sensible people.

A pervasive institution of Soviet life that became exceptionally luxuriant during the Deep Comb-out is that of the 'secret collaborator' (in Russian abbreviation *seksot*, a word meaning an informer for the Political Police). Unlike so much else claimed by the Soviet regime, these secret collaborators are not an invention of the Bolsheviks: it is the totalitarian organization of Soviet society, equipped with modern technology, that has generalized the *seksot* to extravagant dimensions.

The *seksot* is not supposed to be a paid informer; the conception underlying his function is that of civic duty. It is a commonplace of Soviet life to say that one out of every three citizens is a *seksot*; there is, of course, no way of checking this, but there can be no doubt that an awareness of the presence of secret informers is a fundamental factor of Soviet life. The pervasiveness of the institution is such that Soviet citizens have found it natural to regard themselves as being under the surveillance of the secret informers at almost all times no matter where they are. It is also common knowledge that the informers, as part of the all-powerful police network, are vital for the life and liberty of all Soviet citizens.

There are, of course, voluntary informers – people who out of some perversity, perhaps viciousness or a mere liking for tale-bearing and being on good terms with the authorities, become voluntary monitors.

More common are those who have been forced into tale-bearing by the Political Police itself. They may also be characterless, or may have some special reason to be afraid of the Police or some special reason to mollify it, perhaps in the hope of rescuing friends or relatives.

During the Deep Comb-out some of the *seksots* were bona-fide idealists, who had offered their services out of sheer devotion to Bolshevism.

But no matter how conscientious an informer might be in this period, no matter how idealistic his resolve to behave in a completely objective manner, it was impossible to satisfy the Political Police through objectivity alone.

In the case of these sincere idealists, indeed, it is plain that their idealism was sustained precisely by this assumption that the Party was really sincere when it said that the class enemy had to be checked up on for the sake of the Revolution. Like other innocents undone by the spectacular development of the Political Police under Stalin, they failed to grasp the inwardness of the notion of class enemy: this consisted not in the objective evaluation of people who might have been genuinely hostile to the Soviet regime, but in extending the institutional effectiveness of the Political Police itself as a tool for the manipulation of the populace.

Because of this, and because of the complex ritual applied during the Deep Comb-out, the Police insistence on 'real' information actually meant a contribution to the construction of fictions that could be used not as part of a judicial procedure, but as part of an administrative routine.

Hence sincere informers were obliged to go far beyond the reporting of discontent, which was, of course, both notorious and ubiquitous.

Sincere informers generally took a long time to grasp the fact that the 'actions', as opposed to mere gossip, that they were asked to communicate to the Political Police were themselves mere fictions composed by the Police themselves: the assassinations, acts of wrecking, 'diversions', etc. were woven out of whole cloth by the Political Police in order to give a *raison d'être* to their repressive measures and also to justify the growth of their own apparatus. They served two goals – the justification of the ritualist, mythological propaganda of the Party, and the expansion of the power of the Police.

What the *seksots* never grasped, even at the height of the Deep Comb-out, was this cardinal point: the Political Police had no interest at all in the objective truth – it had an institutional requirement for reports regardless of whether the reports corresponded to anything else.

Hence a sort of tug-of-war began during the later thirties between the secret informers and the Political Police – the informers had mere words to report, and the Police wanted deeds, that is, *reports* of deeds. The secret informers were naturally told they were under suspicion – perhaps *they* were soft-pedalling plots!

The result was foreseeable. The secret informer found himself giving not merely an objective account of a conversation, but deducing conclusions from it: thus a remark that nothing could be bought in the shops would find its way to the Police as the expression of 'dissatisfaction with the Party's economic policy'.[6] A remark to a foreigner about the housing shortage would be converted into proof of espionage; anyone who relayed a quip about Stalin would be reported as the 'instigator of a terrorist state of mind'. Coteries of friends and colleagues would be converted into groupings of one kind or another – political organizations, political groupings . . .

This in itself did not amount to very much in the way of information either, though in the case of the idealistic *seksots* it did perform the function of obliterating the distinction between truthful reporting and the concoction of fantasies. Thus it destroyed the moral fibre of those informers who had, at least in the beginning, volunteered out of genuine idealism.

As the Political Police began living up to the aims of the Deep Combout, such reports, though they harmonized with the Police fantasies, did not produce much meat. What the Police wanted was not mere attitudes or mere potentialities, but reports on 'real' groups and 'real' spies. At the same time ordinary people kept becoming more and more cautious even in their day-to-day conversation, making it increasingly difficult to deduce anything in any case.

By the time this point was reached, of course, the way was long since open to the construction of outright inventions. The only limiting factor to such wholesale fabrications was plausibility, but in Soviet conditions that itself sounded like one more element of fantasy. The criterion for a given invention was really its conceivability: if the invention was about a given person, the only question to be asked was whether such a person could *conceivably* have embarked on such-and-such a plot. If it was conceivable – again through the prism of the Political Police, which found any number of things perfectly conceivable for its own purposes – then it could be forwarded to the Police.

The element in these constructions that vanished almost immediately, as devoid of the smallest interest either for the informer himself or for the Police, was whether a given individual had *in fact* done what he was reported to do.

It was on the foundation of these systematized fabrications, gathered by the Political Police from its countless sources, that it built up its remarkable network of anti-Soviet conspiracies, organizations, wreckings, espionage – providing the interrogators with a solid body of material on the basis of which they could then extort confessions tailored to suit the 'objective material' in the Police dossiers.

One *seksot* was finally discarded, and wound up in gaol like millions of others because he could not get over a curious inhibition he had about this question of plausibility. Though a sincere idealist who believed that the end justified the means he could not, somehow, overcome his reluctance to report utterly inconceivable uprisings and plots that had no verisimilitude *at all*. Because of this he was finally considered by his superiors to be derelict in his duty. In prison, of course, he had to make up for this shortcoming by now confessing in earnest to the reality of all the things he had been faithfully reporting as though they were merely potential.[7]

What is perhaps most extraordinary about the Police technique at this time is that it never resorted to the classical device, so well-tried under the Tsarist regime, of the *agent provocateur*. Nothing would have been simpler than the creation – if necessary out of nothing – of bona-fide acts of wrecking, sabotage, plotting, explosions, uprisings and so on. Even if, let us say, the Police could not use trained *agents provocateurs* to heighten the universal discontent in the Soviet Union, what could have stopped it from putting on plots and acts of sabotage that were factual, even though contrived, and thus have obtained genuine evidence?

This never happened. The requirements of the Political Police remained limited to paperwork – reports claiming to report facts whose utility revolved merely around their being elements in dossiers used for the extraction of confessions. The operation was on such a gargantuan scale that it must have seemed superfluous, indeed wasteful, to try to contrive *genuine* plots, *genuine* explosions, *genuine* acts of sabotage, when these, too, would have to figure, eventually, as mere reports on paper.

It is doubtless an indication of the curiously dreamlike quality of the entire operation of the Charades and Comb-outs, a Pirandello-like equating of appearance and reality that indicates more clearly than anything else that the prime source of the slaughters was psychological.

The further implication, of course, is that in spite of the general discontent, there were in fact no instances of genuine plots or genuine uprisings, hence that the Political Police was perfectly willing to be satisfied with the fantasies of the *seksots* and of the prisoners under interrogation. That is what it wanted and got. There was no need at all for it to go to the trouble of creating extraneous and irrelevantly genuine facts of its own.

The first thing entailed by a denunciation was the loss of a job. Whoever fell into the established categories of ostracism became untouchable. Whatever his qualifications might have been, however numerous or powerful his connexions, he would be ostracized as a political leper the moment he found himself ejected from his office. He would rove about from one office to another doing his best to rehabilitate himself by an appeal. No one could help him: that in itself would have been taken as a sign of counter-revolution. In any case this state of mere joblessness generally came to an end with an arrest; indeed, many people would finally beg to be arrested, since the status of political and moral untouchability and the *de facto* impossibility of finding another job often proved unendurable.

Aside from its scope, what distinguished the Deep Comb-out was the prominence of the victims. They were no longer mere hangovers of the previous pre-revolutionary past, 'former people' or kulaks – but the managers, Party people, secretaries of the Party in regional and district committees, the key personnel of the vast Soviet governmental apparatus, the topmost figures of the Red Army and the summits of the State.

When such prominent people were taken, no immediate announcement was as a rule made: it became a Soviet habit during this period to keep a careful look-out to see whose pictures vanished from the walls or whose work disappeared from bookshops and libraries. When books and pamphlets began vanishing it was understood that their authors had been arrested; at the height of the arrests and massacres, textbooks vanished *en masse*. The pace of arrest at one time became so rapid that entire editions were returned for pulping even before being distributed; the arrest of their authors meant that the editions had to be destroyed. For years, in fact, schoolchildren had no school books at all and had to write out all their lessons. (The big banknotes, at this time, had been signed by five superior officials; since they were all arrested, the few notes that came out in 1938 were unsigned altogether.)

Similarly, if artists were arrested their works also quietly disappeared, but in the case of technicians, sensibly enough, the work that might have been done by them was not wiped out but merely transferred to someone else's credit. A prisoner who had done some work on physics together with colleagues saw his own identical account of the work appear in two technical reviews ascribed to the only two members of the team still at liberty.[8]

Arrest meant total isolation from everything outside the Police milieu: it was followed by interrogation, after a completely unpredictable period varying from a day or two to a whole year (the regulations provided for a maximum interval of ten days).

As the Deep Comb-out snowballed, the same factor that had involved the secret informers in the progressive elaboration of fantasies was applied to the handling of the population as a whole. The principle that had been so strikingly demonstrated in the Great Charades – the extraction of 'sincere' confessions – was generalized. The confessions required for the Political Police dossiers did not require the same degree of elaboration achieved in the Charades, but they had to constitute materials for the same sort of libretti – routinized, standardized, and homogenized as the Deep Comb-out attained monstrous proportions.

A standard gambit in opening the interrogation was to ask: 'Do you know why you have been arrested?' If the prisoner said, as he was bound to, that he didn't know, the interrogator would then ask: 'Well, tell me the hypothesis you have formed of the reason for your arrest.'

This of course imposed a special problem on all political prisoners; since mere denial would itself be interpreted as indicating hostility to the authorities, he had to say something or other, and that something or other was indicated to him, at least in the early days, in the form of an outline of the expected confession and later on, when the arrests had become a deluge, by prison gossip quickly supplying the fantasies required by the interrogators.

Though this technique has reminded many people of the identical method in use by the Spanish Inquisition, it is no more than a natural reaction to a situation in which an interrogator has no information of his own. It is followed even in an ordinary criminal case, if the investigator has nothing to go on but a name and is obliged to bluff his way towards some information by a leading question put to the person he is interrogating.

There was no such thing, of course, as a defence counsel; in the great bulk of cases there was never any question of a defence at all. In the Great Charades the 'counsel for the defence' were themselves simply assigned to play a certain role in the libretti ordered by Stalin.

The theory of the interrogation was simple: it could not be finished except with a confession, which was, in fact, its aim.

There were hardly any cases in which the arrests were linked to an actual occurrence – an accident of some kind, or for that matter even the real expression of a dissident opinion. The Political Police might, rarely, use such an event, but only as an element in another completely fabricated context. Since the scope of the fabrications was very broad there was no need for actual events to be interwoven with the comprehensive confessions required. Just as bona-fide events – i.e., deliberately staged atrocities – were too much trouble to bother about in assembling the material gathered by the secret collaborators, so it was generally not worth the trouble to make use of *de facto* situations.

The general method applied in the given circumstances was a matter of common sense: it was known at this time as the Yezhov method throughout the Political Police; it consisted of granting the prisoner a free rein in the creation of his own particular legend. It was evidently impossible to create batches of fabrications in central headquarters and then have them tailored to fit each prisoner, hence it was more sensible for each man to do his own creating and do it, moreover, by personalizing the legend as much as possible and even linking it to real occurrences.

The creation of complex legends had to be contrived with some detail, and also to sound important, since if they were turned down by the examiners as too trivial or too incredible the interrogation would simply go on.

The prisoners had to cudgel their wits to contrive plausible, important-sounding crimes with a political content. The real flights of fancy necessarily had to come from relatively well-educated or well-placed prisoners. Mere peasants could escape with a rather simple statement that they had sneered at some defect or other in the Soviet system in order to promote 'subversion'. This could be called 'counter-revolutionary agitation' under the Soviet code; it was good for between three to seven years' forced labour.

Some amusing instances of creative imagination have been recorded:[9] A workman from Kiev, in order to show sabotage, gave a detailed account of his attempts to blow up a bridge a kilometre long with several kilograms of arsenic; he abandoned the project because it started to rain. Another worker explained at length his activities in an organization aiming at the construction of a number of artificial volcanoes in order to explode the entire Soviet Union. A Greek physician, to show espionage, said that in writing home he described some small fish that were being bred to fight malaria mosquitoes; another prisoner admitted that he had informed the Polish consul of the weather as shown in a forecast put up regularly every day in a public park; a professor engaged in 'self-criticism' at a public meeting, admitted that he had indicated the depth of the Dnieper River in a textbook; on this basis he was arrested as a spy and in prison confessed that he had done this to help the Germans in wartime; another professor had indirectly conveyed to the Japanese consul some reports concerning the political views of some Jewish children.

Of course it was often difficult for even very imaginative people to create plausible legends quickly; sometimes the prisoners would be helped by the examiners themselves; sometimes a whole cell would co-operate to build up as good a confession as possible. Prisoners became specialists, indeed were often used by the examiners themselves to perform this function in one cell after another.

The interrogation technique of the Political Police had been worked out in some detail over a long period of time. It was quite specific and in its broad outlines laid down by central headquarters; this is indicated by the simultaneous use of identical techniques throughout the Soviet Union.

They first made it clear to the prisoner that he was being called upon to testify voluntarily to his own guilt; he was assured that afterwards he would be freed or in any case leniently treated. The examining magistrate would vary the technique of persuasion to suit the individual before him. The initial phase of persuasion would last quite a long time, followed if necessary by various forms of intimidation. The very fact that the prisoner was refusing to confess would be made the subject of still another criminal charge – holding up justice; he would be threatened with harsh consequences.

As in the Charades, accordingly, from the very outset the relationship between the prisoner and the examiner was one of negotiation. Since it would evidently be unreasonable for the authorities to promise someone immunity for having planned to blow up the Soviet Union, the object of negotiation was to persuade the prisoner not to confess his guilt in the normal sense – which for such grave crimes would obviously entail severe punishment – but *to sign a confession of guilt*. In return for such a signed confession the prisoner would be made promises implying in the nature of things that the confession was, in fact, worthless, or indeed meaningless as far as its ostensible content went; it was plainly required for some quite different purpose.

The actual process of persuasion would be framed by all sorts of psychological devices: allowing screams of agony to be overheard, fabricating bogus courtroom scenes with sentences of death changed at the last minute and so on.

The most effective weapon was the threat of reprisals of all kinds – including torture and death – against members of the prisoner's family. Prisoners would be told that their children would be hidden away under unknown names in orphanages and never be seen again; mild forms of punishment for families would consist of eviction, deportation orders of varying degrees (forbidding them, for instance, to live in the fifteen largest cities of the country, in the forty largest cities and so on, in addition to the specifically designated deprivation areas in Central Asia or

Siberia). If an upper Party or government functionary was arrested his wife generally was, too; their children were often sequestered in special asylums.

The social ostracism that almost invariably followed imprisonment was actually a tribute to the strongest, as it were positive element in the government's manhandling of the population; psychologically it implied assent to a claim that was, in fact, instinctively acknowledged – mainly, no doubt, by the ideologically committed part of the population – that the intentions of the regime were essentially justifiable, that there was, in fact, something in it.

All contact with the newly disclosed 'enemies of the people' was avoided. Not, it would seem, through mere fear – though there must have been that, too – but through an emotional identification with the Party that could withstand all factual reality. Prisoners' relatives were also as a rule given the sack; prisoners' children would be tormented by ostracism at school. A wife might sometimes be helped after the prisoner confessed, but although this apparently was rare it was often held out as bait to the prisoners.

The Political Police would sometimes break prisoners' morale by moving them around from one cell to another, to show each prisoner the varying degrees of torment possible. A stubborn case would be left for months on end in some peculiarly disagreeable cell, or a cell full of prisoners still undergoing the effects of the beatings-up that were a part of the interrogation procedure; the recalcitrant prisoner might then be moved to still another cell with prisoners all busily composing their confessions in an atmosphere of relative merriment.

The Political Police disseminated all sorts of encouraging rumours about the charms of exile after confession: for instance, one would be allowed to go on doing one's own work, even be joined by one's family, or benefit by a general amnesty to celebrate the twentieth anniversary of the Bolshevik putsch.

The beatings-up were not the most effective torture device; stoppage of sleep was. Police personnel would operate in shifts; if necessary they could keep a prisoner sleepless, standing on his feet, for many days at a time. Known as the 'conveyer', this technique had been so refined that it was almost invariably successful. It was the only form of torture used up to the second half of August 1937; beforehand physical violence had not been used much; threats and beatings were enough. Afterwards, to be sure, as the arrests became epidemic, a certain amount of torture was applied, though never so systematically as in the Gestapo prisons.

When sleep is needed the desire for it overrides all other bodily requirements. It is agonizing; it also obliterates moral resistance, partly by dissipating the ability to concentrate. Hallucinations become commonplace; the feet of people standing more or less immobile for hours and days swell up monstrously.

Few could or did resist this treatment, but some could survive it for days or even in some cases weeks. Sleeplessness, together with the threat of its application to the families of the prisoners, proved to be a quite irresistible technique.

All such methods – moral torment, sleeplessness, psychological devices – were called 'cultural' by the Political Police, i.e., in the Soviet nuance, 'civilized', 'well-bred'. The more violent methods consisted in the main of beatings-up, done in a preliminary stage with fists alone but later on with objects that were used precisely because of their *improvised* nature – especially chair-legs, for instance. Whips, blackjacks, truncheons and so on were apparently not available, doubtless as a method of pretending that each beating was somehow on impulse, not an established routine. This fiction was further sustained by the fact that it was only the examiners and their assistants who beat up the prisoners, not the regular staff of the prison; this fortified the illusion that it was not part of the organization, so to speak, but a personal caprice.

A high functionary of the Political Police said that beatings were not part of the training manual, even though they were applied throughout the country: trainees were simply told that a confession had to be secured at all costs and given to understand that beatings-up were perfectly all right. Pains were also taken that no visible damage was done; what happened within the body was of course another matter (kidneys were often permanently damaged).[10]

Hardly anyone could resist the interrogations for more than a month; the rare exceptions that did hold out were simply killed. None of the interrogators or, after a while, the prisoners themselves, could bother asking themselves the meaning of the procedure: such a question was itself a sort of luxury that was possible only in the phase before the arrests became torrential. Those officials who felt they were doing no more than loyally carrying out the commands of the Soviet authorities simply put their heads down and pushed on. Hundreds of thousands were wrung through the machinery of interrogation, including famous heroes, people whose physical courage was celebrated, devoted long-time revolutionaries, to say nothing of the still more idealistic foreign Communists who in some cases were put through even more. If the example of a famously courageous man like Mrachkovsky could be held up to initially recalcitrant prisoners, what hope could there be?

Many faithful partisans of the regime lost their faith after their arrest. Those who had been in the Party itself or the State machine had perforce done all sorts of harsh, repressive things as part of the discipline required for the implementation of an ideal. Thus they had willingly borne some of the guilt for the criminality of the regime; when arrested they had no moral reserves to sustain their faith.

Hence officials were often the easiest of all to make confess; having been devoted supporters of the regime they lacked any motivation, still less any energy to resist. Many functionaries confessed out of a kind of discipline. Even after arrest they would be willing to confess in order to preserve the authority of the State while at the same time blaming all sorts of peripheral factors for their actual arrest – blunders of all kinds, even sabotage *within* the Political Police and similar mishaps.

One of the methods deliberately applied was the systematic use of the foulest possible language; at a time when Soviet domestic propaganda was much concerned with a sort of suburban priggishness, the Political Police made obscene abuse part of the technique of cowing prisoners.

Psychological reversals were also cultivated: an interrogator, for instance, would suddenly start screaming at a prisoner at the top of his lungs, in a way that looked demented; then he would be transformed, and start chatting pleasantly with a colleague.

The extravagances of the mass arrests and slaughters of the later thirties had nothing to do with the psychopathic qualities of the Political Police. As an *élite* corps, for all its savagery, it had a sense of allegiance to principle. Though the idealists who had abounded in the summits of the organization at its inception did not last beyond the Deep Comb-out, and were replaced by run-of-the-mill bureaucrats, the psychopathic cruelty associated with the Nazi regime was never present in the Soviet Union. The brutality shown by the Police in extracting confessions was not generated by perverse emotionalism, but was a reflection of the extraordinary conditions of the regime.

Though the conditions may have been equally severe under both systems, the specifically Nazi perversions – meaningless experimentation on helpless prisoners, the creation of manifestly pointless labour as a technique of humiliation, torture for its own sake – were completely absent. The harshness in the camps was due to the rigours of nature, to general scarcity, administrative incompetence, and a disregard for life, not to the lusts of psychopaths.

This itself highlights the monstrosity of the Deep Comb-out. It was not, for instance, as though there had been an outbreak of some emotional disease, as there seems to have been among the Nazi summits. It was simply called forth through the sort of political logic generated by the evolution of the Soviet state from its conspiratorial origins.

As the Bolshevik Party evolved out of its own ideological prejudices and fixed views and on their basis constructed *ad hoc* solutions of government problems – *within a certain framework* – the logic inherent in the application of such essentially capricious propositions put forth as principles simply generated its own train of events, without ill-will, so to speak, on anyone's part. Hence the Charades and slaughters cannot be explained on the basis of emotional disturbance – epitomized in the dementia freely ascribed at various times to Stalin – but must be seen against the background of the political evolution of the Soviet dictatorship under the impact of the 'Third Revolution' (industrialization and collectivization).

The many Police officials who behaved cruelly without being personally sadistic or even harsh by nature believed wholeheartedly in the Party line, both in its scientific validity and in its moral elevation. This, accompanied by a limitless dedication to what the Party 'represented', in its leaders and in the ensemble of its institutions, created a substitute, in fact, for what would otherwise have been the consciences and intellects of the partisans of the regime.

Outside the performance of their duty as examining magistrates, the Soviet Political Police personnel could be and generally were perfectly sociable, agreeable, helpful, unpretentious, and even friendly; the cruelty they displayed in their official functions, accordingly, reflected the special ambience created in Russia by Bolshevism rather than by the 'Russian character'.

It is plain, in fact, that the police procedures of the Nazi system and the Soviet were not spiritually akin. Whereas Nazi prison guards and ss men, called upon to perform acts of malignant bestiality, would perform them either because individually they were not averse to them – i.e., were psychopathically sadistic – or else really were bound by the chain of obedience to their superiors that they were notoriously to invoke in their self defence later, the Soviet Political Police would refer, not to *obedience*, but, in a more religious way, to the worthiness of their intellectual system as a whole. They would not have pleaded a blind faith either in the hierarchy they were members of or in a mere catechism, but in something founded on science and morality linked by a special logic. To such devoted Political Police officials, Marxism, the Soviet State, and the General Line of the Party were alpha and omega.

In the early stages of the Deep Comb-out it was possible to insist on accuracy in writing down the admissions. A survivor mentions his tenacity in seeing to it that his depositions were accurately taken down; he describes this concern of his – which he shared, strangely enough, with his examiner – as a 'sheer luxury'.[11] Later on the flood of arrests swept away all such questions of detail; countless thousands of prisoners were subjected to the most agonizing treatment for the purpose of constructing out-and-out fantasies.

Formally speaking, the link between fantasy and evidence could be established by a sort of theory that the existence of an idea implies the existence of an organization to implement it. Thus, a (subversive) idea gives rise to a (subversive) remark; that remark could be held by the interrogator to demonstrate conclusively the existence of a (subversive) organization. This declaration of philosophic principle, as it were, gave the interrogator enough morale to hector the prisoner in an apparently rational manner. The semblance of rationalism did not *convince* anyone, but it established flexibility in the linkage between arguments; ultimately it enabled the interrogator to break down the prisoner.

The logical sequence dependent on the acceptance of a necessary link between a remark and an organization was used, for instance, against a prisoner who survived:[12]

His interrogator seemed to want him to admit to something that was harmless – membership in a counter-revolutionary organization, since that could be extrapolated merely from his having made remarks at one time or other. If that was all he wanted, this prisoner could not see, at the time, what the point was. Was he *really* suspected? Did they want nothing but a fictitious confession, like those in the Charades? And if suspected, what was he suspected of – working for the Nazis or merely membership in some Opposition?

But the explanation was even simpler – what the authorities wanted primarily was lists of names, which were just as incredible, to be sure, as the fantasies their owners were supposed to be involved in, but had the charm of utility. They were, in fact, the principal lever needed to manipulate the population.

Lists of names were established by the question that invariably followed the incantational formula: 'How do you account for your being here?'

The standard question bore on the recruitment of agents for espionage: it had the form of a couplet that became celebrated: 'Who recruited you?' and 'Whom did you recruit?'.

The recruitment formula constituted a fundamental moral problem far more painful than the necessity for creating different forms of nonsense that were bound to have a merely abstract quality. It involved, after all, questions of treachery, betrayal, or slander. How far would one be forced to go?

The best way of saving one's skin and salving one's conscience was to produce for both categories of recruiter and recruit the names of people who had either died or left the country for good. An Armenian priest with a good memory simply confessed to having recruited every Armenian he had ever buried during the preceding three years.[13] Sometimes a cell would have ready a list of corpses for use by any prisoner it fitted. It was considered, by and large, perfectly all right morally to denounce people who were already arrested and sentenced, or sometimes had simply been denounced already by others. The examiners, themselves very eager to get their quota of confessions, would naturally help out often by asking for confirmation of other prisoners' depositions.

One of the paramount elements of the Deep Comb-out was its scope: there could be no feeling of solidarity between people who felt selected at random. While this may naturally have made people *hate* the regime still more, on the other hand it eliminated a prime source of opposition. The regime, by atomizing the society it terrorized in order to terrorize it the better, also insulated itself against effective reprisals.

The Political Police technique was bound to reach its limits very quickly. During the flood-tide of the arrests the whole operation had become utterly unreal; people would blithely put down the first name that crossed their minds. A little while later, after anyone was arrested his gaolers would have at least half-a-dozen names of those who would shortly afterwards also find themselves in gaol providing further lists of names at the same ratio.

Even with the overlapping of many of the bogus denunciations, even with the presence of all sorts of blanks in the artificial lists – corpses, émigrés, etc. – the snowballing effect proved to be crippling. Only a few months after the Police technique was applied systematically, tens of thousands of people were flooding the gaols and concentration camps.

The extraordinary mechanism that kept the Deep Comb-out going at a high speed is illustrated by the recorded case of a prisoner whose zeal went too far.[14] Sylakov was a somewhat unhinged railwayman, an authentic proletarian (his father had been a railway guard before him). Wild and temperamental, he found the army unendurable; when news from home got worse (his old mother fell gravely ill, his young wife left him) he decided to desert: leave was out of the question.

But this desertion upset him; he felt he had to be punished. And since at the time the Soviet government was campaigning to have all criminal offenders of whatever kind confess their sins and repent, Sylakov decided to 'volunteer his confession of guilt'; in the atmosphere of the era he thought it sensible to take a chance on accompanying his confession of guilt with an anti-Soviet conspiracy in which he assigned himself a key role.

A modest man by nature, his initial version of the plot was rather modest, too; it began with a scheme in which he and a few friends were going to hold up a post-office for the purpose of stealing money to finance terrorists. This was the point at which, according to his confession, he decided to repent. He thought that in view of his youth and plebeian origins nothing much would happen to him.

He rang up the Political Police and told them that he, both a deserter and an important political criminal, was giving himself up.

The Police had different plans. The moment Sylakov was taken to headquarters they gave him the most severe interrogation possible; they beat him brutally and kept expanding his original confession. They dropped his 'few friends' and forced him to implicate the *whole* of the military unit he had deserted from. He himself, a youthful ignoramus, was not at all the key figure: that was his commanding officer, aided by subordinates. The aim of the plot was correspondingly expanded: it was the destruction of the Soviet regime and the restoration of capitalism under Tsarism. The conspirators were supposed to have allocated each other different positions: Sylakov had been tapped for Governor-General of Moscow.

The preposterousness of this mechanical ramification of Sylakov's modest little original fantasy was outweighed by tragedy. A huge number of people suffered. Very nearly the whole army unit was arrested, and the wives and a great many officers and men were, too, as well as Sylakov's two working-class sisters, his old, crippled mother, his father, and an uncle, a porter, who had seen Sylakov only once. This uncle, under Tsarism once a corporal, was upgraded to general for the purpose of the 'plot'.

When the standard recruitment formula was applied – 'Who recruited you?' and 'whom did you recruit?' – a vast harvest fell into the lap of the Political Police. All the unit officers claimed they had been recruited by their seniors and had recruited their juniors: as a growing number of prominent people were involved this sort of multiplication would, of course, soon have encompassed the whole of the Red Army.

The Political Police abruptly went into reverse, applying the same procedure of forcing prisoners to make confessions, this time with a contrary point.

This affected Sylakov in a strange way: the Police were now demanding that he should withdraw his confession and confess that the whole of the plot he had confessed to was a fabrication. He had been thrashed within an inch of his life to get the false confession to begin with: why should he retract it? In the beginning he thought it was all a ruse contrived by his examiner; he had to be beaten up all over again before getting the new point.

The same thing happened to the hundreds of people involved by their own extorted confessions; one of the soldiers, confronting Sylakov in the reverse position, was very reluctant to go back on the original false confession that had been forced out of him, since it seemed to him dangerous to admit, in the presence of a Political Police officer, that he had lied. He falsely confessed to a serious but imaginary crime, even though the guilt for it was going to lay him open to execution.

Sylakov himself was treated very leniently, as it turned out; he was given a sentence of only three years, merely on the desertion charge; the fabrications in both directions were simply dropped.

By the end of the summer of 1937 the flood of fantasy inundated the country as a whole, though at the same time all forms were complied with. Bundles of warrants would be distributed; it was impossible for any prosecutor even to read the names. The Political Police found itself grotesquely overworked: to comply with the demonic scheme inherent in the very conception of the conspiracies whose non-existence made them bafflingly elusive it was necessary to keep the number of bogus subversive organizations proliferating at almost the same rate as the geometrical progression of suspects.

By the time the repression had reached flood-tide hardly any of the prisoners put up much resistance; as thousands and more thousands of people were processed in the same assembly line, a sort of fatalism seized on the gaols. By this time it was known that the heroes of the Revolution and the Civil War had also been gaoled, had also confessed to fantasies, and had generally been wiped out. By the time a certain point was reached, prisoners might feel that not only was there no point in holding back, but on the contrary – the *more* extravagant the fantasy, the *more* preposterous, the better.

The more intelligent ones decided that perhaps the best way out was to concoct the most unbelievable atrocities and then drag *everyone* into them – the summits of the army, government institutions, sciences, the political apparatus, and thus somehow bring the whole operation down by the weight of its very preposterousness.

By the time that the number of prisoners had swelled into ungovernable dimensions, it was in a way not even dangerous. You could nonchalantly plead guilty to attempts at assassinating everyone, including Stalin; there were thousands at your side. There was no longer even any shame in confessing to espionage on behalf of the Nazis. In 1937 and 1938, according to Political Police charges, Hitler had positively millions of spies working for him, generally for nothing. The picture of life as it emerged in the Soviet Union at the time was that of a strange fantasy in which the topmost figures in the country, men in charge of the economy and institutions of the whole Soviet

Union, though they *seemed* to be tussling with genuine problems were in reality hatching schemes to blow it all up.

The pressure on the Police had the effect of stimulating rivalry within the organization; each investigator had an interest in outdoing his colleagues by getting not merely more but better confessions – i.e. better known people committing more heinous crimes. There was an inevitable competition in the invention of elaborate subversive plans, which came to take in more and more territory in national life – going on from inventing plans to explode trains, barracks and factories to the poisoning of vast numbers of people, preferably army men and industrial workers.

Of course they might have preferred, in the heat of the competition, to outdo their colleagues by producing not merely plans but facts – actual caches of explosives and ammunition – but here, of course, they ran into a snag that could not be got round. It was impossible to produce material evidence of any kind.

There does not seem to have been a single subversive organization in existence – there were no uprisings, no attempts at assassination, no secret caches of arms, *nothing*. With the fanning-out technique of the Police, to be sure, countless bona-fide assassins could have remained unnoticed in the armies of impostors.

The Political Police had a perfectly rational explanation of this that naturally reflected credit on themselves: it was only watchfulness on an heroic scale that had managed to unmask the monsters before they got down to business!

But even though this was rational or at least logical, still, it would have helped, in their intra-mural competition, if someone could actually have found something.

In the absence of real sabotage, what had to be concentrated on was the mass-production of bogus *plans* for sabotage. Counter-revolution was nowhere, counter-revolutionary plots were everywhere. The tiniest village had several groups of terrorists plotting day and night to kill Stalin; every factory was stiff with saboteurs – all on the verge of some atrocity. People with political backgrounds specialized in plotting to dismember the country, in order to hand over various sections of it to various countries – Germany, Japan and so on; members of various ethnic minorities did the same. Among the scientists murderousness was concentrated among the bacteriologists – whose speciality had something magical, mysterious and intangible about it.

Prisoners had no way of following the chain of recruitment back to any real source, by 1937 lost in the mists of antiquity. Since everyone had been undergoing this blanket process of recruitment for months, the original recruiters, known in some gaols[15] as the 'arch-recruiters', were long since dead.

These founding fathers of the recruitment had been processed in 1936 and then exterminated: their progeny were the millions arrested *en masse* in 1937 and 1938. Although one might have imagined that the original source of recruitment – in the *ad hoc* theory deduced from Political Police routine – had been some Opposition or other, it seemed that this was not so.

As late as the spring of 1937 the Political Police seized hold of not only anyone who was in some way connected, however tenuously, or for that matter fictitiously, with one of the Charades, but also anyone whose name was simply mentioned in any dossier at all for whatever reason. Consequently, in the chain of recruitment hammered out by the Political Police, the prime recruiters were also men with no Oppositional past at all. This did not make any particular difference, since they too had to claim to have been recruited somehow, and it was only natural, indeed inevitable, to pick one of the scores of people involved or mentioned in the Great Charades.

In the beginning, apparently, the Political Police arrested all those denounced, but as the flood swelled that became impossible for technical reasons. Some principle of selection had to be applied to the flood of recruits. By the time the automatic working of the geometrical progression entailed by the technique of bogus recruiting was threatening to encompass the entire population – which by the beginning of 1938 or 1939 it would have – it was obviously imperative, in order to cope with the flood at all, to establish some refinement in the round-up. In 1938, after all, a huge section of the population was necessarily listed in some Police file as 'suspect'; it was only natural for the Political Police to begin getting a little restive.

They had, of course, a peculiar problem. It was out of the question *not* to arrest a man who had been scheming for years to kill Stalin, or operating underground as a terrorist agent of Hitler. Despite their awareness of the total fantasy of the whole thing, an open admission of it was clearly impossible. Nevertheless, though the gaolers maintained a solidly credulous front, the magnitude of the mania finally compelled them to do something practical to put some brake on the movement. Inevitably, of course, in the semi-farcical situation of the time, they collided with the dead-pan resistance of the prisoners themselves, who by the summer of 1938 were leaning over backwards to cast the dragnet as far abroad as possible. As examiners began suggesting, sometimes a little sheepishly, that some names might not, after all, be required, the prisoners would fight tenaciously for their own register of bogus suspects; prisoners denouncing a maximum number of people would amuse themselves by picking on all the most conformist Stalinites they could think of.

There was a splendid instance of this over-cooperation: Upon his arrest in the spring of 1938 a doctor with a retentive memory who was the secretary of the Medical Council in Kharkov noticed the procedure in the prison for a few days after his arrest. When his interrogation came up he answered the cardinal question – whom he had been recruiting – by enumerating on a pad of paper the name of every single one of the hundreds of doctors in the city. With a straight face he claimed that all of them had always been enemies of the people, that he had been ordered by his 'organization' to recruit everyone, and that as secretary of the Medical Council he had been very well situated to do so.

When asked to write down only the most important leaders, he refused, saying they were all equally important, and that if an organization had to have leaders he was it, and the only one. When he continued his refusal to thin out the ranks of the enemies of the people he was sent back to his cell as an *agent provocateur* and told to think again. The doctor then accused the local Political Police examiner of trying to shield some enemies of the people; he insisted that the head of the Political Police intervene at once.[16]

Even though no one, by and large, in the Soviet Union believed the actual content of all such investigations and trials, the discontent itself could be thought of as explaining the government's repressiveness *in general*: the regime might be defending itself, in its own way, against the universal hatred. In any case, there was no local authority that was capable of putting a stop to the effervescence.

Abroad, of course, the net impact of the whole movement was so massive that very few people would have been willing to say that *the whole thing* was a fabrication. Exaggerations might be admitted easily enough, but these were then excused as inevitable in a critical situation.

It was child's play for Stalin to maintain his paternal air of bland, good-humoured, sober patience. In his interview with Roy Howard, of the Scripps-Howard newspaper syndicate in America, at a time when thousands of foreign Communists who had fled for their lives from Germany, Austria, Hungary, Italy, Czechoslovakia or Poland, were being tracked down, shot out of hand or exiled to concentration camps, Stalin could say, with his usual aplomb: 'According to our Constitution, political émigrés have the right to reside in our territory. We grant them the right to asylum, just as the United States grants it.'

6
The Deep Comb-out: Results

The effect of randomness arose out of the hypocrisy permeating the whole process, which depended on the pretence that there was a genuine link between an individual and his arrest. This fiction underlay the terror; had a genuine principle governed the selection of victims, those aware of it would have felt safer when outside its range.

The real reason for an arrest, in the vast majority of instances during the Deep Comb-out, was the victim's 'objective characteristic' – his social origins, his personal connexions, his membership in some organization, his nationality.

It was just this objective characteristic that was not acknowledged: the interrogators had to create a case on the basis of a metaphysical construction. Nevertheless, once an individual began to be worked over, the objective characteristic was, it seems, instantly apparent to everyone.[1]

This criterion of selection was logically entailed by a principle embedded in Soviet law – that of collective responsibility. Explicitly applied only in 1938, when the relatives of a fugitive from the Soviet Union were declared liable to detention in a forced labour camp,[2] in practice this principle has always been taken for granted. With its implications of solidarity based on the notion of class, it was a hangover of the Civil War. Ultimately, of course, it is as old as warfare; it has been applied with unusual matter-of-factness in the Soviet Union, and never questioned even by Communist Oppositionists.

This in its turn is an integral part of another Soviet attitude – the utter lack of connexion, in principle, between the arrest of a given individual and his actual conduct (apart, of course, from *real* crimes).

Outside the Soviet Union it is a mere truism that a man must at least be suspected of having done something before he is subject to arrest. There may be instances of wrongful arrest, but there is a systematic procedure in which the two elements, the individual and the deed, are causally connected. In the Soviet Union no connexion is necessary. This was especially manifest during the Deep Comb-out.

The very notion of gaoling someone is understood in a sense that is, as it were, political, hence the arrest of anyone in the Comb-out was in reality dependent on a decision as to how to treat certain categories of people. It is true that not everyone in a given category would inevitably be arrested, but as soon as that category came under a ban imposed on it from above, often for unknown reasons, the probability of someone in the category being arrested would rise geometrically.

In war-time, for instance, all enemy aliens may be gaoled: the rule is applied categorically. In Nazi Germany, anti-Jewish legislation affected all Jews.

It was so in the Soviet Union, except that though the *reason* for arrest – the so-called objective characteristic – prompted the actual arrest, it did not apply in a blanket fashion to everyone within the category.

This was so, doubtless, partly because of the difficulty of applying such categorical criteria effectively to an enormous population, especially when the criteria could not even be acknowledged, and partly because of general conditions – the state of the Political Police files, the multitude of fanciful denunciations, the degree of overcrowding in the prisons and camps.

If someone was in a top echelon, for instance, his chances of escape went down; if he belonged to two categories at the same time – i.e., a top Party official with Polish connexions – his chances of evading the rule dwindled even more sharply.

The administrative procedure, being capricious, was essentially chaotic; it could be evaded by personal agility. A good technique of avoiding arrest was to change jobs and domiciles: it generally took a long time – between six months and a year – before the Political Police could catch up with a newcomer and begin establishing his dossier. The accumulation of secret reports on a newcomer took time: it also took time for him to fill in questionnaires, and for the file from his last place of work and residence to follow him to the new place. All these documents were forwarded not by mail but by special messenger, which involved great delay. Sometimes they were never delivered at all. Tricks of this kind were endless: they included feigning drunkenness, being arrested in advance for petty crimes, etc.

There is also some indication that some individuals would be left untouched in some of the highly vulnerable categories precisely in order to contradict the blanket character of the danger: *some* senior Red Army personnel, *some* foreign eminent Communists, *some* academicians, and so on.[3]

This concept of sociological perniciousness could not, of course, be justified in any conceivable legal system – it was consistently denied by the regime – yet its intra-Party foundations had been laid down long before. Even before Kirov's murder an important measure had given the capriciousness of the dictatorship a quasi-juridical, or in any case administrative instrument. On 12 January 1933 a joint plenum of the Central Committee and the Central Control Commission had ratified a decision, taken on 10 October by Stalin independently, intended to 'ensure iron proletarian discipline within the Party' and to 'purge the Party ranks of all unreliable and unstable elements and other hangers-on'.[4] This was supplemented by another resolution (28 April 1933) enumerating the categories of purgeable Communists.

The initial theory of purgeability had revolved around the 'alien class' nature of those purged, i.e., former landowners, bourgeoisie, kulaks, White Guards and Mensheviks – long since vanished from the country at large, to say nothing of the Party. The 28 April resolution tossed these in, but added three other categories that implicitly justified the expulsion from the Party of any member at all: double-dealers, overt and covert violators of discipline (of Party and State), and turncoats.

The notion of double-dealing laid the groundwork for alleged charges of subversion functioning behind a mask of allegiance that could be stigmatized as bogus; 'violators' were thought of as both failing to carry out decisions and also making others waver by calling such decisions, say, 'unfeasible'; the 'turncoats' were objective allies of 'bourgeois elements', who did not really want to fight the class enemy, who evaded the fight against kulaks, grafters, idlers and robbers of communal property.[5]

It is obvious that these moralizing epithets created an indefinitely wide net that could entangle anyone on a mere say-so. Any Party member whatsoever, of any rank, could be included with ease in one or all of such categories.

In short, the relatively precise description of Stalin's opponents in meaningful terms – such as 'former Oppositionists' – was replaced by a far more capacious and capriciously interpretable word: 'unreliables'. The purge was, quite simply, designed to squeeze all those elements out of the Party that might prove to be disobedient to Stalin. The past jargon of the regime concerning 'socially alien elements' was replaced by this much handier word, while a robust political neologism – proletarian iron discipline – fortified the colourless word obedience.

The January resolution had, through the use of the catch-all word, unreliables, created a philosophical definition of great juridical scope; in the wake of Kirov's murder this was to be generalized still further and given teeth.

On 13 May 1935, five months after Kirov's murder, the Central Committee passed four fundamental decrees, all secret (except for a clause in one calling for a public check-up on Party credentials) and geared to the prospect of war, primarily against Germany and Japan, secondarily against France and Great Britain.

One decree set up a Defence Commission of the Politburo; the other three aimed at eliminating all sources of disaffection in the rear: they dealt with the 'enemies of the people'.

The second decree created a Special Security Commission (also in the Politburo) that established the following operational scheme to achieve the 'moral and political unity of the Soviet people': the whole of the male population and the educated segment of the female population were broken down into three divisions – intelligentsia, workers and peasants. Everyone was supposed to be scrutinized by the Political Police for political trustworthiness.

A percentage of people to be eliminated was laid down, with a 'table of specifications' to be used as a criterion; then a schedule was set up, laying down deadlines for eliminating all individuals involved, working its way up from sub-district to national republic.

Those to be eliminated were as follows:

All remnants of the 'former people' as well as their children. All members of all political parties, hostile for whatever reason to the Bolshevik regime: this lumped together all Left-wing opponents of the Bolsheviks and Right-wing (anti-Soviet) groups, and their children.

Class enemies like kulaks and sub-kulaks; clergy of different denominations; all former Oppositionists, regardless of current membership in the Communist Party or current political attitude; all former nationalists in any national Soviet republic.

These categories might be called objective categories, however unfounded the actual accusation based on membership in such a category might be. But to facilitate the processing of such a huge population, the Political Police felt it to be inadequate as a basis for determining potential enmity to the regime, which from around that time on simply meant Stalin's personal rule.

A further category was devised, described as consisting of people harbouring anti-Soviet feelings. This was the equivalent of the notion of potential 'hostility'; it represented the introduction into a mock-juridical process of an algebraic quantity that could be invoked at will on the part of the Political Police in order to involve anyone; it could be profitably applied on the basis of the denunciations that were to become rife.

These decrees (passed in 1935 in order to 'regularize' the deportation to the Arctic and Siberia of tens of thousands of Party people in the wake of Kirov's murder) had created an indefinitely expansible device: linked to the earlier redefinition of purgeability in terms of unreliability, etc., it was to prove procedurally fruitful.

People arrested initially because of anti-Soviet feelings were later assigned, as the Deep Comb-out developed, to various roles – spies, saboteurs, terrorists, insurrectionists – contrived within the framework of the institutionalized fantasy that blanketed the country during this era.

During the years between Kirov's murder and the start of the Deep Comb-out – 1935–6 – the Special Security Commission, in collaboration with various 'psychologists' attached to the Political Police, had begun compiling the endless lists of enemies – past and future – of Stalin's faction. There was no question of coping with such numbers by means of the regular juridical machinery. Consequently a special tribunal was established under the Political Police Headquarters, with extraordinary three-man tribunals down to the district level in order to try prisoners *in absentia*.

At the same time a systematic campaign was started. By means of the tested device of 'Bolshevik criticism and auto-criticism', the entire population – including all non-Party Bolsheviks – was harangued daily by *Pravda* and the whole of the local Party press to produce 'evidence' – i.e., denunciations – intended to 'unmask and wipe out' the enemies of the people.

Stalin had once said that all criticism was necessary 'even if it contained only 5 to 10 per cent of the truth'; in practice this meant that a denunciation would be acted on if only 5 per cent of its allegations was considered true.

The notion of 'vying with each other' in a sort of socialist competition was applied to denunciations; the table of specifications set up by the Political Police Headquarters in the capital was often outdistanced by local organizations, which set up their own tables of specifications. In March 1939, after the rivers of blood had become rivulets, this was specifically mentioned by Andrei Zhdanov, at the Eighteenth Party Congress, where he referred to one organization that had started to classify 'enemies of the people' in terms of the mere number of denunciations in its dossiers.

The following represents a more detailed articulation of the categories of enemies of the people established by the Special Security Commission as a result of the decree of 13 May 1935. These categories are all based on the objective characteristics of the individuals and might be still further refined, since any given individual might well belong to a number of categories at the same time, in which case his eligibility for gaol would be overdetermined.

In addition, of course, to all members of all former Oppositions (associated with Trotsky, Zinoviev and Bukharin), and all members of all other pre-revolutionary Left-wing parties (Mensheviks, Social-Revolutionaries, Anarchists, Bundists, etc.) – all of whom might be considered bona-fide enemies at least of the Stalin faction, far more came under the axe.

(It is of some interest to note that monarchism or fascism *as such* did not constitute a charge, which was always linked with some 'progressive' ideology that was *then* equated with fascism in an institutional form such as spying for the Gestapo, etc.)

The most unexpected social category to be squeezed through the Deep Comb-out was the Communist Party itself.

Never before had such a thing even been thinkable – that countless numbers of senior Party people should be arrested on the basis of a systematized fiction.

Both the topmost and the intermediate ranks of the Party were swept as by a devouring flame. Between 1938 and 1939, in fact, practically all the top-level Party functionaries were arrested, including all the secretaries of the provincial Party committees, very nearly all secretaries of the lower-level Party committees (regions, districts, towns) and of the 'functional' Party committees assigned to major industrial enterprises, transport organizations, factories, universities, colleges, publishing houses, and so on.

This is all the more significant when it is recalled that in Soviet tradition – i.e., since Stalin expanded the office of General Secretary under Lenin – it is the secretary of a given organization that is its genuine boss.

The Party officials winnowed out of existence by the Deep Comb-out themselves fell into three classes.

The Old Bolsheviks, or the veteran idealists of the early period of the Party who had not joined any of the Oppositions and were reflective, sincere, self-sacrificing, old-fashioned, faithful ideologues. They had, to be sure, concurred in the slaughter of the peasants, but for idealistic reasons; now, to their astonishment, they were being removed.

The second group were authentic Stalinists – unwavering partisans of Stalin's faction, of his General Line, and of himself personally. This was doubtless one of the most devoted large groups in history, if we recall the incredible amounts of blood letting it had justified not through ideological fanaticism like that of the Old Bolsheviks, but through its *esprit de corps* as it swiftly evolved into a bureaucracy. Their mystical devotion was directed at Stalin as the emblem of Party solidarity.

These people made no bones at all about confessing; to them it was a further act of devotion to the Party through its agent the Political

Police; even though they had not been privileged to be informed of the reasons for it, they docilely conformed with Party discipline.

The third group of Party people were the careerists who had come into the Party long after its 'conquests' had been consolidated. Here there was no question of idealism at all, but simply the shrewdness of people on the make, feathering their own nests, and alert to any change in the Party from the exclusive point of view of their own interests.

It was quite impossible for them, too, to have foreseen the singular development of the Soviet State: they were undone just because of the superior positions they had intrigued their way into. In spite of all their organizational loyalty and personal zeal, in spite of their doing every-thing the organization way, they could not keep pace with this particu-lar organization; they found themselves arrested, deported, and replaced by practically identical counterparts.

These top Party officials were arrested with kaleidoscopic rapidity; they gave the impression of relaying each other, sometimes to hold onto their offices for a very short time, partly because their successors were generally corruptible careerists themselves and often exacerbated their own subordinates, extending the scope of the vicious circle.

The Red Partisans were for many years a heroic category in the Soviet Union – it was they who waged guerrilla warfare in the rear of the White armies during the Civil War. They had been given privileges of all kinds, special rations, etc. But even though the phrase is regarded as an honour to this day in the Soviet Union, the whole organization, both its leaders and nearly all its members, were arrested, beginning with 1936, and accused of counter-revolutionary conspiracy.

The same goes for the organization of the former political convicts of the Tsarist period, who had done forced labour (*katorga*) and like the Red Partisans were regarded as Soviet heroes. They also confessed with relative ease: they had not been trained for Bolshevik interrogations by the relatively idyllic conditions of Tsarist exile and imprisonment.

As far as the army was concerned, two main categories of officers were encompassed by the decapitation linked to the execution of Tukhachevsky and the other generals: pre-revolutionary officers like Tukhachevsky himself, and working-class officers who had made their way in the Revolution and the Civil War.

Taken together, these categories represented the whole of the political intelligentsia and the summits of the Party, the State, the army, and the Political Police itself.

By the time the Comb-out was in full swing, membership in the Political Police was an objective characteristic of the most dangerous kind: the higher the rank, the greater the danger.

In 1937 alone more than 3,000 operational officers of the Political Police were killed,[6] including Molchanov, who had handled the interrogations for the first two Charades, two of Yagoda's deputies, and Yagoda himself, in the third Charade. Their children were simply abandoned on the street. The flats of the Political Police officials who had been killed were sealed; no one dared take the children in.

Yezhov and Stalin had to be extremely careful in enticing Political Police officials on foreign assignments back to the Soviet Union: though the service as a whole was soon thrown into a panic, the officers abroad were kept calm by not having their department touched for a long time. Meanwhile they would be called back, especially if they had wives and children in the Soviet Union, given a vacation – from which they would write to tell friends how well everything was going – and then seemingly given some other assignment; in the now classic manner they would be removed from the train at the first stop, taken by car to gaol and killed.

Some forty officers were called back to the Soviet Union in the summer of 1937:[7] only two refused to comply.

Ignace Reiss, one of the last idealists in the Political Police, broke with the regime in July 1937 and tried to escape; his assassination (3–4 September 1937) was organized so rapidly by the Political Police abroad that he couldn't even write the revelations he had been planning.

Walter Krivitsky, the Political Police resident in Holland, had been working in army intelligence until 1935; when called back he fled to Paris with his wife and young son. He was saved only because there had been such a scandal in France about the kidnapping (23 September 1937) of a former Tsarist general (Miller) by Soviet agents that it was considered inopportune to kill Krivitsky in France. He was killed a few years later (1941) in Washington, D.C., though not before he had managed to write a memoir.

Thus, while the Political Police as a whole was raked through very thoroughly, the Foreign Department, under Slutsky, was handled with kid gloves, with a maximum of concealment. But by the beginning of 1938, since most of the old Political Police officers were back in the Soviet Union, there was no need for Slutsky to be kept alive; he was killed in his turn (17 February 1938).

The working out of these principles of arrest was sometimes a little schematic. For instance, one prisoner was a Soviet agent who had come back to Russia after spending eight years in a Rumanian jail on charges of espionage; on his return he was instantly arrested by the Political Police as a *Rumanian* spy, together with the chief of his department in the Soviet espionage service who had sent him abroad in the first place.[8]

In fact, nearly all senior espionage officials were arrested as soon as they came back to the Soviet Union.

The loss of manpower through the arrest of the top personnel in the Political Police had curious effects. At the beginning of 1938 the Political Police still had generals or at the very least colonels as heads of departments. But it was impossible to promote people fast enough to keep up with the arrests of senior officials. There was a steady decline down to majors, captains and lieutenants as department heads. By the middle of 1939 it was routine for interrogations to be carried on by sergeants in positions that in 1937 would have been held by majors at the least.

All the prisoners had seen this process for themselves:[9] during the course of only three years they saw men who had been junior assistants, not even lieutenants, become department heads. Someone gaoled for several years might learn that ten or twelve examiners who had interrogated him had themselves been arrested. Two prisoners[10] outlasted more than ten of their examiners; one of them more than twelve, including the examining magistrate who had had him arrested.

This rapid turnover meant that inexperienced, youthful men of provincial origins would be put in charge of cases whose backgrounds they could not know, not even how the confessions had originally been obtained, and were ignorant to a large extent of the unusual circumstances prevailing before their arrival. Thus the bulk of the youthful, ignorant, and provincial examining magistrates were convinced of the guilt of the 'enemies of the people', i.e., of the authenticity of their confessions.

The Political Police officials were nearly always charged with high treason; expecting to be executed at any moment, they were generally quite twitchy. Once in gaol themselves they were perfectly pleasant – quiet, unassuming, and even comradely, though they never revealed any secrets. Other prisoners had no hard feelings towards them; any vindictiveness was due to special circumstances.

They were treated by their successors much the same as other prisoners, but more harshly. They did not share the optimism that was often common in the gaols; they were, in particular, exceedingly reluctant to confess, since they were naturally more familiar with what lay ahead of them.

Most curiously, they usually admitted that their faith in the Soviet regime had been completely unshaken until their arrest; they used to think of the prisoners, however obvious the legendary aspect of their confessions, as at least *potentially* enemies of the people. Consequently, on first being arrested they thought their own arrests were mere *mis-*

understandings; when allowed to they would write complaints to their own former colleagues now in the role of examiners. There was in fact a very widespread attitude on the part of all these innocent officials that it simply could not happen to *them*: since they were innocent they wouldn't be touched. They realized only gradually that the prisoners they themselves had interrogated were altogether innocent. This peculiar guilelessness explains the voluntary return of so many Political Police officials from abroad.

Apart from the usual guarantees of faithfulness extracted from any Soviet agent working abroad, such as family hostages, small children and so on, this trustfulness was the one overriding consideration that explains why so many experienced, intelligent, hard-headed Political Police officers serving abroad did not break with the regime and flee. Many of them really thought that by going back they would be demonstrating their personal loyalty to and faith in Stalin, who *therefore* would spare them.

The pulverization of the Old Bolsheviks, the Party, the State, and the Political Police was no more than the spearhead of the terror directed at the population as a whole.

Since the population as a whole could not be wiped out, the means of terrorization revolved around the visible summits of society. These were conceived of not only from a political, or institutional point of view, as in the case of the great organisms just enumerated, but by using social function as a criterion.

'Specialists' were decimated. Foremost were the railwaymen, traditionally considered the working-class *élite*. They had always been relatively well-paid, had been well organized in trades unions even before the putsch, and had the high morale of a real caste, often linked to each other by marriage. Though most of the railwaymen had at first been opposed to the Bolsheviks, by the time that all political dissidence was wiped out after the putsch, and as Soviet industrialization staggered forward, the railway system had become crucial.

Though it was not quite so dangerous an objective characteristic as high-ranking officerdom, membership in the People's Commissariat for Transport greatly increased the liability to arrest.

Since 'wrecking' was the most realistic element of all accusations during the Deep Comb-out, it was only natural, during the expansion of the industrialized economy, for all accidents, defects, blunders, etc. to be uniformly interpreted as sabotage, and since these figured more frequently on the great railways, it was equally natural for more railwaymen to be arrested. While all railway accidents were generally interpreted as sabotage, they were generally hidden from public view as far as possible unless they could be made to serve some purpose in one of the Great Charades.

From Stalin's point of view, what had to be done was to break the morale of the transport organization, like that of the engineers shattered a few years before during the proto-Charades that involved the Industrial Party, the Shakhty wreckers and others. Since, like everything else, the railways were working inefficiently, the general policy of intimidation was applied to them too.

Nearly all senior transport administrators were arrested, as were the stationmasters of practically every station in the country. They all confessed to sabotage. Traffic grew even worse afterwards and brought about still more accidents that had to be interpreted as sabotage.

An illuminating case was that of about 40,000 railwaymen, together with their families and associated personnel, who had been stationed in Manchuria, under an agreement with the Chinese, until 1937.

These people figured in two quasi-fatal categories: their profession itself and the fact that they had been 'residing abroad'. When the Japanese had occupied Manchuria the railwaymen had been lauded to the skies as heroes by the Soviet press. Now they were nearly all to be stigmatized as Japanese spies; another charge for them to make a ritual confession to.[11]

The programme of industrialization had required the people to be intimidated; this had become routine, but after the Great Charades, the intimidation, which had been directed beforehand at pre-Soviet vestiges, had to take in everybody. Beforehand – in the early thirties – there were still very few Soviet-trained technicians; in this era, with its show trials aimed at technicians, the sentences had been relatively mild. Many of those tried had been released afterwards and sent back to work in an almost normal way; many had even been promoted. Under Yezhov these same people were all sent back to gaol again, especially those who at that time in the early thirties had refused to confess. This time, they were accompanied by a great many Soviet-trained personnel who had meanwhile come of age and had constantly been eulogized in countless official publications.

It is a curious psychological sidelight on the Deep Comb-out that this time the older ones tended to confess at once, while the younger, trained in Soviet conditions, often showed some resistance.

The biggest single objective characteristic of the Deep Comb-out consisted of any connexion whatever with a foreign country.

Since this group was so far-flung, and was the principal pillar of the attack on 'Trotskyism' – established in the first Charade as synonymous with espionage – it must be subdivided. It contained many real foreigners, including incompetent workers, mostly from Germany, who had come to the Soviet Union under the pretext of idealism but in reality looking for easy jobs. Then there were idealistic helpers in the cause of socialist construction, and a great many political refugees, not always Communists. In addition Moscow housed the members and staff of the Communist International and associated organizations like the Trades-Union International (Profintern) and the Peasants' International (Krestintern). Those sympathetic to the Soviet regime were in acute danger.

In fact, the Stalin regime distrusted most of all any loyalty based on conviction; it favoured material interests and fear.

A foreign specialist who simply kept insisting on getting more money and putting up increasingly extravagant demands was in no danger; the worst that would happen would be his expulsion. The older generation of the Russian *élite* (scientists and scholars), completely alien to the regime, was also relatively safe. What was suspect was idealism *as such*.

Many people who had fought for Republican Spain came to the Soviet Union after Franco's victory; they were immediately labelled Franco agents and wound up in gaol. After Hitler occupied Czechoslovakia the Czechs immediately became German agents.

A case is reported[12] of a Czech confectioner who had been in Russia since the First World War. In gaol, he was forced to confess that even before the collapse of the Russian monarchy he had, as a Czech, been recruited by the German intelligence service to spy against the Soviet Union – i.e., a national of a non-existent state was recruited to spy against another non-existent state on the long-range assumption that the first state would eventually be occupied by Germany!

Though there were no Japanese in the Soviet Union, there were a great many Chinese. They had come after the outbreak of the First World War, when the Tsarist government had recruited some 2,000,000 of them for timber work. Some had stayed on, marrying Russians and sometimes enlisting in the Red Army; they were to be found in many occupations, including the laundry business, where their abilities enabled them to survive. They were all accused of being Japanese spies. Their morale in gaol was remarkably high: they never lost their dignity and were always extraordinarily clean, generous, fair-minded and tranquil.[13]

The Assyrians were a small community scattered, like the Armenians, throughout the Soviet Union; they were generally bootblacks. They were mostly turned into Turkish spies or sometimes agents of British imperialism – they had promoted their intrigues by cleaning shoes with poor polish, to provoke dissatisfaction with Soviet-made shoes!

There were also many individual cases against completely random foreigners in the Soviet Union for any one of a variety of reasons. A curious case is reported of a Viennese café-owner who had invented some kind of coffee-machine: his Left-wing clientele in Vienna had predicted a big market for it in the Soviet Union, and he had made a trip to Moscow as an ordinary tourist to show it to various government departments.[14] He never quite grasped what had happened to him.

It did German Jews no good at all to be Jews; their position was summed up by an examining magistrate: 'Jewish refugees are Hitler's agents abroad.'[15] Indeed, as the result of an agreement with the Nazis after the signing of the German–Soviet pact, all Germans in prisons and camps were taken to Moscow – between September 1939 and spring of 1940 – and a large proportion then turned over to the Gestapo. They included Jews and anti-Nazi refugees, many who had taken Soviet citizenship, and also many deprived of German citizenship. The Jews and other anti-Nazis were put in German prisons and concentration camps, including Auschwitz.

Most skilled foreign workers were simply arrested; Germans, Austrians and Poles (followed by Italians) were in the greatest danger. Whole blocs of flats assigned to foreigners were cleaned out *en masse*.

A category even bigger than that of real foreigners was that of foreign agents. This was immensely capacious. The sub-division of native foreigners took in everyone born abroad, including those of Russian descent born in the Tsarist provinces lost to Russia after the First World War, e.g., Poland, Finland, the Baltic States. These people were often completely russified, unable to speak a word of the foreign language they were supposed to be associated with.

Latvians always had a special position: they had come during the First World War, partly when the big industrial installations were transferred from Riga, and partly with the retreat of the Red Army in 1920. They were important in the Civil War – even more than the Chinese – and also played a special role in the secret services of the Police and of the Red Army. Now, in the Deep Comb-out, all Latvians were accused of being members either of Trotskyite or of nationalist organizations.

Since accusations had to be contrived on the basis of fantasy there was often a sort of logical extrapolation:

A Latvian fitter from a locomotive factory, accused of subversion, found himself confessing that under the orders of the Latvian Secret Police he had been promoting a Greater Latvia, which was supposed to include a large portion of European Russia as well as Moscow.[16]

The *logical* character of this is evident: since there was in fact no such organization, its functions were deduced from the consideration of the phrase Latvian nationalism, i.e., what *could* such an organization be working for?

There was for some reason a huge proportion of Latvians in the foreign department of the Political Police; thus, as people began to be arrested on the basis of their objective characteristics these people were recalled and gaoled, either because they were of foreign origin, or had been abroad, or were in the Political Police itself, so that there were far more Soviet agents in the gaols than agents of foreign powers.

Soviet citizens who had travelled abroad, scientists who had gone on behalf of various institutions to Germany, England, the United States and so on, were in great danger, as were engineers and members of Soviet buying and selling missions.

Many of these were, of course, completely dedicated Communists, working abroad for the Soviet Union in a variety of ways. An important engineer is reported as giving a lecture to the whole of a big cell on engineering abroad; he had just come back from America, where he had signed contracts for millions of dollars for the construction of a rolling-mill; he explained to his cellmates that the lecture had originally been intended for the commissar of his department.

Industrial relations with foreign countries were precarious. The government organization known as VOKS, which handled cultural relations abroad, arranged visits of foreign scholars, promoted propaganda for Soviet achievements and managed international congresses and foreign organizations of intellectuals, was suddenly charged by the Political Police with being no more than an espionage network. The whole staff, accused of having been recruited by the German, Polish, Rumanian or Japanese espionage services, were arrested out of hand.

Anyone participating in any international congress (physiologists, geologists, astronomers, etc.) ended up in gaol. Any connexion with anything abroad was dangerous: anyone corresponding with foreign countries; ordinary people getting presents from relatives; scientists with colleagues abroad were all in mortal peril.

More than a million Russian prisoners had been captured by Germans and Austrians during the First World War. Having been 'abroad', they were natural targets for a charge of having been 'recruited' by the German intelligence service. In 1938 ordinary workers and peasants from collective farms began turning up in cells. They were utterly baffled: they had been prisoners of war. The former German, Polish and Austrian prisoners of war who had stayed on in Russia and generally married Russian women were arrested almost uniformly as spies.

In 1936 the Soviet government began systematically wiping out all

German settlements by arresting nearly all male adults of collective villages and accusing them of espionage for Germany. The same thing happened to nearly every Polish, Ukrainian and White Russian family near the Polish border.

The increasing centralization of the Soviet State during the thirties endangered all national minorities; during the Deep Comb-out charges of nationalist conspiracy became common.

The Jews were in a particularly vulnerable position because of the total proscription of Jewish nationalism (Zionism), condemned in the Soviet Union since its inception. There was no overt anti-Semitism as such during the thirties, though Jews were gradually and quietly removed from the summits of the State and Party, while Jewish Political Police officials or Jews connected with the armed forces seemed more likely to be arrested than parallel non-Jews. People would say: 'He's not a Party man and not a Jew – so why has he been arrested?'[17]

The combination of governmental centralization and the necessity for processing the population resulted in the revival of an institution. The mass deportation of ethnic minorities was revived by the Soviet Union for many peoples on its western and Korean borders. Bulgarians and Greeks, for instance, were arrested *en masse* as spies, though for some reason the Bulgarians were charged with spying not for Bulgaria but for Rumania or Germany.

With all these mass arrests it might have been thought that a good opportunity had been provided to catch some real spies. Yet just as real facts – authentic or contrived – had been more trouble to make use of than they were worth in the composition of the libretti for the Great Charades and for the interrogations during the Deep Comb-out, so the question of whether a prisoner was or was not a real spy turned out to be a mere triviality.

Border-crossers were naturally arrested, and equally naturally accused of espionage; it is even possible, though of course beyond enquiry, that there were some real spies among them. This is not wholly unlikely: the Deep Comb-out took in such huge numbers of people that it must, in fact, have snatched up a few bona-fide spies as well. Because of this, even though it has always been difficult to recruit spies among the Soviet population itself – the morale of the 'former people', the aristocracy and the bourgeoisie having been broken once and for all in the wake of the Civil War – one can assume that there were *some* spies in such a big country.

The very generality protected any real spies there may have been; with millions of people confessing to bogus activities it would have been impossible to distinguish between real spies and others. Even if a few real ones had been taken out of espionage their genuine activities could not have been uncovered. Obligatory false confessions had to be accepted, hence the false confessions even of real spies had the effect of involving mostly innocent people, thus hiding in their turn whatever real accomplices they might have had.

There was a feeling in the concentration camps and cells that some of the border-crossers who were picked up were genuine spies; they seem to have been ostracized completely, even though the crimes that they confessed to were just the same as those that so many millions had been gaoled for. The prisoners made a clear distinction between forced bogus confessions and forced true confessions made by people caught in the act.[18]

The definition of espionage in the Soviet Union is very broad: it is defined as the communication of any fact whatever that has not been formally published. The prices of goods, for instance, remarks about their quality, remarks about relations between individuals in the government or the Party and their political attitudes, may be called espionage if passed on to foreigners, or for that matter to anyone who might *see* a foreigner. Telling someone the lay-out of a city, or the name of someone in charge of some collectivized unit, might be turned to use in making out a passport for a foreign agent. Thus, in effect, espionage is what is meant in other countries only by military espionage.

A totalitarian state assumes that it can, by fiat, withhold all information from anyone, to a degree that in a non-totalitarian state would be regarded as merely utopian. This may account for the credulity with regard to primitive fabrications that in a different context would be evidence of paranoia.

But just because this attitude was so pervasive, minor acts of espionage were not a really adequate lever to bring about arrests: they were simply too common and hence, for the purposes of the Deep Comb-out, too banal. Something more positive was generally required for formal charges.

What was dangerous, by and large, was noticeability – prominence very nearly as such. The phrase 'former people', for instance, referred to anyone of any prominence whatever before the 1917 putsch: always a bad thing, and an inevitable tag in all documents, it constituted a mortal peril during the Deep Comb-out. The same fate, curiously enough, was likely to befall anyone associated with celebrities: they were in special danger and were often arrested even before the celebrities themselves.

If amusement can be found in this macabre period, the confusion arising out of the similarity of Russian names – the universal use of often identical patronymics – led to cases of mistaken identity. The technique of extracting confessions being what it was, such people, however mistakenly arrested, found themselves producing the same confessions assigned to the real culprits before the mistake was discovered.

As the Deep Comb-out kept deepening, the geometrical progression implicit in its mechanism very soon reached a limit.

The geometrical progression itself had evolved out of an element in police procedure that might be thought of as quasi-technical.

Originally the tormenting of the prisoners had been intended – in the case of the politically-minded ones – to force them to reveal the names of others who might genuinely have shared their views. From Stalin's vantage-point it was views as such that were reprehensible; the mere fact of having views to begin with implied potential dissidence.

In the beginning, accordingly, the savaging of the prisoners produced a huge crop of people who from the official point of view were guilty of *something* in this very special sense; then, as every one named in this stage of the breaking-down process was arrested in his turn and broken down, the list began to grow.

This method of increasing the number of victims had a mechanical element that was quite independent of the reality of the views held, whatever they were: the mere process of making people confess to the names of their 'accomplices' under duress meant that the limit of the real view-holders was reached very quickly, and since the duress continued the names began to overflow at a geometrical rate. Genuine ideological links became blurred to the vanishing point: as the duress grew far more ferocious, people began to play up to the heartlessness of the interrogators and to use that playing up as a form of resistance.

When the very procedure was travestied, and prisoners began incriminating everyone they could remember, from corpses to famously slavish Stalinists, it was clear that the machine was being circumvented; it was a sort of *grève de zèle*, a strike of overfulfilment; since it had been built into the routine procedure and fortified by a growing terror, there was no way out. The only thing that could, in fact, halt the automatic operation of this geometrical progression was fiat from above.

Thus the technique based on the denunciation of more and more people by more and more people finally reached a stage in this progression that took in some eight or nine million people. The next wave of accomplices would have involved literally the entire population.

The Deep Comb-out stopped abruptly. It simply came to an end – unforeseen and unexplained. What was perhaps for Stalin a minor tactical problem was solved by replacing his creature, Yezhov, by L. P. Beria, who had become conspicuous in the Georgian Political Police and then in the Party machine.

Beria had been made Yezhov's assistant in July 1938. On December 1938 Yezhov himself was dropped, with no explanation; a few months later his name disappeared from the roster of the Central Committee; he was arrested. It is not known whether he was killed. He was rumoured to have died insane; in the *Great Soviet Encyclopedia*[19] he is referred to as an enemy of the people together with his predecessor Yagoda and his successor Beria.

Around the same time another, and as it turned out final, trial took place in the small Moldavian Republic, tucked away in the south-west of the Soviet Union. The head of the local Political Police and four subordinates were court-martialed on charges of arresting innocent people and extracting bogus confessions by torture.

The charges were, for once, accurate. Even so they were compounded with other charges in the characteristic style of the Deep Comb-out. When the Political Police officers confessed they naturally took pains to keep their own organization out of it: they, too, were merely obeying the instructions of counter-revolutionary organizations. They were found guilty and duly shot.

Nevertheless, though these men had simply been doing exactly what the whole Political Police apparatus had been doing for two-and-a-half years, this Charade broke the pattern: killing these obscure officials seems to have been Stalin's way of calling the whole thing off.

The procedure followed in this rather soft-pedalled conclusion to the Deep Comb-out epitomizes in a curious way the bizarre piece of illogic – quite unnoticed at the time – that highlights the obsessive ritualization of the Comb-out.

When the examiners were arrested in their turn as enemies of the people, no question was ever raised as to the guilt of those whom they had been examining. Granted the criminality of the examiners and the presumption that they had themselves been engaged in sabotaging the State by malfeasance, one might have thought that those they had undone might be rehabilitated.

Nothing of the sort ever happened. No evidence was reviewed, for instance, in the light of the examiner's criminality, nor did his own maleficence ever weaken the validity of any confession extracted by such an enemy of the people. The people still in gaol on the basis of the very confessions whose falseness their examining magistrates were now being shot for did not benefit in the slightest.

The subsidiary further point that they had all been doing this in any case on orders from above was not even mentioned.

In this respect the conduct of the Great Charades and the Deep Comb-out was merely typical of the regime throughout its existence, especially under Stalin. The fact that the ancient notion of the scapegoat was used to bring the Comb-out itself to a close is one more piece of macabre irony.

After a large-scale programme had been applied and had in countless instances misfired, those instances would then be ascribed to irresponsible – and during the Comb-out – criminal individuals. The collectivization programme had been consummated at untold sacrifices; an example was then made of individual officials accused of an excess of zeal or misuse of authority at the very least, and later on, in harmony with the over-all pattern of the Charades and Comb-outs, also accused of sabotage.

So, in the final phase of the Comb-out, the very technique of the Comb-out itself was passed off as sabotage: the extravagances of the whole period of terrorism were themselves laid at the door of 'Trotskyites'! This word, already in general use for anyone described as an enemy, traitor, spy and villain, was now to explain away the explanation, just as the monstrosities of the industrialization process had found a scapegoat in the Trotskyites. The Party could still boast of having rectified the crimes committed by enemies of the people.

The military were an exception; they went on being combed out, though at a slower rate. Arrests and killings reached their peak, like the Deep Comb-out in general, at the end of 1937 and the beginning of 1938, but the military kept being churned up by the characteristic phenomena of the Deep Comb-out – arrests, gaolings, killings – throughout 1938 and later, even after the disappearance of Yezhov. A senior military officer was shot a fortnight before the Nazi invasion in 1941.[20]

Nevertheless the terror as a whole was over – for the time being, it seemed, with no further trials and with no mass arrests. The authority of the Political Police itself was not changed in any way, nor was the system of forced labour for the time being changed at all. The terror itself was never officially denied, nor were its victims systematically and formally rehabilitated, except much later, well after's Stalin death, when batches and driblets were rehabilitated by implication.

In March 1939 the first Party Congress to take place in more than five years laid down an official scab over the gaping wounds of the Charades and the Comb-out. This Eighteenth Congress was a more remarkable display of total passivity than even its predecessors. The principal note struck was again the eulogizing of Stalin. The stenographic report of the Congress is packed with doggerel ostensibly gathered by the delegates from all over the country to sing the praises of the Locomotive.

Stalin, with his characteristic, almost epigrammatically flat prose, said that there had been, it was true, some 'serious errors', and, for that matter, even more 'than might be expected'. But he continued: 'Undoubtedly we shall have no further need of resorting to the method of mass purges. Nevertheless the purge of 1933–6 was unavoidable and its results, on the whole, were beneficial'.[21] This was the signal – though doubtless of problematical value – that the terror was really and truly finished with. (It is of some interest to note Stalin's dates in this curious promise of his: the 'purge of 1933–6' was as nothing compared with the *real* atrocities of 1937–8.)

Zhdanov, one of the three main speakers in addition to Stalin and Molotov, castigated the local Party organizations for their obtuseness and overzealousness: he was very sharp with them because of the bogus evidence, the needless exclusion of countless innocent people from the Party following the exclusion of one spy: outrageously, for instance, 64 per cent of one Party organization had been kicked out.

The only concession made by the Congress on this question was to write a few more provisions preserving the right of appeal against being expelled from the Party, which meant more or less nothing, even though the resolution voted by the Congress pointed out that the Comb-out was ineffective for two reasons: the Party had not caught the real enemy infiltrators, after all, whereas the massive method applied meant some of the 'rights of party members' had been 'restricted'.

In any case there was not the smallest shadow of an Opposition at this Eighteenth Congress nor the slightest question of Stalin's paramountcy. The Politburo contained no one who could have dreamt of questioning Stalin's slightest remark.

The abrupt ending of the Comb-out involved a change of control of the Political Police and a renovation of its personnel; neither its function nor its structure was changed in the least. Many of the people who were released when the Comb-out ended in 1938 were picked up again when the Nazis attacked in 1941; this time they vanished once and for all, though their cases had often been conducted by interrogators who had meanwhile been arrested themselves.

The Political Police remained in the hands of Beria, a thoroughly reliable servant who in 1935 had demonstrated his pliability by recreating to Stalin's taste the history of Georgian Bolshevism.

With Beria the reign of terror continued, but only against the summits of the regime: the mass Comb-outs and killings came to an end. Beria did away with the device of the Charade and simply shot all members of the Central Committee and superior army officers after secret trials without bothering about any confessions by the victims. He sometimes shot such people even after they had been released by the Political Police.

Though Stalin had Beria stop the mass killing and concentrate on the elimination of Central Committee members, top Political Police officers, and superior army officers, Beria zealously carried on another kind of Comb-out.

He exiled whole ethnic groups to Siberia and Kazakhstan – Chechens, Ingush, Karachai, Balkars, Kalmyks, Crimean Tatars and Volga Germans. A whole series of ethnic minorities were torn up by the roots and banished, as were sections of the Baltic population. Khrushchev's Secret Speech in 1956, commenting on these 'monstrous' acts committed on Stalin's initiative, added that the 'Ukrainians escaped this fate only because there were so many of them; there would not have been room enough for them all elsewhere'.[22]

Stalin's onslaught on the Party is graphically illustrated by the condition of the summits. In 1934 the Central Committee comprised seventy-one full members and sixty-eight candidate-members: of these 139 people, ten had been killed or gaoled by the spring of 1937; some ninety-eight had been arrested or shot (according to Khrushchev) 'mostly in 1937–8'. At the very least, some ninety of the topmost Party officials had been got rid of after the February-March plenum of 1937. they included foremost figures in the apparatus of the Party, in the economic structure, in the government machine, and in the army.[23]

Of the army people, in addition to Marshal Tukhachevsky and a number of other topflight generals, Gamarnik, Yakir, the Commander-in-Chief of the Land Forces, and Marshal Bluecher, Commander-in-Chief of the Far East, a vast throng of subordinate officers were wiped out.

All Civil War veterans, with very few exceptions, were killed. Many more senior officers were killed during the Deep Comb-out than throughout the four-year war against the Nazis. By May of 1940 about one-fifth of the unit and sub-unit commanders were missing; 68 per cent of platoon and company level officers had had only a five-month training course for junior lieutenants; by the summer of 1941, when the war broke out, only 7 per cent of officers had received any advanced military education at all; 37 per cent had not finished intermediate training; 75 per cent of the officers had held their positions for less than a year.[24]

Soviet official histories show that all commanders of military districts, all corps commanders, practically all brigade and divisional commanders, about half of all regimental commanders, and all but one fleet commander were removed, most of them killed. By the time the Deep Comb-out had dwindled away, fully one-third of the officer corps – including three of the five marshals, all eleven Deputy Commissars of

Defence, and thirteen of the fifteen generals had been removed, most of them killed. It has been estimated that the total number of losses amounted to about half the total officers' corps – or about 35,000 officers altogether. 90 per cent of all generals were killed; 80 per cent of all colonels. 30,000 officers below the rank of colonel were killed.[25]

During 1937–8 army officers were constantly being arrested, though the higher officers seem to have been purged in two big batches, the second one being eliminated after the middle of 1938, perhaps in order to allow some effort at replacement to be made.

It is not difficult, by referring to the actual figures published by the Central Committee of the Party, to calculate the number of Communists who were wiped out. Of a total of 1,966 voting and non-voting delegates *more than half* (1,108) had been gaoled on accusations of counter-revolution.[26] Stalin himself, in his report to the Eighteenth Party Congress in 1939, circulated an estimate of his own, saying that the purge of 'Party members and candidates which began as early as 1933 . . . was continued until May 1935. It was further decided to cease enrolment of new members in the Party and it was duly stopped right up to September 1936 . . . Moreover, as a result of the dastardly murder of Comrade Kirov, which proved that the Party contained many suspicious characters, it was decided to carry out a check . . . of Party documents, both of which operations were only concluded by September 1936 . . . . The present Eighteenth Congress represents about 1,600,000 Party members, i.e., 270,000 members less than the Seventeenth Party Congress'.[27]

For Stalin to have said this openly, at a time when the consequences of the Deep Comb-out were visible throughout Soviet life, is a vivid demonstration of the potency of a controlled press. Stalin could produce this bland misstatement even at a time when the Soviet press, both national and local, indicated beyond question that the really virulent stage of the Deep Comb-out had not even begun by 1936, that it had taken on dimensions that could soberly be called universal throughout 1937, and that it did not even reach its climax until the third Charade of 1938 (Bukharin, Rykov and others).

Even on the face of it Stalin's figure of a loss of 270,000 Communists, matter-of-factly presented to the cowed Eighteenth Congress, was quite bogus. In his simple calculation of the figure (by deducting the membership of the Eighteenth Congress from that of the Seventeenth) he omitted two cardinal points:

The Party rolls represented by the Seventeenth Party Congress also included almost a million candidate members (935,298) who automatically became full members in the second half of 1934 (after enrolment was resumed).[28] Hence, before enrolment was stopped again in May

1935, the Party would have had 2,809,786, without even including any members admitted from the ranks of new candidates (who were supposed to remain in this status at this time for between one and two years).[29] Moreover the great bulk of the Party members at the Eighteenth Party Congress were not included at all among the members represented at the Seventeenth Party Congress, i.e., they had come into the Party *after* the resumption of enrolment in November 1936.

Stalin was comparing figures with non-comparable time-limits. When the figures and the periods of time are made commensurate it is obvious that:

> Seventeenth Party Congress (members as of 1 May 1935)
> 2,809,786
> minus 1,588,852 members as of 1 March 1939
> ———————
> = 1,220,934 members purged and liquidated (at the time a synonymous operation).

There was a striking increase in the absolute and relative number of Communist Party members ploughed under between 1934 and 1939 (the era of the Deep Comb-out) and all those eliminated beforehand. The official figures are unmistakeable:[30]

1917–22	219,630
1925–33	800,000
1933–4	362,429
1934–9	1,220,934
	2,602,993

Of these only the first figures refer to the period before Stalin's primacy. It was the only purge that could be called voluntary since it was based merely on the re-registration of all Communist Party members in 1921. Anyone who did not re-register was simply said to have voluntarily resigned. The figure of 800,000 refers to the first clean-ups conducted by Stalin: those of 1925, 1926 and 1930. The same list shows that the clean-up of 1933 resulting in the expulsion of some 362,429 is almost the same number as the total Party membership of 1922 (401,000), the figure when Stalin became General Secretary.

Sociologically, quite apart from their numerical weight, it is clear what the figures mean. The whole of the Old Party had been wiped out; a new Party had taken its place.

At the Eighteenth Party Congress, when Stalin said that the Party had been 'able to appoint over 500,000 young Bolsheviks to leading posts in the State and Party',[31] half a million new jobs had plainly not been created for them; they simply stepped into the shoes of all those Party members who had been removed – all secretaries of local committees, all members of governments and central committees of ethnic republics, all managers of the various state enterprises, Red Army specialists in administration and so on.

More specifically, the Central Committee elected by the Seventeenth Party Congress was utterly wiped out:

		By 1939
Full Central Committee members	*Natural causes*	*Liquidated or otherwise punished*
71	4	51
Candidate members		
68		63

Furthermore, of the full members and most of the candidate members of the Central Committee of 1934, those who had been removed by 1939 had been in the Party since before the 1917 putsch.

With respect to the more obscure victims of the Deep Comb-out – the toiling masses! – it is, of course, impossible to achieve much precision. Yet the numbers of victims were so vast that rough statistics are revealing enough.

There was an incredible degree of overcrowding in the Soviet prisons during the Stalin terror. This overcrowding, though in some ways the most excruciatingly painful aspect of life in prison, was not designed as part of the torment, but was a consequence of the muddle bound to attend the unprecedented numbers of people imprisoned. The overcrowding, combined with the knowledge of the number of prisons in a given area, the average period of detention, the term in gaol before a prisoner was removed to a camp, the general figures for the population of the area a prisoner came from and the duration of the Comb-out itself, laid the groundwork for calculating the gross number of people arrested. The estimates show a surprising harmony – between 5 and 10 per cent of the total population.

There were some variations in these averages between those for the individual Soviet republics – Ukraine, Armenia and some others – and those for central Russia; also, the big cities and towns had a higher yield than the countryside. There were some differences based on class and profession: the intelligentsia, the Red Army officers' corps and the railway workers had far more arrests proportionately than other groups.

All the figures, adding up to an estimated grand total, were arrived at by calculating these proportions, on the basis of the knowledge of the many Political Police functionaries who were eventually arrested themselves; the figures were supplemented by calculations made by the railway functionaries from some of the bigger stations; they gave a rough count of the number of people being carried in the prison trains that passed through their stations every day. There are, in any case, no major discrepancies between all these calculations.

Taking the Soviet population at the time to be about 150 million there were, accordingly, between 7,000,000 to 14,000,000 people held by the Political Police around the height of the Comb-out in 1936–8.

Alexander Weissberg, one of the survivors, a gifted scientist, reports his method for calculating the numbers involved in the Deep Comb-out. Simple, and surely basically sound, these figures accord, in addition, with all other sources.[32]

Weissberg was gaoled for some time in the Central Prison for Kharkov and its environs (Kholodnaya Gora); by checking the numbered receipts given each prisoner (for money and for clothing) it was possible to see how many prisoners had been taken in a given period of time. Since his prison was the central one for the area a great many prisoners passed through it on their way elsewhere; they had had their examinations before. Thus, by the time Weissberg left his own prison (20 February 1939) he had calculated that during the preceding two years about 5.5 per cent of the total population of the Kharkov area had been imprisoned.

He and his fellow-prisoners in Kharkov central prison learned that the same basis of calculation had been applied in all central gaols throughout the Soviet Union, with the same approximate results in every case, between 5.5 and 6 per cent of the total population. The first figure establishes a sum total of nine million people arrested.

Weissberg then deducted about two million for people charged with criminal offences. This was a special category: it was not the ordinary number of people actually brought up on some specific criminal charge during this time, but a special category established by Yezhov. He had done this in order to slow down the drainage of skilled workers who had also been winnowed out on the usual charges of 'subversion', and still keep up the flow of manpower to the forced labour camps. These criminals might not have been criminals at all, but simply people arrested years before on some criminal charge who had served their time and had been unmolested by the police since then. Their names still figured in the police dossiers.

Such men did not come before a court at all. They were simply drafted off to the forced labour camps in great numbers: the sentence was either three or five years' 'correctional labour'. (Weissberg never found out the reason for the difference in the sentences.)

Each police district was allocated a certain quota, which the Political Police chief was responsible for. Sometimes the contingent laid down in the arrest plans decided on by the central authorities, could not be filled; for instance, if the people listed in the dossiers at headquarters were no longer there or for any one of a number of reasons. In a case like that it was naturally up to the Police chief of the district to fill the quota somehow; he would do this by picking up ordinary people on one pretext or another. In this way the demands made by the quota system often involved people quite mechanically, without even a bogus political pretext.

The calculations of numbers made on the basis of the numbered clothing and cash receipts could be confirmed by other methods, such as checking with the kitchen staff as to the number of bread rations prepared at any given time: it was also possible to determine the average sojourn at the central prison of prisoners on their way elsewhere; the percentage was the same, and coincided with the percentages arrived at with such general methods at central prisons all over the country. When the Political Police itself began to put its own personnel through the mangling-machine, by the summer of 1938, the figures could be checked with them.

This general method of calculation produces a total of seven million political prisoners for the two years 1937–8. If a million is added to cover politicals who were already in prison during 1936 (based on estimates made by Weissberg from what he was told by Political Police officials who themselves were arrested) there is a general figure of eight million politicals for the two-and-a-half years of the Deep Comb-out. The slight rectifications that might be made for duplication of names in the lists – because of repeated trips of the same prisoners through the central depot prisons – may be considered to be more than made up for by the existence of special prisons in Kharkov and other provincial capitals from which the prisoners were sent off to forced labour camps with no detours. There were, for instance, special prisons for railwaymen.

By the end of 1938, when the Deep Comb-out was substantially over (except for the sustained elimination of the military) Weissberg even records that 100,000 prisoners were set free.

Aware that the bloodletting meant a direct loss of manpower, Stalin took some steps to compensate for it. In March 1937 he sketched a new plan for the intensive training of Party functionaries, the main point of which was the preparation of replacements; second and third secretaries for instance, had to be put through a rapid course of training so that they could step into their bosses' shoes.

A general census was carried out, with tremendous fanfare, at the beginning of 1936: the results were never published. The official explanation was that the figures had been distorted by the usual saboteurs and criminals. But the Political Police estimated privately that the total for the country, including the prisoners in camps and gaols, came to 147,000,000 – i.e., for a decade there had been no net increase in the Soviet population. In other words, the birth-rate was just enough to balance the losses from the killing of the peasants and the mortality of the deportees.

The mass blood-letting had the most disastrous effects on the economy of the country as well as on its armed forces. The Soviet Union was radically weakened by the Comb-out at the very moment that it began frantically rearming against the threat of Hitler. Labour and materials were increasingly diverted into defence measures; factories making tractors and trains began turning out tanks; the building of new houses came to an end in favour of the construction of defence works.

There was a substantial decline in industrial production that may be traced directly to the Deep Comb-out, with the wholesale loss of trained workers from defence industries, factories and design centres. In 1939 there was a steep drop in the production of basic industrial categories (pig iron, steel, rolling metal) that was barely made up for by the time war broke out in 1941, when the level for 1938 was reached again. In 1940 the production of motor-cars and tractors had gone down by more than a quarter.[33]

The weakness of Russia as a result of the Comb-out, especially because of its disastrous effects on the Red Army, could be seen dramatically in the war against Finland, and even more strikingly in the collapse of the Red Armies during the first six months of the Nazi onslaught on Russia itself in 1941. The initial contact of the Russian peasants with the German armies led to wholesale surrender; it was an unqualified success for the Germans. The peasants, driven to despair by a decade of oppression, welcomed the Germans as liberators.

The Nazi colonial policy salvaged the Stalin regime: the Nazi humiliation of the peasants both as individuals and as Russians ('sub-human'), accompanied by wholesale shootings, whippings, and general enslavement, locked the Russian peasantry in the embrace of its own regime.

7
Why?

A traveller woke one morning to find himself entangled in the crown of an enormous tree. Seeing that he could not free himself, he settled down. 'Since I cannot adapt circumstances to my will, I adapt my will to circumstances – I choose to remain here.' (Muslim tale)

The strange situation outlined in the preceding pages is easy to sum up: it is hard to explain. If Stalin was not a maniac, why did he do it? Also, how *could* he do it?

The 'official' explanation was embedded in the Great Charades; in sophisticated forms it was espoused by pious partisans of the regime, who without believing the confessions accepted the general idea of a cleansing of anti-regime elements, either of the Tsarist past or of the turbulent period of the twenties that saw the emergence of the Stalin entourage.

Since such partisans reflected the Party view of the 'Masses' as being far too simple-minded to understand the grand Communist vision, they might also believe that there was something, after all, in the confessions, too. Once a gross rationale for the Comb-out was accepted, it was easy to explain away its excesses, like the atrocities of collectivization, as due to an excess of 'zeal'.

These same Masses produced their own explanations, in countless prison conversations: a collection of current theories was made by a couple of sophisticated prisoners.[1] They illuminate the spontaneous reactions to the Deep Comb-out, which from the point of view of any individual was, of course, like a tidal wave.

Many prisoners, though disturbed by the Charades and the Comb-out, remained enthralled by the official view of life; for them it was possible to believe in the essential rationality of what was happening even while disregarding the specific claims of the authorities.

One theory widely held among the pious Communists who flooded the gaols and camps was based on the assumption that while in the bourgeois world the penal code concerned only criminal behaviour, the youthful Soviet State, still in the grip of its growing pains, had to protect itself against *potential* crime and criminal states of mind.

Thus the Deep Comb-out forestalled, through foresight, the commission of such potential crimes. If someone is known to have incurable kleptomania, why wait for him actually to steal?

Similarly, friends chatting might be saying things in themselves harmless – quipping, reminiscing – but this might *point* to an anti-Soviet attitude that might evolve into readiness to commit a crime; especially in times of crisis, readiness was just a step away from action.

Hence wise guardians identify all those groups that might harbour such potential criminal possibilities; identification, initiated by the *seksots* and rounded out by the objective characteristics, determined the categories of people in whom a hostile attitude might be expected to evolve. If one knew that a whole group was very likely to break out in hostility to the State, it was best to emasculate the entire group.

This theory was thought to be confirmed by the far greater emphasis that was laid on the two cardinal recruitment questions – 'who recruited you?' and 'whom did you recruit?' – than on the details of the contrived legend.

In this view the principal aim of the Political Police was the sociology of the group, not its activities. The confession was supposed to create a pretext that could – later – be used to justify an arrest that would then be in accordance with the penal code. The crime inherent in the composition of a potentially hostile socio-political group was to be converted, later on, into a real crime.

This theory takes for granted the rationale of Stalin's manoeuvre; it accepts the innocence of the prisoners as far as their personal activities were concerned, as well as the utility of the fiction of personal responsibility as a way of enabling the Political Police to operate. It allowed pious Communists to give themselves a convincing explanation of the quirks that made it possible for innocent people, especially innocent functionaries of the Political Police, to be arrested while obviating the need to condemn the Soviet regime as such.

A variant of this theory explained why Party veterans and foreign Communists were especially hard hit. The change of attitude that led to a pact with Hitler could not be openly admitted; yet it was bound to lead to resistance among orthodox Communists. This resistance had to be nipped in the bud. Thus, in 1938 many prisoners were prophesying the Hitler-Stalin pact of 1939 *only* on the basis of the categories of arrests!

Another theory was also rooted in the official idea of 'vestiges': a poetic metaphor, it may be called the theory of the generation of the wilderness – Socialism was the Promised Land, Tsarist Russia was Egypt. All those who had seen Tsarism, who had seen foreign countries, who had dreamed of *pure* Socialism, had to die off in order to allow Stalin's bogus Socialism to be accepted as genuine.

Other prisoners resorted to the 'fascist plot'. This idea, aimed at Trotsky, simply projected the notion of plotting fascists into the generation of the Charades and Comb-out themselves: fascists had wormed their way into the summits of the State with the aim of destroying the regime from within. Thus the Great Charades were explained away on the basis of their own scripts!

This concept was clung to by many staunch Communists, who underwent the entire ordeal without losing their faith.

There was another unofficial Communist reaction – the labour force theory. It was the most popular theory in the prisons. It explained the countless arrests 'materialistically', as due to the need for manpower in remote areas, where people refused to go in spite of the lavish benefits. Since the masses were reluctant to sacrifice themselves, though that was their duty as Communists, the government simply had to force them. The theory was popular since it helped reconcile people to their sufferings and harmonized them with their Soviet faith. It did not explain why the workers on such great projects were called enemies of the people and not praised as heroes. Moreover, the productivity of forced labour was incomparably lower than that of free labour, even under Soviet conditions; the theory disregarded the labour of the Political Police themselves in arresting, questioning, guarding and transporting the prisoners. Also, why should the government employ skilled people at unskilled jobs when it needed them above all for skilled jobs?

Many pious Communists in the gaols and camps gave up any attempt to grasp the incomprehensible horror of it all, and resorted to the Book of Job: God knows best! No one could understand but the topmost leaders – *they* knew: no one else had a right to ask questions.

One popular theory claimed that the very technique of incrimination inevitably entailed a geometrical progression. According to this theory, it had not originally been intended to arrest or kill quite so many people, but the technique of blanket denunciation quickly attained snowballing proportions because of its actual mechanism.

This explains some technical elements in the Deep Comb-out, yet it is plainly insufficient. The 'snowball' might have produced an excessive number of arrests, but that would surely have been foreseeable; also, the theory disregards motivation. It can only explain a part of the vast operation, generally cases like that of Sylakov.

A similar theory maintained that the Deep Comb-out reflected plan and counter-plan, a factor in state economic planning. In its broadest, most abstract version, an economic Plan is composed by the highest authorities and passed on down through subordinate departments till it reaches the lowest echelons, where workers or employees are supposed to volunteer to perform still more than is required by the Plan.

Then the Plan, revised by the voluntary over-subscription of the individuals involved, goes on back to the top, where it is further revised through the incorporation of such over-subscription into what now becomes the definitive Plan, including, as an average, what had originally been a special individual effort. Many prisoners thought this technique of over-subscription functioned for the Political Police, and that it was magnified by the natural evolution of this kind of formalized, though tacit negotiation between the Political Police chiefs and their subordinates.

Since the Political Police files took in very nearly the entire population, with everyone classified in various categories – White Guard sympathizers ('former people'), former Oppositionists, people connected with foreign countries – it was always known very precisely how many people would be produced by a given Comb-out on a given pretext. All the material accumulated by the activities of the Political Police informers, plus the material derived from the confessions to the examining magistrates, would be in the files as well. Each card had notations of the degree of social danger; this depended on how much material was in the files and what its scope was.

To show zeal, an official could heighten the perniciousness of a given individual by moving him from one category to another, from the less dangerous to the more dangerous; in this way he could unmask as an enemy of the people someone who had previously been, say, a mere delinquent. A subordinate could achieve status, promotion, and praise by producing more material on this basis, especially if those unmasked were highly placed.

This theory emphasizes a vital technical element, but does not encompass the process.

All these theories were held by those who did not denounce the Soviet system as such, but gave esoteric explanations of specific functions within it.

A sort of Party struggle theory was hotly defended by Marxist politicals. Stalin, according to this theory, could not carry out an open *coup d'état* against the Party; hence he replaced its personnel with a disciplined organization of people unified not by convictions but by the power he gave them in patronage; he had had to do this because in spite of his manoeuvring he had never won the support of the bulk of the

membership, but had triumphed only by the introduction of police
tactics into Party life. Some claimed that as early as 1934 Stalin had
been asked to resign by a majority of the Central Committee; Kirov was
to have replaced him. Hence Kirov was killed on Stalin's say-so just
before Stalin was going to be replaced.

While failing to situate Stalin within the proper context – the immense transformation of Soviet society – this theory at least points up
the distrust of the regime for all convictions as well as for all idealism. It
accommodates the massiveness of Stalin's repressions; it is also consistent with countless specific incidents. Its cardinal features will be
indispensable for all other critical theories.

The Party struggle theory had a streamlined version that placed the
entire phenomenon of the Comb-out at Stalin's feet, and simplified the
general notion of fascist infiltration of the Soviet State and the
Communist Party.

Another version, 'Bonapartism', maintained that Stalin was doing
everything out of personal ambition, even to the point of aiming at a
throne. This extremely personalized view – in harmony with the cult of
personality – had a certain vogue because of what seemed to a great
many people to be the utter incomprehensibility of Stalin's omnipotence.

One or two whimsical theories have a quaint charm; they show the
extravagances resorted to by prisoners reluctant to denounce the Soviet
system.

A cobbler devised a retribution theory: every prisoner had been
arrested for the expiation of some personal sin. That sin had nothing to
do with what he was charged with, to be sure, but since no man is
wholly free of sin his seemingly political offence was just a reminder of
past transgressions.

One fervent atheist, a former president of the International League of
the Godless, had a still simpler explanation of the Deep Comb-out –
sunspots!

The major theories mentioned above were discussed far and wide
among the prisoners. There were also many improvisations among
specialists, who produced a spate of historical analogies for Stalin's
absolutism, the culmination of which was the Deep Comb-out.

The strangest element in the ferocious repression had been the sing-
ling out by Stalin of his own institutions for ploughing under. One
theory of Stalin's despotism held that the Deep Comb-out was no more
than a revolution of the lower ranks of the Party against the higher. In
other words, the highest authority – Stalin and his intimate associates –
obliterated the topmost and intermediate strata of the Party by relying
on the masses of the people.

They could do this because the masses were, very naturally, imbued with hatred for the jumped-up peasants and proletarians now ruling them so cruelly in the name of a Party that was still preaching, in a ritualistically hypocritical way, both egalitarianism and the primacy of plebeians.

This theory was buttressed by some historical analogies; not merely with medieval feudalism, but even with Ancient Egypt, in which power was defined not through property-holding, but as a function of office, which by conferring the right to the *use* of property constituted the exercise of power.

In the Soviet gaols the educated prisoners amused themselves by making comparisons between temple priests and the secretaries of Party regional committees, between the Emirs of the Muslim Caliphs and the Gauleiters of the Nazis, between the Chinese mandarins and the Soviet managers of industry, between the overseers of the Aztec kings and the secretaries of the Soviet trades-unions.

From this point of view, whether the control of the means of production is exercised in the name of the God-King, of the Caliph, or of Stalinism as the all-inclusive framework of society, it comes to the same thing in terms of function.

Since loss of office in such a state entails the loss of power, there is bound to be a conflict between the central authority and the groups exercising power by virtue of such office-holding; this supplements the natural rivalries and frictions between the various groups of office-holders.

On the one hand the supreme authority tries to get as much power into its hands as possible, on the other the office-holders try to make their offices hereditary; they try to make their *control* of the means of production hereditary. There is also a natural antagonism between the various levels of officialdom in the bureaucratic state – lower, medium, higher.

The evolution of European feudalism is a classic instance of struggle between the central power and the nobility, both greater and lesser. Originally the land had been the property of the central power, both theoretically and practically. But the nobility managed to consolidate its right of *control* into an hereditary right, i.e., possession. It was not until the end of the Middle Ages, with the growth of the urban bourgeoisie, that the central power, relying partly on the bourgeoisie and partly on the lower strata of the destitute nobility, broke the power of the great feudal lords, bringing about a new form of dominion – absolutism. This struggle was consummated in France by Louis XI, in England by Henry VIII, in Spain by Philip II, in Russia by Ivan the Terrible.

Characterized everywhere by extreme brutality, its essential feature was the union between the central authority and the masses. To cement this union what was necessary was a special social formation, a kind of militia elevated above all social strata and directly subservient to the central authority and to no other group.

Ivan's regime was a genuine parallel to Stalin's, which in its drive for consolidation was naturally opposed by the higher Party and government officials, who consequently had to be smashed.

The Bolshevik Party was still encumbered by the Old Bolsheviks – the hangovers of the ideological Oppositions who were necessarily hostile to the divergence of the regime from the original ideals of socialism while it had still been a mere theory, uncontaminated by administration. Moreover, these Old Bolsheviks, Red Partisans and political ex-convicts (the *katorga* group) had long since been exasperating everyone by preening themselves on their personal pasts; they were felt by many people to be standing in the way of a younger and better-qualified generation.

Yet it is plain that the Deep Comb-out went far beyond anything that can be explained by the need to eliminate the Old Bolsheviks and their pretensions.

The bulk of the Party officials who had been arrested were in fact devoted to the General Line; untroubled by any socialist past whatever, they could wallow in luxury as representatives of a new generation of office-wielders who, in the growing absolutism of the Stalin regime, enjoyed enormous power by virtue of their indispensable function.

It was natural for these parvenus to push themselves forward – they had often married beautiful women from the 'former people' – and try to create a new high life revolving around the Kremlin court. It was just these intermediate Soviet careerists who constituted a new *élite*, cut off from the bulk of the people by an insurmountable barrier not merely of luxury – fantastic compared with the life of the masses though rather mingy compared with the West – but by social pretentiousness.

This *élite* revolved around the Party, the topmost army, the topmost Political Police, the *élite* intelligentsia of the theatre and cinema, engineers, scientists, and so on.

Its tendency to consolidate its position could be seen in the growth in the number of special schools – the equivalent of the former cadet schools – that handled the education of the youth, and in the increasing nepotism shown to the children of the new *élite*.

The Soviet version was infinitely more exclusive than any capitalist *élite*: it consisted of a series of concentric circles, each of which tried to keep itself untainted by the striving vulgarians below.

The *élite* in the capitals was paralleled by the growth of a provincial *élite*, made up of Party secretaries and the top officials of regional Committees and individual Soviet republics.

The new *élite* was detested by its inferiors and the masses, especially since it had almost exclusively proletarian origins, which made the inequalities seem grotesque and, more particularly, *unjust*. Similar hatred was felt by lower officials for higher. Because of this built-in social insecurity the new *élite* was on a quest for safeguards; it was natural for the central power to obliterate them.

Here Stalin could count on the sympathy, in a sense, not merely of vast masses of subordinate Party members – now with a new career opened up to them – but of the masses, who had suffered so much from the ferocities of the regime as a whole and had also been outraged by the unjustifiable exaltation of their own kinfolk.

This view seems to do justice to three fundamental factors: on the one hand the underlying apathy of the bulk of the population, and on the other, two dynamic forces – the summits clinging to their power, and a parvenu officialdom hoping to perpetuate its privileges on the basis of something more enduring than the performance of certain functions.

From this point of view, the Deep Comb-out would have to be considered successful, since local foci of authority were broken up and diffused within an amorphous administrative structure. The functions of the dozen principal People's Commissariats, for instance, were taken over by a Ministerial Council representing almost a hundred ministries; a similar process took place within the Central Committee of the Party. Concentrations of power beneath the level of the topmost office, that of the dictator himself, were counteracted.

If this theory were an adequate explanation it would have to explain how the same new men, inheriting the old interests, were now bound to carry on with the same old campaign for the same goal – the perpetuation of their power.

This neo-absolutist theory can be supplemented by the social supply theory.

The destruction by the central authority of the new mandarin caste threatening it was necessary in order to keep to a minimum the exploitation of the people by a new ruling class, i.e., to prevent the new rulers, just below Stalin, from consolidating themselves, and at the same time to keep on infusing the caste with new blood. Stalin left the structure of the newly evolving bureaucratic state unaffected; while changing its personnel he kept them all in a state of high tension.

On the one hand, he flashed the prospect of a brilliant career before the eyes of the oncoming younger generation, the hosts of subalterns who would otherwise have had to wait for years, even decades, before winning coveted promotions; on the other, by coupling their advancement with a maximum of unrest and insecurity, he kept the masses from crystallizing their hatred of their masters in a dangerous form.

Why, after all, envy mandarins just because they were mandarins, when everyone knew they were on tenterhooks the whole time, waiting to be packed off to gaol and death? Everyone knew that the most powerful bosses generally had two small suitcases ready – one at home and one in the office, in readiness for the day they would be snatched.

According to this theory of social supply, the system of social replacement, or circulation of the *élite*, provided for under Stalin's veiled management, was much the same as in the capitalist system, where advancement is attended by, say, the disappearance through bankruptcy of the various entrepreneurs shaken off the capitalist tree by successive crises and replaced by new people coming up, without a radical change in the structure of society itself.

This theory applied the same criteria to the Soviet system. There, too, despite the 'socialist ideology' of the summits, there was no channel by which the universal drive to get ahead could be satisfied as it could be under capitalism through the techniques of personal aggrandizement. Nor was there any highway to success *via* political activity, in the capitalist sense of elections.

From this point of view what the Deep Comb-out did was to make room for new people. The intellectual workers, trained at vast expense and with great difficulty by the Soviet system, were to be found vegetating in the forced labour camps, contributing to the incalculable reservoir of manpower used very wastefully from a purely utilitarian viewpoint.

This theory aptly describes the relaying process by which room is made for those of the offices above. The upshot is that it is out of the question for anyone to think of settling down, in the philistine capitalist sense of giving himself and his family the security that is the hallmark of any bona-fide ruling class.

The social supply theory, accordingly, explains how the Soviet system performs the same function as the destruction-plus-healing of capitalist competition, while at the same time ensuring the circulation of the *élite*. This does not include the summits themselves.

Because of this the potential explosiveness that might otherwise characterize a system in which so many people on bottom hated the milieu of the happy few on top, is obviated; the resentment of those who are exploited has nothing to cling to. The rate of change is too fast: the people who are in the favoured milieu at any given time are obviously not going to be there long. There is no enduring coterie of people, the functional equivalent of the aristocracy or bourgeoisie, that can be singled out for the resentment doubtless felt by the sufferers. The coterie at the actual summit is small enough to be protected without much difficulty, especially since the rapid turnover also affects the strata just below the summit and thus makes it difficult for the energies of immediate subordinates to be rallied effectively. Personnel supply crises are thus inevitable in the Soviet State. They have nothing to do with the malevolence, sadism, or paranoia of the rulers, but evolve on the basis of a characteristic dynamic in the social process.

This may explain the curious facelessness of the whole Soviet system. Social relations, abstract, perhaps, in their nature, become still more abstract in the Soviet Union: the ruling class is established there not as a milieu of people, but as a formal pattern of relationships – in fact, as an idea. Even the group of people that had to carry out the Deep Comb-out could not protect themselves against the working out of the idea they were in the process of implementing.

This theory is repeated with slight variations by recent escapees from the Soviet bloc.

It seems to be a Soviet-style, 'Marxist' way of defending the autocracy by ascribing to it an impersonal, materialistic mechanism absolving the ruler from any responsibilities for his own decisions. Moreover, even assuming that this mock-Marxist, quasi- or pseudo-sociological explanation of the Deep Comb-out as constituting a replacement of the generations is correct, how could it be causally linked to Stalin's decisions, which were, after all, what started the whole process? How did the pressures relieved by the replacement of whole strata of the population make themselves felt on *Stalin? He* was no sociologist!

Most recently (1974) a different type of 'global' explanation has been advanced by the writer Alexander Solzhenitsyn.[2] Essentially it seems an original sin theory, the original sin being embedded in the nature of Marxism, which shaped Solzhenitsyn's youth and against which he later revolted with great violence.

According to Solzhenitsyn, now an old-fashioned, religious Russian patriot, Marxism began extracting macabre consequences from its premisses the moment it was installed by the Bolsheviks in 1917; for him there was no evolution with the Soviet system at all – all was black and has remained black.

This approach fails to grasp the dynamic development of the Bolshevik monopoly; the graph going from thousands in the twenties to millions in the thirties remains incomprehensible. To accommodate the timelessness of his conception Solzhenitsyn has recourse to equally timeless factors – human nature,[3] Russian history.[4] He even goes back to Catherine the Great for precedents! Disdainful of analysis, obsessed with condemnation, infuriated by the primitive Marxism he was brought up in and impatient of ideas other than religious generalities, Solzhenitsyn, despite his passionate sincerity, sheds no light on the rationale of the grotesque Soviet experience.

Stalin advanced a view of his own; it has a certain interest! He expressed it a little informally (in an interview with an actor and a film-director)[5], to the effect that Ivan the Terrible – generally considered a demented though brilliant sadist – was fatally soft-hearted. Though he was a 'great and wise ruler', he had failed to carry through to a successful conclusion his otherwise admirable struggle against the divisive activities of the great feudal families. True, he liquidated some, but between bouts of personally torturing various opponents he would then spend so much time on prayerful atonement that he failed to 'liquidate the . . . remaining great feudal families'. It was this 'failure to fight the feudal lords to the end' that led to the terrible Time of Troubles after his death. Far from being ferocious, Ivan was not ferocious *enough*; it was his gentleness that led to disaster.

After this interview of Stalin's, his tame historiographers, in an abrupt reversal of fashion, began praising Ivan the Terrible as a progressive ruler.

Stalin's excursion into history-writing did not constitute an actual theory of the Charades and the Comb-out; it merely explained his own ruthlessness as tailored to a certain historical task. Since he had devised both Kirov's murder and the resultant Charades and Comb-out, we may assume the operation was meant to benefit himself.

Yet how could the slaughter of so many people have benefited him?

It seems sensible to begin by disentangling the real from the mythological elements in this unusual enterprise.

Real elements – those with a certain pedestrian, tangible, more or less obvious utility – plainly played a role in Stalin's long-range planning. One of the factors highlighted throughout this frenzied era was, for instance, sabotage. A general affliction of the Soviet regime had always been its inefficiency. There were countless cases of accidents, botch-ups, corruption and waste. It was easy to blame them all directly on the victims of the Great Charades and the Deep Comb-out. Wrecking, in fact, was their most realistic aspect; at least *something* had actually happened and could be demonstrated, in contrast with the accusations of subversion, dismemberment of the country, and similar myths.

The most cursory examination of the Soviet press shows that all the alleged crimes involving sabotage that came up in the Charades – wrecking, diversions, etc. – were merely the results of the slipshod management of industry following the breakneck acceleration of the Five-Year Plans.

The disclosure during the Charades of the notorious shortages, wastage and so on, was plainly a rather pathetic attempt to blame them on Trotsky, who could not even conceivably have had anything to do with them. The acts of sabotage mentioned in the scripts of the Charades were quite different from individual terrorist acts: the sabotage paraded by Stalin was on such a massive scale – mines, railways, factories – that the whole government apparatus would have had to be involved. The collaboration of many thousands of people was plainly indispensable.

The Charades and the Deep Comb-out created a scapegoat for the acute suffering the Soviet population had been steeped in.

Another 'human' by-product of the terror was the attainment of personal goals. Arbitrary denunciation was obviously useful for paying off grudges, securing promotion, even getting a flat!

This became particularly evident in the remarkable industry displayed by young people and all kinds of junior officials in 'unmasking' everyone above them. It was this element in the general campaign of terror that was given the sociological interpretation noted above – as a mechanism for social turnover, as an outlet for ambitions, a device for easy promotions and a way of thinning out a top-heavy bureaucracy by getting rid of the older generation.

Psychologically, in any case, this procedure of capricious denunciation explains what might be called the positive element of the Soviet terror – its stimulus to selfish desires in the bureaucratic summits.

Denunciation was, in the nature of Soviet Police procedure, its own justification: the mere fact of its having been made gave it weight. Thus by making the country a jungle in which every man's hand was raised against everyone else, Stalin was elevated still further beyond controls.

There were also fringe-benefits, in the way of timing, in foreign affairs strategy. Stalin had timed the first Charade in August 1936 to have its impact just after Hitler had marched unopposed into the Rhineland, and a little while after the People's Front, with massive support, had become the government of France. This enabled Stalin to extract a maximum of support for his first Charade; it was a form of blackmail of the labour movement as a whole and more particularly of the Left-wing and liberal intelligentsia in Western countries.

Once again he was benefiting from his built-in strategic position as the inevitable and sole leader of anti-Hitler forces. At this time, abandoning Stalin implied the break-up of the People's Front, which in its turn im-

plied, perhaps, handing over the whole of Western Europe to a rapidly
re-arming Germany.

For that matter the very dementia of the Charades, by perplexing
intelligent enquirers, made it impossible to criticize them with understanding: in such a critical situation many people preferred to swallow a
mystery, however nightmarish, rather than take a chance on denouncing
it.

As the People's Fronts demonstrated their impotence, Stalin's ap-
proaches to Hitler finally bore fruit in the form of the Stalin-Hitler Pact
signed in the second half of August 1939. Stalin hailed the Pact by saying, on 24 August 1939: 'I know how much the German people loves its
Führer. I should therefore like to drink his health.' A few days later an
eminent German newspaper could explain part of the background of the
Pact: '. . . The removal from the social life of the Soviet Union of that
upper layer who go by the name of Trotskyites, and were on that ground
removed, was indubitably an essential factor in the rapprochement
between the Soviet Union and Germany.'[6]

Though Stalin's trustfulness *vis-à-vis* Hitler was cruelly frustrated, he
was to be salvaged by a factor that transcended politics – the patriotism
of the Russian people.

Yet it is plain that these mundane, banal, human factors played a
secondary role in the conception of the Charades and the Comb-out. The
perspective that must govern their understanding is essentially a fusion
of theology and sociology. The Great Charades and the Deep Comb-out
established a theological framework *for a certain population*.

In theory the conspiratorial Bolshevik nucleus was supposed to be
governed by 'democratic centralism' – free discussion within the
enclosure; outside, a united front.

Yet it was plain, as the Bolsheviks became bureaucrats, that this
notion, quite unreal even before the putsch, was bound to turn into one
more element of state hypocrisy.

From the outset the Dictatorship of the Proletariat was no more than
the dictatorship of the Bolshevik nucleus, and moreover of a handful of
men within it. With Stalin's paramountcy this tendency towards
concentration achieved its maximum expression.

It was only with the Stalin dictatorship, in fact, that another
Bolshevik fetish – Party unity – was finally attained, together with the
spontaneous generation of the orthodoxy that had grown up during the
squabbling of the twenties.

This orthodoxy had become all the more indispensable since all pre-
suppositions of Marxist doctrine were being left far behind at the very

moment that it was necessary to pretend that true Marxism was forging ahead more vigorously than ever.

In the twenties 'Trotskyism' had been invented as the counterweight of this swiftly forming orthodoxy. It was devised as the antithesis of Marxism-Leninism. Trotsky, representing an unfashionable echo of Marxist tradition, had to be made guilty of something *alien*. His ideas – all of them mere applications of Marxism – had to be denounced as the polar opposite of Leninism, proclaimed to be the property of the Stalin coterie. It was because the criticism of Trotsky's personality and career had to be made annihilating that the idea of one General Line, flowing inevitably from a unique set of premises and entailing a unique set of conclusions, had to be anchored in the minds of the Party and the public.

This idea implied that no variation was an 'accident' – it was wrong in essence. Every 'error' had its 'roots' in personal qualities. Thus Trotsky, like *all* opponents, was damned by his Original Sin.

It was in the elaboration of that Original Sin that the cardinal feature of Soviet theology may be seen.

It consists of the Manichean polarization of the universe into Light and Darkness, the consequent projection of an Evil Adversary, and the calcification of an orthodoxy whose authority is encased in the solemnity of a state lie, buttressed by an apparatus of terror.

Trotsky had to be turned into a Trotskyite – a fountainhead of Wrong. Mere rationality might have made this seem difficult – Trotsky was known for his own orthodoxy – but the factional squabbles revolving around life-and-death issues created the formula.

Trotsky began to be systematically undermined in the early twenties by means of the mechanical exegesis that had become routine as Bolshevism was transformed into a State Church. As the parvenu cult turned what had been a discussion of ideas into the petrification of enforced conformism, Trotskyism was fabricated in order to facilitate the destruction of Trotsky and *all other opponents* by a theological demonstration that only the dominant coterie was *truly* Marxist.

Thus the invention of Trotskyism and its concomitant satanization were a necessary stage in the evolution of Stalinism, itself one of the countless ironies of history, since Stalinism, which actually does describe an authentic institutional complex, was never acknowledged in the Soviet Union even at a time when the cult of Stalin the Genius was in full flood.

The campaign of the mid-twenties was paralleled, on the reverse side, by the stereotyped recantations of Oppositionists, who from the very beginning of these recantations in 1924 were obliged to abjure Trotsky specifically when applying for re-admission to the Party. By the end of 1927 the ritual was already fixed.

But Stalin's personal, or factional, interest also reflected a fundamental tug of Soviet society – the need of the *élite* to consolidate the regime as such. Stalin's movement to fortify his own position was the inner circle enclosed by a much larger concentric circle: his location at the apex of the pyramid entailed the consolidation of the pyramid itself.

The movement initiated in the early thirties implemented the potentialities inherent in a society ruled by Bolshevik terror. Since this contradiction between rulers and subjects was explicitly obliterated by official doctrine, the consolidation of the regime inevitably took a special form.

During the NEP period that began in 1921, the precariousness of the Bolshevik position was dramatically highlighted by the very success of the NEP, a major surrender of socialist principle. It meant that the Bolsheviks were more dependent than ever on their mortal enemy – the masses of the people.

Granted the vulnerability of the dictatorship, there was only one way out of the dilemma. The peasantry had to be nationalized – uprooted and made dependent on the State, instead of *vice versa*. Only brute force could nail down the peasants; only brute force could keep the collective farms in existence at all.

The violence unleashed by the Political Police hit the vast bulk of the countryside – the peasantry still made up between 60 and 70 per cent of the population – and had to be systematically applied for years.

The famine of 1932–3 and the slaughter of the peasants also played a cardinal role in the disillusionment of the workers, themselves only a short jump from the countryside and with innumerable connexions with their peasant kinfolk.

Unlike the famine of 1921, which was not blamed on policy, the ferocity of the collectivization campaign, the forcible eviction, expropriation, starvation and butchering of a huge segment of the peasantry under the slogan of liquidating the kulaks, could be blamed only on the Party.

In declaring a total war against the bulk of the population, the Party was more isolated than ever. The expropriation of more than twenty million peasant households and the herding of the survivors into collective farms constituted a drastic social upheaval. The spiritual isolation of the Party in the twenties, the original source of Stalin's power *within* the Party, was strengthened incalculably during the early thirties. The straitjacketing of the peasantry did not solve the farming problem technically – to this day it is a running sore – but it reinforced the dictatorship immeasurably by an economic monopoly. By the time the campaign had been fought to a successful conclusion, the country was on a new course.

After collectivization had smashed the peasantry, a lull seemed possible, especially since the industrialization of the country soon showed results. Both phenomena taken together held out the hope that a period of peaceful consolidation was now conceivable. Sergei Kirov embodied the general hope for reconciliation within the Party.[7]

It was just this that disquieted Stalin. If the strain of war had kept the Party yoked to his discipline, willingly accepted, the relaxation of strain might imply an erosion of discipline that on the one hand would be premature and on the other would, in any case, be dangerous for Stalin personally. The killing of so many people, the increasing brutality of the intra-Party clean-ups left a heavy mortgage of hatred to pay off.

The concept of the Deep Comb-out and its umbrella, the Great Charades, is to be linked to Stalin's defeat in the Central Committee plenum of 1932 over the killing of Riutin, who had called for Stalin's removal as the foremost task of the Party. This reflected the threat to his supremacy posed by Kirov and the policy of conciliation. (It is no doubt the explanation of a slightly cryptic phrase in a telegram sent by Stalin to some Politburo members on 25 September 1936, referring to a lag of 'four years' in the 'unmasking' of his enemies (the Trotskyite-Zinoviev bloc).[8]

Hindsight indicates that the view of Kirov and his supporters was essentially utopian: it was based on the assumption, after all, that the draconian measures applied during the implementation of the first Five-Year-Plan had been successful, that society was *changed*, as it were organically, and hence that socialist construction could proceed in future without too many upsets.

Stalin, doubtless more intelligent, must have seen that the question of socialism in the Soviet Union was a mere chimera; what had to be done was *to stay in power* – a different question altogether!

By the end of 1934, when Stalin brought off Kirov's murder, he had come through a severe ordeal: a formidable rival had been eliminated, the first Five-Year-Plan had been more or less fulfilled, the peasantry was shackled, and the practically constant purging process had cowed the Party, as it seemed, completely.

Conformism of the most systematic kind seemed to prevail; it encompassed the entire *élite*. With the new intellectual framework established by the end of the twenties, the word Trotskyite could be applied to anyone who fell foul of the shifting stereotypes rapidly congealing, one after another, in the General Line.

Yet the tension had to be sustained; the country was still being churned up by the State. The Party straitjacket was not enough to contain the bloodletting of the collectivization, the menace of Nazism, and the growing chasm between the Stalin dictatorship and the older, still ideologically minded former Party leadership and their sympathizers.

Conformism, hallmark of the new orthodoxy, was not as yet applied outside the Party with full rigour. Censorship based on historical falsifications still lacked bite. Nonconformism had to be supplemented by charges of criminality, subversion and treason; the process of satanization, when given teeth, inevitably transformed the quality of despotism.

As early as 1928, when Trotsky was deported to Siberia, officially because of his preparation of an 'armed insurrection', this official reason was never, in fact, given to the public. By the end of 1929, 'Trotskyites' were already being charged with wrecking, sabotage, and so on, yet at that time no trials were staged.

This type of charge was initially also conceived of on a purely literary plane: with hindsight, one can see it as the first step in a gradual process leading from a merely literary slander to bogus charges leading to real executions. There was a logical road along which the dominant faction travelled: the initial repressions rooted in factional differences had to be justified by charges that obviously could not be based on *merely* factional differences: the charges in their turn had to be justified by being made more and more ferocious.

Thus there was a logical sequence from the initial calumniations of the Trotsky coterie in the twenties to the systematically articulated impostures of a decade later. The labelling of Trotsky as a deviationist in the middle twenties and his stigmatization as the Father of Evil in the middle thirties are linked, indeed, by a grand evolutionary arc whose final segment was rounded off during the Great Charades themselves.

Yet the grotesque amplification of 'Trotskyism' must be put in its proper perspective. Conceived *en bloc*, the overriding aim of the Charades was the destruction of *all* deviations from Stalinist orthodoxy.

By 1936–8 there could be no serious question of a *flesh-and-blood* Opposition: individual Oppositionists had long since been expelled from the Party or were being physically annihilated during the Great Charades, together with *all* variants of opinion and whole strata of the population assigned to some *ad hoc* category. The leaders of the Opposition were no longer leaders in any sense; they were, without exception, shattered men with no prospect of political recovery, and plainly, moreover, without the will or ability to reverse their destinies.

Trotsky's ideas, having proved incapable of influencing events, were now quite irrelevant. There was no revolution in Germany, Great

Britain, or France; in Spain the Republic was crushed; despite the most painful convulsions Stalin's entourage had emerged triumphant; it was even to survive the Nazi onslaught Stalin did nothing to forestall, soften or deflect.

At the very moment Trotsky's name had become the equivalent of Satan throughout the spiritual realm controlled by Stalin, Trotskyism had become completely inconsequential. It was merely a label used to lump together all divergences from the dominant faction, and for that matter *everything* pernicious.

The temptation to recall the parallel between Stalin and the early Church Fathers is irresistible.

When the Kingdom of Heaven – Jesus's original message – failed to materialize, its place was taken by the Church that had arisen in his name. Bolshevism took on the same structure. The utopia promised by the seizure of power did not materialize, nor could it in Russia. But the regime could not admit this; to justify it a special way of treating the sacred tradition had to be devised.

Just as the Roman Catholic Church corrects and controls, through its own tradition, the Bible as a whole, while Protestant sects impose a fashionable interpretation of key passages, so the Stalin regime came to control the interpretation of its own sacrosanct progenitors. The satanization of Trotsky had to be 'philosophized' by lumping Trotskyism together not merely with all divergent Left-wing opinion, but with fascism, Nazism, militarism, capitalism, Wall Street, bourgeois nationalism and for that matter – in our own day – Zionism and the State of Israel.

This polarization is the cardinal feature of the whole process: it represents the creation of a new world order, a modern version of the ancient division of the universe into Light and Dark. The creation of a category of Evil has institutionalized Heresy.

It took only a few years for the terror that in the early thirties had begun spreading within the Party to reach its logical conclusion – the physical annihilation of enormous strata of the rank-and-file.

At first this sweeping conclusion might have been thought to have a more or less practical rationale: the intensification of the Party terror was bound to take in everyone who might be considered a rival or *potential* rival of Stalin's.

Yet the logical progression from a small to a big terror *within* the Party had a still more sweeping and even more 'logical' conclusion of its own.

The very mechanism of the terror, its automatic fanning out, its actual momentum, meant that anyone who could be suspected of opposition to the State (Stalin) was already charged with it: that meant, in effect, *literally* everyone. Terror became ubiquitous.

If conciliation within the Party, under the leadership of someone like Kirov, was dangerous, the alternative was evidently terror, and halfway terror is obviously more dangerous than terror all along the line: as Machiavelli pointed out, hurting an enemy grievously is dangerous, killing him may not be.

Hence Stalin found it necessary to eliminate not only all Old Bolsheviks, but whole strata of the population that had already been shaped by history *in the wrong way*. The leadership of the Old Party were not merely veterans of Party theory and of Marxism, but had also had first-hand experience of a way of life in Western Europe and elsewhere. Compared with the home-grown product of the Bolshevik Party in the Soviet Union after the October Revolution, they were dyed-in-the-wool cosmopolitans.

After the Soviet regime began its great retreat from the hopes bound up with October, that is, after the initial wave of idealism ebbed into the quagmire of millennial brutality, such people were perfectly capable of perceiving and broadcasting the remarkable divergence between the new Soviet society – based on the lies and tortures of the Stalin faction – with the life of the West, the life of Tsarist Russia, and for that matter civilized life in general.

This process could also be described innocuously, even flatteringly: Bukharin,[9] for instance, thought the Old Bolsheviks were no longer useful for constructive purposes simply because they had all been brought up to be negative critics of everything. Trained to pour scorn on all aspects of the *status quo*, to analyse it with 'ruthless' Marxist logic, they were naturally like fish out of water when it came to building even a dam. Hence, to Bukharin's mind, they were destroyers: construction did not call for critics but devoted hod-carriers.

And if – in Bukharin's version of Stalin's reasoning – these Old Bolsheviks were no longer a help but merely a hindrance on the road of construction, why – they had to be got rid of. In a caste of people that constituted the *de facto* administration was simply an obstacle, it had to be eliminated – ruthlessly, since what had to be performed, after all, was a surgical operation.

Perhaps Stalin was a sociologist after all! He had already installed a new generation of men who owed nothing to the past and everything to him; this new generation was bound to be sustained and magnified by the extinction of the old.

One might claim Stalin's behaviour to be a form of Marxism! If a new society had been brought into being, then the people still in the grip of the ideas, habits and institutions of the old society were obviously out of place, indeed were misfits, socio-technically speaking, and dangerous *per se*.

The Great Charades and the Deep Comb-out constituted two elements of a real revolution. It was not the mere putsch in 1917 that had been the Revolution: contrary to Soviet mythology, that had nothing to do with the proletariat. The decisive revolution was the one made by Stalin at the end of the twenties and consummated by the restructuring of the Party and of society at large during the thirties. It set its stamp on the Soviet Union for an unforeseeable length of time to come.

The herding of the peasants into the collective farms, the large-scale industrialization of the country, were one element: the other was the obliteration of all elements of intellectual independence *via* the attack on the Party and the Comb-out of the population, and the consolidation of Stalin's personal entourage as a Party now more monolithic than ever.

There was obviously a contrast between the Old Party people and the new generation of managers, bosses, and bureaucratic cattle-men created by the break-neck collectivization and industrialization.

In a sense Stalin was applying Kirov's policy of conciliation in his own version. Kirov had intended to broaden the Soviet base by involving a variety of non-Party workers and peasants in the support of the Party. Stalin took over this basic policy of amalgamating the ruling caste with the population, except that he subtracted the personnel of the current ruling caste and filled the vacuum with new elements. He created, in short, a new ruling caste over the corpses of the old.

There is some indication that Stalin formulated this idea explicitly: in the spring of 1937 Krivitsky was told by his Political Police superior, Slutsky: 'Stalin has said that the entire pre-revolutionary and war generation must be destroyed as a millstone around the neck of the Revolution.'[10]

Stalin was making a sort of logical extrapolation from the strange regime generated by the primordial decision to monopolize power in a country like Russia.

He obliterated the generation still in the grip of early Bolshevik idealism, made obsolete by the fruition of the new regime. Simultaneously, he pruned the population as a whole to tailor it to the new situation.

It is just at this point, between the traditional terrorizing of the Party and the application of the terror to the population at large, that the ritualistic technique of the Deep Comb-out becomes understandable.

Stalin had all his instruments at hand – the Police, the heresy, the plot, the 'wrong people', the scenarios, the Charades. Yet these instruments were not very refined, nor was there a manual of instructions for their use. Dossiers composed on the basis of bogus confessions – the primary mechanism of the Deep Comb-out – were indispensable; once set in motion a geometrical progression was inherent in their logic.

The institutional necessity of the bogus dossiers also explains the purpose of the confessions.

After all, what was their point? Some novices in the Political Police might, to be sure, have thought their prisoners guilty of *something*, but since they had complete power over their prisoners anyhow, what was the sense of the whole rigmarole?

By the time of the Comb-out there was no longer any question of eliminating classes of people genetically hostile to the regime – monarchists, industrialists, priests, etc. Indeed, even such hostile social hangovers, though slaughtered on occasion with remarkable ferocity, were never wiped out as such: they were accused of specific hostile action. The hostile social vestiges were not in the position of, say, Jews, gypsies, Polish intellectuals and various other *Untermenschen* under the Nazi regime (though here, too, the Final Solution of the 'Jewish problem' was kept as secret as possible).

The only class of people to be destroyed as such was the kulaks; even there the slaughter was an unforeseen consequence of a reckless policy. The peasants were supposed to be 'educated' out of their class background and turned into model Soviet citizens in the new economic structure.

At the very height of the Stalin blood-letting the theory of social equality was reinforced, when Stalin said the son was not responsible for the father. The Stalin constitution, altogether bogus as it was, proclaimed that no hostile classes existed in the Soviet Union any longer, and that anyone who now opposed the regime was merely perverted or criminal.

Yet the rationale of the bogus dossiers was profound.

First of all it was a curb on the enforcers. Since the theory of guilt was a fiction to begin with, the only thing that could prevent a breakdown of restraint, the transformation of the security organs into a mob of berserk rioters, was just this obsession with form. Inherently nonsensical material *had* to be presented in a symmetrical shape – depositions, confessions, trials.

More generally, with respect to objectives, it was vital to devise a ritual to make it seem that individuals were being dealt with for their own crimes. Consequently, though the *real* reason for anyone's arrest was his 'objective characteristic', the fiction was sustained with great tenacity that he had done *something*.

An examination of the objective characteristics of the throngs of prisoners makes it plain that Stalin thought in actual categories, only partly influenced by the primitive groupings of classical Marxism: they were categories that required obliteration in terms of his own blueprint, in which the maximization of the power of the apparatus was part of the maximization of his control over it.

But these categories could not be blazoned forth: hence, though the prisoners were in fact arrested because of their objective membership in secretly proscribed categories – comprehensive enough to make the principle of the arrests seem very nearly random – this fact had to be hidden.

And it could be hidden only by hiding the individual culpable categories in the mass of the populace at large, by losing each tree in a huge forest.

The necessity for this was all the more inescapable since many of the proscribed categories, perhaps most, were theoretically still looked up to in Soviet mythology as the most heavily laden with honours – the senior officers' corps, the Old Bolsheviks, the Red Partisans, indeed the entire *élite* that Stalin had decided must be obliterated.

Stalin's *potential* opponents ran into the millions; they had to be wiped out, but wiped out by going through a form of judicial procedure. Since there were no crimes, the only form of judicial procedure possible was the form of confession; this provided a judicial form suitable to the nature of the operation envisaged by Stalin – the destruction of social categories under the mask of punishing the misdeeds of individuals.

The insistence on confession was no novelty: many instances spring to mind – the trials for witchcraft, the charges in heresy trials under the Inquisition, and so on, though there was a cardinal difference between these two instances and the Soviet practice of the thirties: people really believed that witches and heretics existed, including, doubtless, the witches and heretics themselves.

As a lever of control, the technique of bogus dossiers was remarkably apt. The Political Police, through its possession of instantly available 'material', could at any time charge anyone they wished to with *something*, and could claim a legitimate basis for it in their files.

The mass of denunciations – which by 1938 already comprised, because of this snowballing technique, very nearly the whole of the adult population – thus created a situation that formally speaking resembled normal police procedure elsewhere: the Political Police could claim that on the basis of 'information received' it might with a perfect show of legality hold any individual for interrogation. It could, in short, arrest anyone it liked whenever it liked, and do so, above all, with no appearance of caprice.

The Political Police seem to have had a file on every functionary of any consequence, charging him with espionage and treason. Even after Yezhov was replaced by Beria in 1938, and even after the Deep Comb-out proper seemed to have come to a complete stop, prisoners were specifically asked for statements inculpating eminent scientists and scholars of espionage at the very moment they were being handed Soviet awards like the Stalin Prize. These denunciations were not necessarily acted on; they were made as a preparation 'in case', and were thus a modality of terror, since if anyone was to be arrested he would know in advance that the Political Police already had 'evidence' against him.

If the atomization of society is regarded as the logical extension of the process of levelling off all rivals that is a prerequisite for the emergence of absolutist rulers, Stalin's despotism may be thought of as the perfection of totalitarianism.

It was necessary – from Stalin's despotic point of view – to fortify the Comb-out of the Party with a much vaster, more pervasive and seemingly more irrational, not to say demented terror directed at the entire populace. Not merely were the conspicuous groups in society culled for victims, but even the peasantry, the people *as such*, was given a sharp lesson whose very irrationality was the source of its efficacy.

The ultimate perfection of this seemingly irrational mangling of the population lay in its engulfing just those solidly established individuals who might have thought themselves, for a moment, secure because of past faithfulness and docility. Actually, no one in any metier whatever who had had time to accumulate status, prestige, authority and connexions was untouched.

It was, in fact, the element of dementia in the very phrase 'enemy of the people' that made it such an effective instrument of intimidation.

The phrase, which Stalin made so characteristically his own, is no more than the lapidary formulation of a situation inherent in the very premises of the Bolshevik dictatorship.

If the Party took power in the name of a programme that was bound to be directed at the way most people in the Soviet Union were actually living, the term 'enemy of the people' is really no more than a summing up of the relationship between the Party and the people – the Party was the enemy of the people!

But how could it acknowledge this? The equation simply had to be reversed. Once reversed, what it made possible – as Khrushchev said years later in an understatement to be expected from one of the heirs of the process – was the 'use of the most cruel repression . . . against anyone who in any way disagreed with Stalin, against those who were only suspected of hostile intent, against those who had bad reputations. This concept "enemies of the people" actually eliminated the possibility of any kind of ideological fight or the making of one's views known on this or that issue, even those of a practical character.'[11]

The 'theory' underlying the concept of treachery has the unmistakable hallmark of paranoia; it was outlined by Stalin himself in a speech to the February–March plenum (1937), when the slaughter was already in full spate.

Criticizing the Party for its lackadaisical attitude towards 'spies and saboteurs', Stalin attacked the 'rotten theory' that a skilful worker necessarily had to be considered loyal: on the contrary, the real 'wrecker' must naturally put on a good show in order to divert suspicion: the 'chatter', said Stalin, to the effect that action against such 'wreckers' would militate against the economic plan must cease.[12]

This was, of course, the same theme as that amplified in the 'unmasking' of lifelong Bolsheviks.

This delusional element may pinpoint the transition from a merely oppressive to a totalitarian regime That transition may be located at the point where real enemies have been vanquished, and mythology begins to be created to justify the quest for enemies who, being imaginary, make the quest endless. Anyone, after all, may be called a potential enemy.

In its broad outlines, accordingly, the paranoid obsessiveness of the Stalin dictatorship with 'potential enemies' may be conceived of as a necessary psychological concomitant of its large-scale projects for the reconstruction of society.

The extirpation of Stalin's own partisans served an essential purpose by providing a dramatic, blood-curdling illustration of the total insecurity of all society below the summit. If personal relations meant nothing, if pull became meaningless, if institutional authority became meaningless, if rank, loyalty and toil safeguarded nothing, then all society had plainly become an appendage of the dictator's omnipotence.

It was as though a frontal lobotomy had been performed on the mind of the Soviet community: its political memory had been excised. It is true that, beginning in the sixties, individuals of great moral fibre have emerged, notably the scientist Andrei Sakharov, and Alexander Solzhenitsyn, to say nothing of the numerous writers whose names are associated with the somewhat chaotic and unorganized underground press (*Samizdat*). Yet with all their courage, amounting in many instances to heroism, they represent outcries of personal conscience, not the reactions of social groups.

Stalin's enterprise reflected the logic of the Soviet system as it evolved on its own set of premises. It was not his caprices that generated the enormities of the Charades and the Comb-out, but the singularity of Bolshevism, brought to fruition by his talents.

In 1956, when Khrushchev abruptly presented Stalin as arch-culprit for the horrors of the thirties, admitting that for a quarter of a century the country had been in the hands of a monster, he blamed the 'cult of personality' and Stalin's personal qualities. This explanation is plainly identical with the 'cult of personality' itself – in reverse.

This was necessary, no doubt, partly to salvage the Soviet regime, and partly, also, to retain at least the figure of Lenin as the linchpin of Soviet orthodoxy.

Yet the unprecedented power concentrated in the Stalin dictatorship had its roots in the decision taken by Lenin and the Bolshevik nucleus to run a backward country monopolistically in a certain direction: it was that decision that led to the Political Police – today the KGB, begotten by the MVD, begotten by the MGB, begotten by the NKVD, begotten by the OGPU, begotten by the Cheka, begotten by Lenin in a personal decree (20 December 1917).

It is fair to acknowledge Stalin's personal qualities, but it is unrealistic to divorce him from Soviet history. The idea is repugnant to commonsense: how could Stalin do so much alone?

It is significant that in Khrushchev's emotional denunciation of Stalin for his manhandling of the Party he failed even to mention the Deep Comb-out, with its extermination of millions of peasants, workers and intellectuals quite outside the Party. The wiping out of all these people was not, after all, Stalin's personal handiwork, but that of the apparatus as a whole.

Khrushchev said: 'In 1937–8, 383 lists (of people in the Party and State summits marked for death) were sent to Stalin with the names of thousands of Party, Soviet, military, Young Communist and industrial or agricultural workers. He ratified those lists.'[13]

This passes over in silence the millions killed by the Extraordinary Tribunals throughout the country during the Deep Comb-out, as well as the vast numbers of rank-and-file Party members. Nor did Khrushchev mention the hundreds of thousands expelled, arrested and killed between 1934 and 1939.[14]

Khrushchev's reticence, and the total silence of Soviet spokesmen since his downfall are doubtless due to the historic involvement of the current leadership in all these crimes.

Stalin's deadliness functioned within the deadliness of a capacious structure – the Dictatorship of the Party and the Political Police terror. His career represented a distillation of Bolshevism.

Lenin's aphorism that 'politics is concentrated economics', demonstrating the paramount role of volition, established the rationale of the 1917 putsch. It was Lenin's high spirits, indeed, that made the Bolsheviks a world force. Yet as soon as the consequences of the putsch in rural Russia could be articulated they manifestly entailed Stalinism. This could only mean that 'scientific' Marxism – Marx's idea that the cosmic surge of economics was the Motor of History – was a mere misunderstanding. But since Marxism, the framework of orthodoxy, could not be challenged, the conclusion was unmistakable:

Russia had been unfit for Socialism, but the due harmony between the economic base and the spiritual superstructure – the cliché of early Marxism – would be restored once Russia was *forced* into Socialism. If Marxism did not fit Russia, Russia could be made to fit Marxism.

Stalin's achievement was formidable. In contriving a mechanism to consolidate his personal despotism as part of the consolidation of the Soviet regime, he had created a new orthodoxy, a new Party, and a new church. He had created a new State.

Truly a Masterpiece!

Epilogue

The techniques of incrimination and 'confession', developed during the Great Charades, were not exhausted. The concept of Charades, of fantastic plots and of degrading confessions has never been abandoned.

The Great Charades have never been disavowed in public; their victims have been rehabilitated only tacitly and by implication. Khrushchev's Secret Speech, demonstrating the fictitiousness of the Great Charades, was addressed only to an *élite* group, the Communist Party summits.

Long after the Second World War a Charade was staged that was stopped only by Stalin's death in March 1953. Known as the 'Doctors' Plot', it seems to have been fabricated by Stalin personally during the winter of 1952–3.

On 13 January 1953 it was announced that several dozen of the most eminent physicians in Moscow had been arrested. Of the nine doctors mentioned in the communiqué six were Jews. The group included the most outstanding specialists at the Kremlin hospital, who were responsible for treating Stalin himself and most of the Soviet leaders. They were all officially accused of killing some of their patients.

Unlike the medical performers in the Great Charade of March 1938, the physicians were charged in 1953 with murdering their patients on the orders of their superiors in the British and American 'intelligence services'. This element – complicity with foreign powers – makes it clear that another Charade was in the offing, doubtless directed at the heads of the Political Police (primarily Beria, Yezhov's successor).

The day of the announcement, the Soviet press launched an overtly anti-Semitic campaign: Zionists, a Jewish relief organization (the Joint Distribution Committee) and Jews as such were systematically attacked. Jews were labelled Zionists and hence agents of 'American imperialism'.

The Doctors' Plot launched a flood of denunciations, gaolings and demotions of Jews all over the Soviet Union: trials were prepared against prominent Jews; huge numbers of ordinary Jews were denounced, sacked, arrested, imprisoned or sent to concentration camps. A 'Zionist plot' was also 'uncovered' in Eastern Germany; there was a mass deportation of 'alien and unproductive elements' from the cities of Hungary and Rumania; it brought about the gradual starvation of thousands of Jews. All this was accompanied by a torrent of propaganda demonstrating that Jews were by nature traitors, spies, embezzlers, imperialist agents and out-and-out murderers. The persecution of the Jews throughout the Soviet Union as well as in most of its satellites swelled into a vast though muffled pogrom.

There were even authoritative rumours (recorded by Alexander Solzhenitsyn) that Stalin was preparing a genuine, blanket pogrom against all Soviet Jewry. Stalin, according to these rumours, intended to have the population incited against the Jews, then have the Political Police 'rescue' them from the mob, in order to eliminate them altogether while they were under guard.[1]

Stalin's sudden death in March 1953 brought the Doctors' Plot Charade to a halt at once. Beria released all prisoners; the Charade itself was officially denounced as a fabrication. This was in sharp contrast with the silence concerning the Great Charades themselves.

The anti-Semitic element in the Doctors' Plot, aside from acting as a safety-valve for anti-Semitism in general, was another scapegoat device to drain off the hatred for the Soviet apparatus, which had a disproportionate number of Jews, generally in the intermediate strata of the bureaucracy, where they came into the most immediate contact with the people. This attracted and reinforced the anti-Semitism still prevalent among the population and to a large extent among the Party and State summits too.

It is not known whether Stalin died of natural causes or was simply removed in time to abort the Doctors' Plot. Whatever the explanation, it is clear that the termination of the Great Charades at the end of the thirties was not definitive.

The concept of Charades has remained a living device of Communist statecraft: apart from the abortive Doctors' Plot, the Great Charades were duplicated, both in spirit and in structure, in Charades in the Soviet satellites long after the Nazi defeat, though these were not so elaborately prepared nor so extensively scripted.

There was the Charade involving the Hungarian Party leadership (the Budapest Show Trial of Rajk and others in 1949), the Show Trial of the Bulgarian Party heads in Sofia of the same year (Kostov and others), the Czech Party upheaval that was disclosed in the Prague Show Trial in 1951–2 (Slansky and others).

These Charades in the Soviet satellites were modelled so closely on the Great Charades of the thirties as to seem very nearly like carbon copies. There was a profound conceptual identity between them and the Great Charades, while the added features – notably the reversion to classical anti-Semitism as an outstanding element, especially in the Slansky Charade – heighten the demonological motif underlying the whole process.

S.M.—8

There were fourteen defendants in the Slansky trial, of whom eleven were Jews. The name of each Jewish prisoner was followed in the indictment by the phrase 'of Jewish origin': This phrase is the keynote to the whole motif of this neo-Charade: since Jewish prisoners could not be described as Jews in the religious sense, and since they could not be called of Jewish nationality – civically they considered themselves Czechs or Slovaks – the words 'of Jewish origin' could only be taken to mean a racial differentiation: people were Czechs or Slovaks on the one hand, and 'of Jewish origin' on the other.

Very few of the Jews had ever been Zionists; the few who were – including Slansky himself – had been members of scout groups as children thirty years before. Throughout their adult life they had all been violent opponents of Zionism and indeed of Jewish nationalism generally. Thus the mere reference to them as Zionists, aside from being a manifest lie, could have only one purpose – to stigmatize them as members of a world-wide Jewish conspiracy that is itself one of the most durable elements in classical anti-Semitism. Its implications were clear: no matter how anti-Zionist a Jew might *seem*, he was secretly involved in a Zionist plot.

The prosecutor was intent on proving that a Jewish conspiracy – world-wide – led by American Jewish leaders and the State of Israel, making use of the Israel diplomatic service, Jewish relief organizations, and a network of Jewish agents throughout the world had been working for 'imperialist' sabotage and espionage services for years before the Second World War. The prisoners were called 'Trotskyite-Titoist-Zionists' and 'bourgeois nationalist traitors'.

The 'conspiracy' had a number of supporting points; one section said the sabotage was in the interest of destroying socialism and restoring capitalism by deliberate blunders in planning, the creation of artificial shortages, and so on. Another section of the indictment linked Zionist and Jewish organizations with American imperialism and its 'reliable agencies'.

The Slansky Charade was modelled not merely on the Great Charades, but on the notorious forgeries of the Protocols of Zion as well, with a further link between this motley assortment and the Free Masons.

The prisoners' behaviour was also modelled on the Great Charades. They reviled themselves in the classical, hysterical style, without apologizing or pleading mitigating circumstances. Their confessions were the sole evidence. Each prisoner blamed his bourgeois and Jewish background for his crimes.

Though the trial was called public, no correspondents from any but Soviet-bloc countries were allowed in. The proceedings were not broadcast from the courtroom but arranged and selected for transcription, and only later broadcast; the remaining parts were given out in the announcer's summaries. The courtroom was packed with 'workers' delegations' and police agents. The Slansky trial was a tissue of the same absurdities as those of the Great Charades.

Like the Great Charades, the Slansky Charade was never disavowed, nor was its sequel, the second Slansky trial in Prague in May 1953.

It is doubtless significant, also, that the campaign against the Jews in the satellite countries, which seemed to have been launched by the Doctors' Plot, went on uninterruptedly even after all the 'charges' had been officially withdrawn.

Eleven prisoners of the first Slansky Charade were killed on 3 December 1952. In March 1969 one of the three survivors, Eugene Loebl, told the story of his imprisonment and interrogation: it is a complete confirmation of all accounts of Soviet procedure during the thirties, for both the Charades and the Deep Comb-out.[2]

The second Slansky Charade was staged in Prague seven months after the first, on 26 May 1953. The sentences were milder: Slansky's brother was merely given life imprisonment. The charges were like those in December 1952; but in the second Charade everything was conducted in secret; a short communiqué announced the outcome.

The conceptual structure that was only partially disclosed in the abortive Doctors' Plot was presented far more amply and nakedly in the Slansky Charades. The process initiated on such a massive scale by Stalin – the satanization of opponents – was articulated very smoothly, somewhat more smoothly, indeed, than in the Great Charades themselves, in which the technical aspects of the process hampered to some extent the tidy unfolding of the myth itself.

The over-all mythical theme of the Moscow Charades of 1936–8 was that of the Bolshevik turned traitor – essentially, of course, the idea of Judas – which swiftly evolved into the conception, still more mythological, of the Bolshevik-*born*-traitor.

Since it is impossible to know just what the leaders of the Communist Parties actually *believe*, this theory of the 'traitor within' may be taken as a handy administrative device, in the sense of a procedure to be followed in order to simplify political realities for their primitive followers, both for the masses and for the lower levels of their own apparatus.

The schema outlined, for instance, in Gottwald's speech on Slansky to the Central Committee of the Czech Party (6 December 1951), streamlines slightly this image of Bolshevik-traitor.

The streamlining was necessary to accommodate an important fact in postwar Eastern Europe: Communist Parties subservient to Moscow were dominant everywhere. Consequently, the Party had become even more of a target than before. Its monolithic character was conceived of as being threatened – 'objectively', again – by leaders guilty of the worst of crimes – 'factionalism' as distinct from ideological deviations, the mere idea of which had by now long since been obsolete. Such factionalists among the leadership naturally had to be 'unmasked' as soon as possible.

Procedurally, the destruction of enemies within the Party would naturally take place in two stages: the first would be the attribution of serious mistakes, the second would be the unmasking of the 'traitors within' as enemies because of the mistakes that would then be ascribed a sinister motif.

Stalin's success in satanizing all his opponents created a mythological departure from reality in two different ways: first of all, fact was dropped altogether. There had been many double agents in the history of the Russian revolutionary movement. Indeed, the dual nature of such individuals (Azef, Roman Malinovsky) was one of its outstanding features. Such dual personalities were able men who while working for the Tsarist Secret Police became so adept, and in complex ways so persuaded of the moral value of what they were doing on behalf of the revolutionaries that they were able to summon up an immense amount of authentic spiritual energy. They were genuinely *double* agents, in fact, not merely men sincerely working for one side while wearing a mask for the other. When such men were finally caught they were regarded with horror as freaks.

These complicated idealists, or psychopaths, naturally vanished under Stalinism, yet it was under Stalinism, at the same time, that this potent myth was evolved.

The myth made it seem normal, in fact inevitable, for leaders of Communist parties to be leaders only in appearance, in reality remaining fanatical enemy agents. This was not conceived of on an individual basis: it often became habitual for whole groups of Communist leaders to turn out to have been enemy agents from the very inception of their careers.

By expanding the primordial Judas-image to take in whole groups of alleged enemies, the satanizing process, collectivized, becomes useful as an instrument of national policy. It can create charges against all enemies, within the Soviet bloc or elsewhere, who might be thought of by the innocent as natural allies – Chinese, Yugoslav, Albanian Communists – but really are natural enemies. This was to be so with respect not only to the Titoists in Yugoslavia but to the various factions that managed to undo the leaderships of a number of satellite Communist Parties.

Lenin had defended the 'objective' utility of the double agent, Roman Malinovsky, by claiming that Malinovsky, surrounded in spite of himself by Bolsheviks, had to help them in order to be of any use at all to the Tsarist authorities; since history turned out to have been on the side of Bolshevism Malinovsky's deception of Lenin was merely trivial.

Such a defence plainly becomes irrelevant when it is alleged that the whole government of some Communist state has sold out to the enemy. As a collective action it can be far more effective than an individual aberration.

The metaphor contrived to explain the defection of Party leaders enjoying *power* was just this conception of their role. The victory of the Party, after the merely apparent defeat of the bourgeoisie – especially in the Soviet satellites after the Second World War – is supposed to be what maddens the bourgeoisie, in its death throes, into infiltrating the Party and perfecting the corruption of the inherently corruptible leaders.

This was the substance of the 'charges' in the Sofia Charade (Kostov) of 1949 and the Budapest Charade of the same year (Rajk). In the Rajk Charade a description was given of the 'highly ramified organization of spies and agents-provocateurs' set up by Rajk and the Yugoslav 'intelligence service' after the Second World War.

There was a significant contrast between the Great Soviet Charades of the late thirties and the satellite fabrications after the Second World War. In their own way the librettists of the Great Charades went to a great deal of trouble to substantiate the charges, plainly monstrous, that people thought to have been lifelong Bolsheviks had always been enemy agents. The working out of their personal motivations was in fact the chief obligation of the script-writers and the prosecution during the Great Charades. Once their motivation could be thought of as established, there was no need to go into the motivations of the secondary characters, who in this respect were generally neglected altogether.

It is true that the librettists did a rather sloppy job; only a very primitive audience could be expected to take seriously the trumped up, artificial, and completely silly explanations of motive they achieved. But they did their best: it was plainly felt to be called for.

In the neo-Charades of the Soviet satellites after the Second World War, on the other hand, no time was wasted on motivation at all. The mythological elaboration had already advanced to the point where it was possible to take the category of Judas-Bolshevik for granted, as an established fact that merely had to be referred to in order to project a sufficient motivation for an individual Bolshevik. Once the idea of a Bolshevik having been a spy from birth was taken for granted, there was no longer any reason to wonder why he had become one. The role of Party leader was his natural mask, just as spying was his nature.

This is, of course, the element that was Stalin's original contribution to Marxism. It was his satanization of opponents that made it natural to avoid any discussion of or even reference to the ideologies of the deviationist leaders: the docile audience of the Communist dictatorship knows in advance that ideologies are meaningless – no matter what the unmasked leaders *say*, they are merely obeying the orders of their superiors in the enemy's intelligence services.

This notion of 'intelligence services' also became a mythological stereotype in the neo-Charades of the Soviet bloc. There are, after all, flesh-and-blood intelligence services in existence, yet for the purposes of popular mythology what was needed was not a naturalistic, even a bogus naturalistic account of their activities, but a sort of adolescent dream-work – *spies*!

It is plain that the institutionalization of Stalinism, which has survived the death of its architect, led to a complete blurring or indeed obliteration of all naturalistic images in the desire to homogenize the mythological process.

The irrelevance of naturalism in this mythological development can be seen from the utter indifference to practical details: Judas-Bolsheviks often work for a whole slew of intelligence services. Rajk was said to have been a Hungarian agent in 1931, then an agent for the Gestapo and American intelligence services in 1939–40, and after 1945 a Yugoslav and American agent.

Institutionally speaking, this indifference to naturalism seems to have been the final Stalinist addition to the primordial Bolshevik image of the Soviet paradise being encircled by an anti-Soviet coalition: the very phrase 'imperialist intelligence service' is plainly a piece of mumbo-jumbo that just because it is so senseless in real life makes it handy for myth-making.

As part of this mythological structure the admissions that were extracted from the prisoners, in the Great Charades, in which specific elements had to be dropped in the course of the negotiations because the prisoners would simply baulk, became, in the Rajk Charade of 1949, routine, lifeless and matter-of-fact, just as blackmail had become a fixed element in the stereotyped explanation of motive.

The mythological harmony of the concept of Judas-Bolsheviks has, in fact, made all elements stereotypes. The notion of recruitment, dealt with even in the Great Charades in a thoroughly happy-go-lucky manner, became if possible still more routine in the neo-Charades of the satellites: any contact of *any* kind with enemy police or intelligence could be regarded by itself as a sufficient occasion for recruitment into the service of the enemy. In the same way official representatives of any foreign government were *all* intelligence agents; *all* information given to the outside world by an unmasked leader was espionage information.

Even though the spy-stories circulated in the neo-Charades after the Second World War were even more preposterous than those of the Soviet Great Charades, they were told in a completely routine, stereotyped, matter-of-fact style. They sounded thoroughly undramatic, partly because, in the satellite context, the contrast there had been between the characters and histories of the Soviet Bolshevik leaders and their 'crimes' was not so sharp.

Though the listless performance of the prosecution in these neo-Charades – in sharp contrast with Vyshinsky's fireworks, partly due to his personal hatred of Old Bolsheviks – might have stemmed from a fundamental disbelief in the whole enterprise, it is possible to deduce nevertheless a sort of belief on the part of its stage-managers

The top Party people in Moscow might not have believed that at the time of the break with Tito the entire Yugoslav leadership was made up of people who had been in the pay of the imperialist secret service since boyhood; their clash had to be given a moral colour. It was natural to translate their power squabble with Tito into mock-Marxist terms: thus Tito's behaviour was 'objectively' the same as it would have been if directed by their imperialist enemies. In this way their esoteric belief, which occasionally broke through the façade for mass consumption, might have been sincere.

The prisoners in the Prague Charade of November 1952 would often refer to their performance of Party duties in the past as instances of subversion, if the General Line had changed in the meanwhile. On the question of the State of Israel, for instance, the Soviet Union had sponsored its establishment in 1948; as part of this general policy of backing Israel the Czech government in a quiet way sold some arms to Israel for its fight against the surrounding Arab states.

By the time of the Prague Charade, however, that policy of support for Israel had long since evaporated; it was replaced by the sponsorship, still effective, of the Arab front against Israel. In 1952, accordingly, Slansky was obliged to highlight this switch to a pro-Arab Moscow orientation by testifying that his support of Israel at that time – in 1948, together with the Kremlin! – had been a sign of his treachery.

This device of regarding as subversion the performance of a duty carried out during the preceding zigzag of the Party Line was carried in the neo-Charades of the Soviet satellites to lengths that in the disregard shown for the intelligence of the audience transcended even the Great Charades.

In the Great Charades, for instance, when Krestinsky said the German Reichswehr had given him some money for Trotsky, and used this as an instance of his espionage on behalf of Germany, he was referring to the well-known collaboration during the early twenties of the Red Army and the Reichswehr (the Reichswehr rented some facilities from the Red Army). At that time only a few highly placed Party people knew this arrangement; hence it could easily be put about later on that Krestinsky and Trotsky had been spies. The public could not be expected to know much about this point.

In the Prague Charade of 1952, however, the average man in Prague was called upon to forget even well-known matters that had taken place in broad daylight only a short while before. Slansky explained, for instance, that he had supported the idea of a specific Czechoslovak 'road to socialism' – a mere cliché in Soviet satellites during the immediate postwar period; he could present that as an indication of his counter-revolutionary fiendishness: the Party Line had changed – in only five years!

By the time of the Prague Charade the Party leadership must have felt that absolutely anything would be swallowed.

Part of the contrast between naturalistic distortion and mythological satanization could also be seen in the theory of the overthrow of the State. The original Bolshevik concept of the assumption of power had revolved around the 'smashing' of the State from without, both in the case of the bourgeois State and in the case of the Soviet State itself (in the scripts of the Great Charades a plan was referred to involving the seizure of the whole of the Seventeenth Party Congress of January 1934).

By the time of the Rajk Charade in Prague this naturalistic theory was replaced by the far more arbitrary, and mythologically suppler, device of infiltration. Wearing the masks of orthodox Party members, the conspirators were supposed to be moving ahead by having themselves appointed, both by each other and by 'good' Communists, to all the top positions. Once they had arrived at their destinations in full force the impersonations were supposed to be ended: the masks would be torn off – Satan would stand forth. They would then seal their triumph not by the old-fashioned technique of setting up a new political regime, but in the new-fangled modern way, by killing off the true Bolsheviks who had defeated them.

But what is surely the cardinal contribution of the post-Stalin evolution of Stalinism is the overt exploitation of anti-Semitism, both in the neo-Charades of the Soviet satellites in the fifties and in the governmental campaigns against the Party and the public in Poland and Czechoslovakia during the late sixties.

The reversion to classical anti-Semitism at the Slansky Charade must be considered another step along the path inherent in the Bolshevik notion of expediency as the sole criterion of behaviour. By the autumn of 1952 what had been a more or less effective taboo on the exploitation of vulgar anti-Semitism was simply dropped.

The terrain had been well prepared. In the later forties, the official Soviet organ, *Literaturnaya Gazeta*, in a campaign against 'passportless wanderers' and 'cosmopolitan intellectuals', had made a point of giving in parentheses the Jewish names behind the conventional Russian pseudonyms of Party people.

The Slansky Charade amplified the use of this device: the Charade was cast in the form of an attack on Jews as such. This attack was different in quality as well as technique from previous practice. It had always been conventional to attack Zionism as 'Jewish bourgeois nationalism', in much the same spirit as the general attack on nationalism, while refraining from the pejorative use of the words 'Jew' or 'Jewish'.

The atmosphere changed altogether with the complete elimination of this taboo in the Slansky Charade. A few remarks, purely formal, were made condemning anti-Semitism, but there were not only hundreds of pejorative remarks about Zionism and Israel, there were just as many references to the prisoners in this Charade as being Jews, all these being systematically coupled with the charges in such a way as to explain the prisoners' criminality.

The doublet 'Zionist and Jewish nationalist' kept cropping up; no reference was made to any non-Zionist Jewish nationalists, such as adherents of the former Jewish *Bund* in Russia. There was no mention at all of any Jew as such in a good or even neutral sense. The theme outlined in the original Soviet campaign of the later forties was buttressed in detail in the Slansky Charade, which made much of the change of names: in Slansky's script he told how he would advise other 'witnesses' to make their Jewish names sound Czech. An attempt was plainly being made to establish a 'racial' solidarity that overrode all other considerarions.

The Slansky Charade of 1952 marked an obvious progression from the political destruction of the Trotsky Opposition in 1927 and its physical annihilation during the era of the Great Charades and the Deep Comb-out in 1936–8. In 1927, when the Trotskyite and Zinovievite Opposition was eliminated, a substantial number of Jews were affected, yet in the autumn of 1927 the word 'Jew' or 'Jewish' was never used in open polemics. Even at the height of the Yezhov Era, when the charges had taken on a nightmarish fantasticality, Jewish origins were not harped on.

Stalin may have disliked Jews: this would seem indicated by his liking for anti-Semitic jokes and still more classically, perhaps, by his reference to Trotsky as 'Judas' in the interview he gave Lion Feuchtwanger in 1937.[3] Nevertheless, despite the horrors of the late thirties, explicit anti-Semitism was never publicized.

By the end of the forties this had all changed: in the neo-Charades in the Soviet satellites, in the Soviet press itself, and in the open anti-Semitism displayed by the governments of many of the satellites since the late sixties, anti-Semitism has evidently become a standard ingredient of political harassment. The ancient stereotype of the Jew as agent of Satan, the fundamental formula of medieval anti-Semitism, has been absorbed into the mythology of contemporary Soviet society, and lies there ready for use.

This has been confirmed repeatedly, notably in the violent outbreaks against Jews as 'Zionists', 'American imperialists', and 'tools of Israel' that characterized politics in Poland and Czechoslovakia towards the end of the sixties. These attacks merely reaffirmed the more or less constant display of anti-Semitism in the provincial Soviet press and have latterly played a special role because of the current alignment of the Soviet bloc against the State of Israel.

Overt anti-Semitism supplements the formula of satanism forged during the Great Charades and the Deep Comb-out. The basic element – 'anti-Soviet' or 'counter-revolutionary' – can easily absorb 'Trotsky-ite', 'Jew', 'Zionist', 'tool of Israel', 'tool of Wall Street', 'tool of American imperialism'. . . .

Thus the theological structure established by the Bolsheviks in the wake of their putsch, absorbed and streamlined by Stalin as he engulfed the Party apparatus, has now evolved a supple and remarkably pivotal instrument for the use of any Communist administration.

It is a crowning irony of history, perhaps, and surely of Marxism, that this instrument should have been plucked from the Middle Ages.

Notes

(References are to books listed in the Select Bibliography.)

Introduction

1 Carmichael, chapters IV, VI, VII
2 Lenin, *What Shall We Do?*, ch. IV, part C, p. 119
3 *Pravda*, 25.7.52
4 Trotsky, *Our Political Tasks*
5 *Pravda*, 6.11.18
6 Stalin, *Trotskyism*, pp. 68–9

Chapter 2

1 Stalin, *Voprosy*, pp. 306–26
2 *KPSS*, vol. II, pp. 594–603
3 Schapiro, part III, p. 390
4 Churchill, vol. IV, pp. 447–8
5 Nicolaevsky, p. 75
6 The conflict about the treatment of the Riutin people is attested by Bukharin (quoted in Nicolaevsky), Krivitsky, p. 203, and Ciliga, pp. 163, 219; also in the Secret Speech – Wolfe, *Khrushchev's Speech*. Though the Secret Speech has yet to be published in the Soviet Union, there is no reason to doubt the version circulated in a text published by the US State Department on 4 June 1956, since this has never been contested by the Soviet government and has, in fact, been tacitly acknowledged as authentic by Communist Parties throughout the world. *Pravda* (27.6.56) reprinted an article on it by the American journalist Eugene Dennis; it called the report of the Secret Speech authentic. The major points of the Speech were ultimately embodied in a decree of the Central Committee (30.6.56). The Speech can be found in full in *The Anti-Stalin Campaign and International Communism*, a Selection of Documents edited by the Russian Institute, Columbia University, New York City.
7 Secret Speech; Wolfe, *Khrushchev's Speech*, p. 230
8 *Pravda*, 27.11.34
9 Secret Speech; Wolfe, *Khrushchev's Speech*, pp. 126–62
10 Orlov, Krivitsky
11 Moscow 1957

Chapter 3

1 Nicolaevsky, p. 46
2 Ibid.
3 Ibid., p. 47
4 Nicolaevsky, Orlov, Krivitsky, Avtorkhanov
5 Orlov, p. 22
6 Suggested by Ciliga and Serge
7 Nicolaevsky, p. 54
8 Ibid.
9 Ibid., p. 48
10 *Pravda*, 1.3.35
11 Nicolaevsky, p. 57
12 Ibid.
13 Orlov, chapter IV
14 Ibid., p. 126
15 Ibid., p. 129
16 *The Case of Leon Trotsky*, pp. 300–4
17 Wolfe, *Khrushchev's Speech*, p. 124
18 *The Case of Leon Trotsky*, p. 101
19 Krivitsky, pp. 219–25
20 Avtorkhanov, p. 229
21 *Pravda*, 29.2.28
22 Schapiro, p. 381
23 Ibid., p. 284
24 Orlov, pp. 344–5
25 Ibid., p. 353

Chapter 4

1 *Pravda*, 10.10.36
2 *Terrorist Centre*, pp. 105–6
3 *Bloc*, pp. 287, 796
4 *Terrorist Centre*, pp. 139–40
5 Ibid., pp. 132–3

6 Ibid., p. 122
7 Ibid., pp. 793–4
8 *Bloc*, p. 298
9 Ibid., p. 677
10 *Trotskyite Centre*, p. 510
11 *Bloc*, pp. 287, 796
12 Orlov, pp. 57–8
13 Ibid., pp. 182–7
14 *Trotskyite Centre*, p. 512
15 *The Case of Leon Trotsky*, p. 466
16 *Terrorist Centre*, p. 104
17 *Trotskyite Centre*, p. 36
18 Ibid., p. 180
19 *Terrorist Centre*, p. 135
20 Ibid., p. 144
21 Ibid., p. 20
22 Leites, p. 207
23 Ibid.
24 *Terrorist Centre*, p. 98
25 *Bloc*, p. 575
26 *Terrorist Centre*, p. 99
27 *Trotskyite Centre*, p. 245
28 *Terrorist Centre*, p. 20
29 *Trotskyite Centre*, p. 513
30 *Terrorist Centre*, p. 68
31 *Bloc*, p. 44
32 *Trotskyite Centre*, pp. 129–30
33 *Bloc*, pp. 366–7
34 *Trotskyite Centre*, pp. 358–9
35 Lenin, *Sochineniya*, 3rd ed., vol. 17, p. 482
36 Stalin, *Sochineniya*, vol. 10, p. 58
37 *Trotskyite Centre*, p. 111
38 *Terrorist Centre*, p. 103
39 *Trotskyite Centre*, p. 235
40 *Terrorist Centre*, p. 123
41 *Trotskyite Centre*, p. 74
42 *Bloc*, p. 257
43 *Terrorist Centre*, p. 131
44 *Trotskyite Centre*, p. 380
45 *Bloc*, p. 333
46 *Trotskyite Centre*, p. 125
47 Ibid.
48 *Bloc*, pp. 310–11
49 *Crime of the Zinovievite Opposition*, p. 19
50 *Terrorist Centre*, pp. 80–3
51 *Bloc* (ed. Tucker): Introduction
52 Nicolaevsky, pp. 26–65
53 Stalin, vol. XII, 1949, p. 69
54 Carmichael, 'Stalin: Two or Three Echoes', *South Atlantic Quarterly*, July 1954
55 *Terrorist Centre*, p. 166
56 *Bloc*, p. 771
57 Ibid., p. 738
58 Ibid., p. 324
59 Feuchtwanger, p. 113
60 Orlov, pp. 251–5
61 *Terrorist Centre*, p. 34
62 *Bloc*, pp. 796–7
63 Krivitsky, pp. 156–8
64 *Bloc*, p. 786
65 Krivitsky, pp. 184–5
66 *Bloc*, p. 574
67 Nicolaevsky, pp. 61–2
68 Souvarine, p. 655
69 *The Case of Leon Trotsky*
70 Muggeridge, p. 246
71 Feuchtwanger, p. 127
72 Carmichael, notably chapter XIII

Chapter 5

1 Krivitsky, Hoettl, pp. 79–87, Churchill, vol. I, p. 225
2 *Great Soviet Encyclopedia*, 2nd ed., vol. 50, pp. 419, 424
3 Orlov, p. 85
4 Beck and Godin, p. 140
5 Orlov, pp. 214–6
6 Beck and Godin, p. 176
7 Ibid., p. 177
8 Ibid., p. 33
9 Ibid., p. 46
10 Ibid., p. 54
11 Weissberg, p. 117
12 Ibid., pp. 148–9
13 Beck and Godin, p. 47
14 Ibid., pp. 166 *et seq.*
15 E.g. prisons mentioned in Weissberg
16 Ibid., pp. 310–2

Chapter 6

1 Beck and Godin, pp. 45 *et seq.*
2 Soviet Penal Code, Article 58 (1a)
3 Beck and Godin, p. 89
4 *KPSS*, vol. II, pp. 782–3
5 *Great Soviet Encyclopedia*, 1st ed., vol. 61, pp. 654–5

6 Orlov, p. 219
7 Ibid., p. 225
8 Beck and Godin, p. 138
9 Ibid., p. 145
10 Ibid.
11 Ibid., p. 99
12 Ibid., p. 109
13 Ibid., pp. 110–1
14 Ibid., p. 109
15 Ibid., pp. 114–17
16 Ibid.
17 Ibid., p. 127
18 Weissberg, pp. 456–7
19 *Great Soviet Encyclopaedia*, 2nd ed., vol. 50, p. 424
20 Bialer, p. 63
21 Stalin, *Voprosy*, p. 594
22 Secret Speech; Wolfe, *Khrushchev's Speech*, p. 190
23 Schapiro, p. 417
24 Bialer, p. 63
25 Ibid.; Conquest, p. 485
26 Secret Speech: Wolfe, *Khrushchev's Speech*, p. 124
27 Stalin, *Voprosy*, p. 593
28 *KPSS*, vol. 11, p. 472
29 Ibid., p. 778
30 Avtorkhanov, p. 242; the author estimates 1,220,934 eliminated between 1934–9; cf. Brzezinski.

31 Stalin, *Voprosy*, p. 597
32 Weissberg, p. 320 *et seq.*
33 Bialer, p. 59

Chapter 7

1 Beck and Godin, chapter VII
2 Solzhenitsyn
3 Ibid., pp. 409–11
4 Ibid., p. 281
5 Cherkasov, pp. 380–2
6 *Frankfurter Zeitung*, 29.8.39, nos. 438–9, 'Von Litwinow zu Molotow', p. 1
7 Nicolaevsky, pp. 32–3, as told by Bukharin
8 Secret Speech; Wolfe, *Khrushchev's Speech*, p. 134
9 Nicolaevsky, p. 61
10 Krivitsky, p. 151
11 Secret Speech: Wolfe, *Khrushchev's Speech*, p. 106
12 *Pravda*, 29.3.37
13 Secret Speech; ibid.
14 Avtorkhanov, p. 242

Epilogue

1 Solzhenitsyn, p. 92
2 Loebl
3 Feuchtwanger

Select Bibliography

ANON., *The Dark Side of the Moon*, preface by T.S. Eliot, London 1946

AVTORKHANOV, ABDURAKHMAN, *Stalin and the Soviet Communist Party*, London 1959

BALABANOFF, ANGELICA, *Impressions of Lenin*, Ann Arbor 1964; *My Life as a Rebel*, London 1938

BARMINE, ALEXANDER, *One Who Survived*, New York 1945

BECK, F., and GODIN, W., *Russian Purge and the Extraction of Confession*, London 1951

BIALER, S. (ed.), *Stalin and His Generals*, New York 1970

BLUNDEN, GODFREY, *A Room on the Route*, New York 1947

BRZEZINSKI, ZBIGNIEW, *The Permanent Purge*, Cambridge, Mass. 1956

BUBER-NEUMANN, MARGARETE, *Under Two Dictators*, London 1949

CARMICHAEL, JOEL, *Trotsky: An Appreciation of his Life*, London 1975; *Case of Leon Trotsky, The* (The Dewey Commission), New York 1938

CHERKASOV, N.K., *Zapiski Aktyora*, Moscow 1953

CHURCHILL, WINSTON, *The Second World War*, London 1948

CILIGA, ANTON, *Au pays du mensonge déconcertant*, Paris 1937

CONQUEST, ROBERT, *The Great Terror*, New York and London 1968

DALLIN, D.J., and NICOLAEVSKY, B.I., *Forced Labour in the Soviet Union*, London 1948

DEWEY COMMISSION, REPORT OF THE, *Not Guilty: The Case of Leon Trotsky*, London 1937

DEUTSCHER, ISAAC, *Stalin*, London 1949; *The Prophet Unarmed*, London 1959; *The Prophet Outcast*, London 1963

DJILAS, MILOVAN, *Conversations with Stalin*, London 1962

EASTMAN, MAX, *Since Lenin Died*, London 1925; *Heroes I have Known*, New York 1942

EHRENBURG, ILYA, *Men, Years, Life*, London 1962

FAINSOD, MERLE, *Smolensk under Soviet Rule*, London 1959

FEUCHTWANGER, LION, *Moskau*, Amsterdam 1937

GINZBURG, YEVGENIYA S., *Into the Whirlwind*, London 1967

HOETTL, WILHELM, *The Secret Front*, London 1953

KRAVCHENKO, VICTOR, *I Chose Freedom*, London 1951

KRIVITSKY, WALTER, *I Was Stalin's Agent*, London 1940

LEITES, NATHAN, *A Study of Bolshevism*, Glencoe, Illinois 1953

LEITES, N., and BERNAUT, ELSA, *Ritual of Liquidation*, Glencoe, Illinois 1954

LENIN, V.I., *Sochineniya*, 4th ed., Moscow 1941–50; *What Shall We Do?*, New York 1929

LOEBL, EUGENE, *Sentenced and Tried*, London 1969

MUGGERIDGE, MALCOLM, *1930–40 in Great Britain*, London 1941
ORLOV, ALEXANDER, *The Secret History of Stalin's Crimes*, London 1954
NICOLAEVSKY, BORIS, *Power and the Soviet Elite*, New York 1965
SCHAPIRO, LEONARD, *The Communist Party of the Soviet Union*, 2nd ed.,
    London and New York 1970
SERGE, VICTOR, *From Lenin to Stalin*, London 1937; *Memoirs of a
    Revolutionary 1901–1941*, London 1963
SOUVARINE, BORIS, *Stalin*, London 1939
SOLZHENITSYN, ALEXANDER I., *The GULAG Archipelago*, London and
    New York 1974
STALIN, JOSEPH, *Foundations of Leninism*, New York 1932; *History of the
    Communist Party of the Soviet Union (Bolsheviks), Short Course*, New
    York 1939; *Sochineniya*, Moscow 1936–51; *Trotskyism or Leninism*, 1928;
    Voprosy Leninizma, 11th ed., Moscow 1947
SCHACHTMAN, MAX, *Behind the Moscow Trials*, New York 1936
TROTSKY, LEON, *History of the Russian Revolution*, New York and London
    1932; *My Life*, London 1930
TUCKER, ROBERT C., (ed.), *Transcript of the Anti-Soviet 'Bloc of Rights
    and Trotskyites'*, Moscow 1938. Introduction by R. Tucker, *Stalin*, New
    York 1973
ULAM, ADAM, *The Bolsheviks*, New York 1965; *Stalin*, New York 1973
WEISSBERG, ALEXANDER, *Conspiracy of Silence*, London 1952; US title,
    The Accused
WOLIN, SIMON, and SUSSER, ROBERT M, *The Soviet Secret Police*, New
    York 1957
WOLFE, BERTRAM, *Three Who Made a Revolution*, New York 1948;
    Khrushchev's Speech and Stalin's Ghost, New York 1957

PERIODICALS:
Bol'shevik, Byulleten' Oppositsii, Izvestiya, Pravda, Sotsialisticheskii Vestnik,
Kommunisticheskii Internatsional, Internationale Presse-Korrespondenz,
Unser Wort, Permanente Revolution

TRANSCRIPTS OF THE 'MOSCOW SHOW TRIALS':
Stenographic *Report of the Trotskyite-Zinovievite Terrorist Centre*, Moscow
    1936 (referred to in Notes as 'Terrorist Centre')
Stenographic *Report of the Anti-Soviet Trotskyite Centre*, Moscow 1937
    (referred to in Notes as 'Trotskyite Centre')
Stenographic *Report of the Anti-Soviet 'Bloc of Rights and Trotskyites'*,
    Moscow 1938 (referred to in Notes as 'Bloc')

OTHER SOVIET GOVERNMENT PUBLICATIONS:
KPSS v Rezolyutsiakh, Vols. i–ii, Moscow 1953
The Crime of the Zinoviev Opposition, Moscow 1935
Great Soviet Encyclopaedia, Moscow 1st edition 1926–31, 2nd edition 1950–8

Index